Making Candles & Soaps

FOR

DUMMIES®

Making
Candles & Soaps
FOR
DUMMIES®

by Kelly Ewing

WILEY

Wiley Publishing, Inc.

Making Candles & Soaps For Dummies®

Published by
Wiley Publishing, Inc.
111 River St.
Hoboken, NJ 07030-5774
www.wiley.com

WILEY

About the Author

Kelly Ewing is a writer and editor who lives in the wonderful community of Fishers, Indiana, with her husband Mark, her daughter Katie, her son Carter, and furry canine friend Cheyenne. She has coauthored several books, including *The Internet All-in-One Desk Reference For Dummies, PCs All-in-One Desk Reference For Dummies,* and *Direct Mail For Dummies.* She has ghostwritten several books and edited more than 75 books on a variety of topics. She also writes articles on sports, travel, and human interest for several newspapers. In her spare time — when she can find it! — she enjoys spending time with her kids, reading, walking, writing, scrapbooking, cooking, and doing crafts.

Dedication

To Mark, Katie, and Carter. You mean the world to me and bring smiles to my face every day of my life. With each passing day, you make me a better and even happier person.

Author's Acknowledgments

First of all, I'd like to thank my husband, whose support, patience, and understanding have enabled me to write this book. He also provided the photographs throughout this book as a personal favor to me.

I also want to thank my young children, Katie and Carter, who understood that Mommy needed to write in the "office" and that when I was done, I would be all theirs to play with and cuddle.

A big thank-you goes to Lois Hensley, my aunt, whose kindness and generosity early on enabled me to write from home on a once-a-week basis while she bonded with my little ones. She willingly gave up a day each week to come to my home and play with her great-niece and great-nephew while she also worked full-time as a nurse.

I'd also like to thank my mom, Judy Steadham, and sister-in-law, Megan Ewing, and her friend Jake Metz for helping me concoct candles and soaps in my kitchen. They came from Plainfield, Bloomington, and West Lafayette, Indiana, to help out.

My sister, Shannon Ryan, deserves a thank-you as well. She put her computer degree to good use researching resources for these appendixes.

Another thank-you goes to Wiley Acquisitions Editor Tracy Boggier, who approached me about writing this book last fall. Other Wiley staff members who deserve a big thanks include Project Editor Allyson Grove, for her wonderful edits and insight, and Copy Editor Chad Sievers, for his eagle eye and humorous suggestions.

I'd like to thank Wiley's Composition Services staff, who transformed the electronic files into an actual book. Project Coordinator Nancee Reeves guided the book through Composition. A big thank-you also goes out to the PLTs, proofreaders, and indexer.

Lastly, a thank-you goes to the book's reviewers. Edward Stephens III, Darryl Chapman, Cliff Rayman, and Karan Hall reviewed the candle information. Michelle Lewis and Kathy Miller reviewed the soap-specific material. Their suggestions and collective experience added to the quality of the book.

Publisher's Acknowledgments

We're proud of this book; please send us your comments through our Dummies online registration form located at www.dummies.com/register/.

Some of the people who helped bring this book to market include the following:

Acquisitions, Editorial, and Media Development

Project Editors: Allyson Grove, Georgette Beatty

Acquisitions Editor: Tracy Boggier

Copy Editors: Chad R. Sievers, Jennifer Bingham

Technical Editors: (candles) Edward Stephens III, Darryl Chapman, Cliff Rayman, Karan Hall; (soap) Michelle Lewis, Kathy Miller

Media Development Specialist: Kit Malone

Editorial Managers: Michelle Hacker, Jennifer Ehrlich

Media Development Manager: Laura VanWinkle

Editorial Assistant: Elizabeth Rea

Cover Photos: Royalty Free, © Infocus International/Getty Images/ The Image Bank

Cartoons: Rich Tennant, www.the5thwave.com

Composition

Project Coordinators: Maridee Ennis, Kristie Rees, Nancee Reeves

Layout and Graphics: Denny Hager, Michael Kruzil, Lynsey Osborn, Jacque Roth

Proofreader: Andy Hollandbeck

Indexer: TECHBOOKS Production Services

Special Help
Elizabeth Netedu Kuball

Publishing and Editorial for Consumer Dummies

Diane Graves Steele, Vice President and Publisher, Consumer Dummies

Joyce Pepple, Acquisitions Director, Consumer Dummies

Kristin A. Cocks, Product Development Director, Consumer Dummies

Michael Spring, Vice President and Publisher, Travel

Brice Gosnell, Associate Publisher, Travel

Kelly Regan, Editorial Director, Travel

Publishing for Technology Dummies

Andy Cummings, Vice President and Publisher, Dummies Technology/General User

Composition Services

Gerry Fahey, Vice President of Production Services

Debbie Stailey, Director of Composition Services

Contents at a Glance

Table of Contents

Introduction

I don't know about you, but I've discovered that as I get older, my interests change. Now that I'm a mom with two small children, I'm starting hobbies that I wouldn't even have considered ten years ago. I now look forward to the 40 and 50 percent coupons from my two local craft stores printed in the Sunday newspaper. A while back, I would've just tossed them. Now, I'm sure my local craft store employees know me by name, thanks to my weekly ventures.

Thanks to all my new hobbies these past few years, I know that starting something new isn't always easy. Take candle and soap making, for example. If you're just starting, you probably have a long list of questions. What should you buy? What's a waste of money? What's the best material to use? What should you avoid? And how do you make professional-looking candles and soaps in your own home?

That's where *Making Candles & Soaps For Dummies* enters the picture. Consider this book everything I know about creating simple and elegant candles and soaps — or rather, everything I think you'll *want* to know. Whether you're engaging in candle and soap making for the first time and looking for basic techniques or you're a pro searching for new ideas or information on turning your hobby into a business, *Making Candles & Soaps For Dummies* offers you practical tips and how-to advice.

About This Book

In this book, you find out not only what supplies and equipment you need to get started, but you also discover how to make simple and advanced projects. Color, scent, embellishments, and other decorative touches enable you to take your candle- and soap-making ventures to new heights. I even devote a chapter to troubleshooting common problems that candlemakers and soapmakers — both beginners and gurus — encounter and how you can counteract them.

Sure, you can discover many candle- and soap-making secrets on your own. But why waste the extra time, effort, and money when you can find out what you need to know in one place: *Making Candles & Soaps For Dummies?* Sit back, relax, and enjoy!

How to Use This Book

If you've ever purchased a *For Dummies* book, then you're probably familiar with this award-winning series. True to the series' reputation, I tell you only what you need to know: in this case, how to make functional, attractive, and professional-looking candles and soaps. You don't find a lot of theory or technical info in this book. Instead, you get to jump right in and try your hand at creating dozens of simple and advanced candles and soaps. I give you the guidelines for candle and soap making and show you the tricks of the trade, but then you get to take it from that point to concoct just the right creation for you.

And if you're interested in something in particular, don't feel like you have to read the entire book from the first to last page. All *For Dummies* books are reference tools, meaning that you can jump in and out, and *Making Candles & Soaps For Dummies* is no exception. You don't have to read the book from cover to cover if you don't want to. (Of course, I won't mind if you do, and the book makes perfect sense that way, too!) Just look up the topic you want to discover more about and peruse the pages at your leisure.

Conventions Used in This Book

This book doesn't have a lot of conventions, but be aware of a few points before you get started.

All temperatures given in this book are in Fahrenheit. Likewise, all weights in this book are in ounces or pounds. If you need a metric equivalent, then you can refer to the following tables.

Liquid Weight	Metric
.16 ounce (oz)	5 milliliters (ml)
.5 oz	15 ml
1 oz	30 ml
2 oz	60 ml
4 oz	120 ml
6 oz	180 ml
8 oz	240 ml
1 pint	480 ml
1 quart	1 liter

Dry Weight	*Metric*
.083 oz	3 grams (g)
.25 oz	7 g
1 oz	30 g
2 oz	60 g
3 oz	85 g
4 oz	115 g
6 oz	170 g
8 oz	230 g

Finally, I just want to remind you that you should read the entire recipe prior to making your candle or soap. You never know what will come up after you've already started — and you can't do much about buying extra wax when you're already in the midst of melting it. So before starting, get *all* your supplies ready to use. *Now* you can start that recipe.

Foolish Assumptions

I always do my best writing when I picture my intended audience. This book is no exception. No, I'm not talking about assuming that you're a busy parent with two young children or a corporate hotshot looking for a rewarding hobby. Instead, I'm referring to your background and skills.

I don't assume that you're an expert. In fact, I'm guessing that this book may be the first time you've even thought about candle or soap making. (Or maybe you didn't think about it, and you received this book as a gift from your mom, who thinks that you have too much time on your hands, or your spouse, who thinks that you're spending too much money on candles and soaps!)

At the same time, I don't assume that you're a neophyte, either. Although I give you all the basic information you need to know, such as descriptions of the different types of waxes and steps on matching your wick to your candle, I also give you details on making more advanced projects and even starting your own business.

How This Book Is Organized

I love to plan, so organizing this book was a lot of fun. I cover the basics as well as any additional information you may want to know as you progress into more advanced material. Then I gathered it all up, organized it into logical parts, and divided it into chapters based on topics. The following sections describe what parts you'll read in this book.

Part I: Getting Started in Candle Making

If you're just getting into candle making or you've been at it for a while but you're self-taught, then you may want to begin with this part. Chapter 1 reveals the basic equipment and materials you need to start. You also find out how to work safely with hot wax, as well as what to do if you spill wax. Chapter 2 explains all those different waxes and wax additions on the market.

Chapter 3 discusses all your mold options, and believe me, you have several. Not only can you buy ready-made molds, but you also can make your own by recycling household objects — within limits, of course — into candle-forming vessels. In Chapter 4, you delve into the topic of wicks — believe it or not, they're the heart of your candle, and you need to make sure they're the perfect match for your wax.

And Chapter 5 gives you a chance to actually try your hand at the hot stuff; you get to melt wax into some basic molded and dipped candles, as well as roll a beeswax candle.

Part II: Jazzing Up Your Candles

When you feel you've mastered the basics or if you've already been making candles for a while, you'll enjoy Part II. This part takes you beyond the basic projects into more advanced candles and decorative touches. Chapter 6 shows you how to change the look and smell of your candles with color and scent.

If you love going the extra mile, then you'll love Chapters 7 and 8. You find out how to add embellishments, paint, stamps, and stencils to your candles in Chapter 7. Chapter 8 offers you recipes for more advanced projects, such as cracked candles, floating candles, layered candles, and multiwick candles.

Chapter 9 gives you ideas for caring for and displaying your creations. If you like to share, then you'll be especially pleased with the information on giving your candles as presents.

Lastly, Chapter 10 tackles candle woes, such as appearance and wick problems, poor burning, and color and scent issues.

Part III: Tackling Soap-Making Basics

If you've never made soaps, then you don't want to miss this part. Chapter 11 not only gives you basic safety information, but it also covers organizing your workspace and securing the proper equipment and ingredients.

You can make soaps in several ways, and Chapter 12 is where you discover the advantages and disadvantages of two popular methods: hand milling and melting and pouring.

Note: You may have heard about the cold-process method of making soap and wonder why I don't cover it in this book. Not only can cold processing occasionally require hours of stirring, but it can also be dangerous if proper safety precautions aren't taken when handling sodium hydroxide, which is a caustic necessary to the cold process method. While many people have mastered the technique of cold process and find it most gratifying, I have chosen to omit it from this book, which is geared for beginners. Most instructors at local craft stores teach the melt-and-pour method. However, if you're intrigued by the idea of this more complicated process and want to find out more about it, take a look at Appendix B. I've listed some Web sites you can visit to find more information on cold-process soap making.

Chapter 13 offers you the inside scoop on soap ingredients and additives. If you feel that you're comfortable with all that information and you're ready to get started, then you can jump into Chapter 14, which provides instructions for creating basic soaps.

Part IV: Fancying Up Your Soap

Giving you a squeaky-clean feeling is only one benefit of soap. Serving as a decorative accessory is another. In this part, you find out how to make your soaps beautiful. Whether you decide to use them on your body or place them around your home for decor, you'll still admire the looks of these functional yet attractive soaps.

In Chapter 15, you discover the secrets of color and scent. Chapter 16 tells you how to go beyond basic soaps and into the sublime. You create embedded soaps, soap balls, stenciled soaps, and three-dimensional soaps, to name just a few projects.

And if you love to relax in the tub, you'll love Chapter 17, which clues you in on how to make a home spa. Bath spas, body lotion, bubble bath, massage oil, shampoo, and shower gel are all at your soap-making fingertips, and this chapter shows you how to make them, using easy steps.

Lastly, Chapter 18 covers what to do when your soap-making adventures go awry. If you're doing something wrong, chances are you'll find answers in this chapter.

Part V: Moving On in the Candle- and Soap-Making World

After you're a candle- or soap-making guru, you may think that you're finished with this book. Sorry, but I have some more great tips to share with you in Part V.

Chapter 19 talks about taking scents to the next level: aromatherapy, which uses scent to affect your body and mind. You find out about essential oils, as well as some great scents for both candles and soaps.

And if you're finding that making candles and soaps keeps taking up more and more of your time so that it's almost a full-time gig and friends and family keep begging for more of your creations, then you'll like Chapter 20. It gives you important information about turning a hobby into a business. You find out high-priority info regarding regulations and business plans, as well as tips on how to market and package your products.

Part VI: The Part of Tens

No *For Dummies* book is complete without the irreverent Part of Tens. This lighthearted and short part offers you additional information in the form of top-ten highlights. Chapter 21 gives you ten holiday decorating ideas (did I say they were easy?). Chapters 22 and 23 offer you great gift suggestions and super projects for kids. And Chapter 24 covers ten must-dos for attending a craft show.

Part VII: Appendixes

Ever see a great new product and wonder where someone bought it? Well, now you don't have to wonder. Appendix A lists candle- and soap-making suppliers. Whenever they're available, I list 800 numbers, Web sites, and addresses. You don't have to wonder anymore!

And if you're now a bona fide candle- or soap-making junkie, don't skip Appendix B. Here, you find an abundance of additional resources for your reading pleasure.

Icons Used in This Book

If you've thumbed through this book, you've probably noticed those funny little pictures in the margins. These little guys, called *icons,* offer you a separate path to get information you're really interested in. Here's a look at what the icons mean:

This icon marks text that gives you a quick-and-easy way to do something. If you're in a hurry to get started on your candle- and soap-making projects, you may want to go through this book and just read these tips. Who knows how much time you'll save?

When you see this icon, you'll know you need to pay special attention to the words next to it. This icon highlights information that you'll want to remember down the road.

When you see this icon, *please be careful.* Hot wax and soap can be dangerous, so I use this icon to point out dangers or problems that may have a detrimental effect on you or your project.

This icon marks projects that are especially appropriate for doing with your kids. Not every project in this book is safe enough or short enough to match a child's skills or attention span, but whenever one is, I make sure to highlight it.

Gel candles are a relatively new trend in candle making, and you can't always make them the same way you make paraffin or beeswax candles. The wax also has a higher melting point, which means an entirely new set of considerations. This icon highlights things you need to think about when making gel candles.

If you've been making candles and soaps for a while and feel like you need more advanced tips or projects, then just look for this icon. It tells you how to take your hobby to the next level or tells you something you may not already know.

Where to Go from Here

Keep in mind that this book isn't designed to be a novel, but a reference book. I don't want you to feel like you have to sit down and read it cover to cover, although you can if you want and it'll still make perfect sense. But if you're interested in a particular topic, just look it up in the table of contents or index, flip to that page, and jump right in. You can read any chapter in any order, or even any section or part of a section. If you come across a topic you haven't heard about, you'll either find a cross-reference to the chapter that covers it, or you can look it up in the index. Who knows the places you'll go? But no matter what, make sure that you enjoy the process. Isn't that what hobbies are all about?

Part I
Getting Started in Candle Making

In this part . . .

1f you're new to making candles, then you'll enjoy this part. You find out what equipment can help you make attractive candles, as well as the safety issues you need to keep in mind. You discover the different types of wax and how to create a perfect wick and wax combination. You also can try creating simple projects, such as taper candles, beeswax candles, and my personal favorite, container candles.

Chapter 1

Stocking a Safe and Efficient Work Area

In This Chapter
▶ Assembling your equipment and supplies
▶ Preparing your workspace
▶ Making candles safely

Making candles can be a relaxing and rewarding hobby. Nothing quite compares to the feelings of pride and pleasure that come from looking at a beautiful, burning candle and knowing that you created it with your own two hands.

Because today's supplies and materials make creating attractive candles easy, you don't need to purchase them. And because candle making isn't an expensive hobby, you can decorate your home with candles, as well as give them as gifts. (See Chapter 9 for more information.)

I get you started off on the right foot in this chapter by explaining what you need, from basic equipment to everyday supplies. I also tell you how to prepare your workspace so that you have minimal cleanup and how to safely melt wax and transform it into candles.

Stocking Up on the Basics: Equipment and Supplies

Making candles doesn't have to be expensive. You can use many items that you already have at home, or you can buy them cheaply at garage sales. If you do need to buy anything at a store, you can almost always find coupons for it in your Sunday newspaper. If you don't have what you need on hand and don't want to drive to stores, you can also order what you need via the Internet. (For suppliers, see Appendix A.)

I suggest getting only the barebones equipment when you start out. As you venture into the hobby more, you get a better feel for the types of candles you want to make and the equipment you need.

To help you get started, the following sections walk you through the basic equipment and supplies required to make candles.

Lining up your equipment

What you're basically doing in candle making is melting solid wax over your heat source. So the first item you need is some type of heat source. Your stove, of course, is perfect for this function, but some people use a small camping stove. In fact, it doesn't matter whether your stove is gas or electric.

Don't use a microwave to melt your wax because the temperature is too hard to control, and you can easily overheat the wax.

Finding your (melting) pot

After you have a heating source, you need something to melt your wax in, a melting pot, if you will. Wax heats up quickly and can explode if it gets too hot, which is why you almost always must use an indirect method of melting it. In other words, don't melt your wax in a pot directly on your burner. Instead, you need some type of double boiler system (see Figure 1-1). A *double boiler* is basically a large pot with a smaller pot inside.

Figure 1-1:
You need a double boiler or some type of improvisation to melt your wax. A small pot, mounted on a trivet inside a larger pot, works just fine.

If you don't have a double boiler (preferably metal), don't think that you have to rush out and buy one. I personally don't have a double boiler. You can use a small pot placed inside a larger pot to get the same effect (refer to Figure 1-1). The small pot needs to be propped up in some way so that it doesn't rest on the bottom of the larger pot. You can use a *trivet,* a three-legged stand that slightly lifts your pot or, if you don't have one, several small tin cans resting on the bottom of the larger pot. You want the top, smaller pot to be at least ½ inch above the base of the larger pot. I didn't have any pots that I wanted to melt wax in, so I just bought some cheap ones at a garage sale.

You probably are pouring your wax from the top pot into your molds (unless you're dipping your candles). A *mold* is simply a hollow object into which you pour your melted wax; as the wax cools, it hardens and takes on the shape of your mold. Craft stores have metal melting containers with a handy little pour spout. As I became more involved with this hobby, I purchased one of those containers, which made cleanup and pouring a whole lot easier.

Collecting the necessities

When you have your heating source and double boiler out of the way, you're ready to get some other necessary items, including a

- ✔ **Mold.** Your first candles probably are ones you make in a mold. The type of material your mold is made of doesn't matter. In fact, you have many mold options, from store-bought ones, to molds you recycle from items around home, to molds you make yourself. Chapter 3 offers you a wealth of information on molds.

  My only suggestion here is to wait before you buy a lot of molds. Just purchase a few basic ones at first to get a feel for what you like. Then, after your creativity is stimulated, you can probably find many additional mold options around your home that you can use for free.

- ✔ **Thermometer.** You can purchase a specialized wax thermometer or use a candy or cooking thermometer as long as it has the appropriate temperature ranges on it. You want the thermometer to register temperatures ranging from 100°F to 300°F.

  I can't stress the importance of a thermometer in candle making enough. Don't even try to make candles without one, because it's too dangerous! (See the section "Playing It Safe" later in this chapter for other safety tips.) Wax gets hot quickly, and unlike items you cook, you can't eyeball wax and know by sight that you've overdone it. The only way to properly guarantee the temperature is with a thermometer.

  You can find thermometers that attach to the side of your melting pot. Check your local craft store, cooking store, or online candle-making resource. (For a list, see Appendix A.)

✔ **Dipping can.** If you're going to be dipping taper candles (see Chapter 5 for the technique), then you want some type of metal container that's wide enough and tall enough to dip your wicks into (see Figure 1-2). Of course, you can purchase these cans, but you can also use something from home. You may not even need to purchase or find another container if your melting pot is at least 12 inches wide. You can just use it to dip your candles.

✔ **Ladle or large metal spoon.** As the wax melts, you need to stir it occasionally. A ladle or large metal spoon works well. As long as you don't leave the spoon in the wax mixture, you can even get by with a long-handled plastic spoon, which is easy to clean and doesn't absorb wax or scent. (The likelihood of melting increases when you're working with gel wax, which requires a higher melting point. To find out how to make a gel candle, see Chapter 8.)

If you look at the preceding list, you can see why making candles is so inexpensive.

Figure 1-2:
For dipping tapers, you need some type of a dipping can that's at least 12 inches wide.

Adding other helpful items

Of course, if you like gadgets, you can always find more equipment to spend your money on. As you continue making candles, you may want to buy some of the following items. None is mandatory, but these items may make your candle-making adventures more enjoyable.

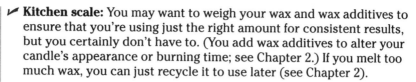

✔ **Kitchen scale:** You may want to weigh your wax and wax additives to ensure that you're using just the right amount for consistent results, but you certainly don't have to. (You add wax additives to alter your candle's appearance or burning time; see Chapter 2.) If you melt too much wax, you can just recycle it to use later (see Chapter 2).

If you do opt for a scale, a digital postal scale is much more accurate than a spring-type diet scale, especially for weighing additives and fragrances, but they do cost more money.

✔ **Baking pan:** You can clean your molds and other equipment in many ways, but I suggest using an old baking pan lined with aluminum foil. Just be careful with your molds because if you use too high a temperature or heat them for too long, it may begin to melt away. For more details on cleaning methods, see Chapter 3.

✔ **Scissors, razor blade, or craft knife:** Sharp tools enable you to trim your wick and cut your wax. Because I hate sharp things, I find that scissors work just swell for me.

When you cut off the amount of wax you need from your block of wax, make sure that you have something underneath it so that you don't damage your countertops.

✔ **Hammer and/or screwdriver:** Sometimes you need to break your slabs of wax apart, depending on their size. You can place a screwdriver in the wax and hammer the end of it to make the job easier. Again, place a protective surface, such as a cutting board, on your countertop before hammering — unless you don't mind the possibility of a gouge in your countertop from a slipped hammer or screwdriver!

Other items you may want on hand include measuring cups and spoons, extra spoons if you want to add fragrance or dyes (see Chapter 6), and possibly a tape measure if you plan to measure your candle mold or finished candle.

Gathering your supplies

I consider *supplies* anything that you need to replenish after you start making candles. That includes candle waxes, wax additives, and wicks. Those items are so important to candle making that I devote Chapter 2 to waxes and wax additives and Chapter 4 to wicks.

The following are a few other supplies you need:

✔ **Mold sealer:** You may also hear *mold sealer* referred to as *wick sealer*, and the latter name gives its function away: You use it to close up the hole where you thread in your wick so that the wax doesn't leak out.

✔ **Releasing agent:** You may also hear a *releasing agent* referred to as a *mold release* (see Figure 1-3). You can purchase silicone spray specially formulated as a releasing agent at any craft store, or you can raid your kitchen and use everyday vegetable oil. The latter works just as well as any releasing agent I've ever purchased. All you do is spray or apply a thin amount of spray or oil to the inside of your mold so that you can remove your candle easier.

✔ **Wax glue:** If you decide to get decorative with your candles, you may want to purchase wax glue so that you can attach embellishments or pieces of wax to the sides of your candle. For more advanced projects and decorative finish ideas, see Chapter 7.

✔ **Wick tabs:** If you buy untabbed wicks, you may want to purchase *wick tabs,* which are thin metal bases that attach to the bottom of your wick. (Untabbed wicks are simply wicks that don't have the tabs.) These tabs are usually used for votives and container candles because the bases help support your wick so that it stands up straight. You can also use them for molds that don't have a hole in the bottom for the wick because they help your wick stay at the bottom of your candle when you pour the wax. (See Chapter 4 for more tips on working with wicks.)

Accuracy counts

One of your most valuable tools in candle making is an accurate thermometer (see figure). You can purchase a wax thermometer from a craft store or make do with a candy thermometer, as long as it gives the correct temperature range. It doesn't matter what type of thermometer you get as long as:

✔ It's accurate.

✔ It lists temperatures in both Fahrenheit and Celsius.

✔ It gives temperatures up to 300°F.

✔ It doesn't melt.

Just as in cooking, whenever you're gauging temperature, you need to wait until the thermometer stops rising to read the temperature. When you're purchasing your all-important thermometer, make sure that you purchase one that does not contain mercury.

Figure 1-3:
Spray your
mold with a
releasing
agent so
that your
finished
candle is
less likely
to stick to
its mold.

If you're going to go beyond making basic candles, you may want to purchase supplies that enable you to color and scent your candles. Wax dye, which you use to color your wax, comes in a variety of forms, including powder, liquid, and solid chips. You can also add fragrance using essential oils, synthetic scents specially formulated for candles, and herbs. Chapter 6 gives you all the details about buying dyes, as well as essential oils and readymade candle scents.

Getting Ready for the Dirty Work: Preparing Your Workspace

If you've ever had a burning candle drip on your carpet, then you know how difficult removing wax from things you don't want it on can be. As a result, make sure to prepare your workspace so that you're not stuck ending an afternoon of candle making with the unpleasant task of scraping wax off your countertops and removing stains from your clothes.

The kitchen is the best place to make your candles simply because that's the most likely place for your heat source, the stove. The following steps explain how to prepare your work area:

1. **Choose an area near the stove where you have enough counter space to work.**

   You need to be able to arrange all your supplies nearby, as well as have enough room to work. The closer you are to your heat source, the better off you are.

2. **Line your countertop with aluminum foil, wax paper, or even an old dropcloth or sheet.**

   Someone may have suggested that you use newspaper to line your countertop. Don't! Although newspaper is indeed an inexpensive alternative — especially if you subscribe to a daily one and you're going to toss it or recycle it anyway — the heat from the wax may cause the newsprint to get on your countertop.

   If you're using aluminum foil or wax paper, turn up the edges at least an inch to prevent runoffs from leaky wax.

3. **Tear off a few extra sheets of foil or paper.**

   You can always use extra foil or paper, so have it ready now, before you need it. For example, after you pour your wax into the mold, you can use these extra sheets to place your mold on for extra coverage.

4. **Get out anything else you may need, based on the project you're making.**

   You can use your time better by having more out than you need rather than wading through drawers looking for something as your wax is heating. Good items to have on hand include potholders, and paper towels. And just as you would when making a recipe, also make sure that you read through the project you want to make and get those supplies ready now as well.

   Okay, I don't want to be an alarmist, but having a fire extinguisher on hand is a good idea, too. Not that you'll need it, but you know what they say: As soon as it's not around, you will!

Believe it or not, you also want to get dressed for the occasion. Didn't know candle making had a dress code, did you? Although you don't have to wear a specific candle-making uniform, you do need to put a little thought into what you're wearing. Wear something that you don't mind getting a little wax on — forget your favorite jeans and sweater — and be extra safe by wearing an apron. If you do get wax on your clothes, see the section "Treating spills," later in this chapter, for tips on removing it. You may also want to avoid wearing clothes that shed. You don't want your candles to have a little extra fur, do you?

Just as with anything else, continual maintenance is better than a major overhaul. In other words, clean up your mess as you make your candles so that you won't have a bunch of work facing you when you're finished. You can find the equipment and supplies you need a whole lot faster, too. Plus, if you don't have that extra can or container in the way, you're less likely to dump it over!

Playing It Safe

Whenever you work with anything hot, you need to take the proper precautions. I suggest wearing thick potholders whenever you're removing your double boiler from the stove, as well as when you're pouring your wax. The following sections also give you valuable safety information for when you're heating wax, treating spills, or putting out a fire.

Don't overlook eye protection. Safety goggles can go a long way in protecting your eyes from splashes. And if you find yourself making lots of splashes, you may even want to consider wearing long sleeves and pants.

Heating wax

Unless you're rolling beeswax candles (see Chapter 2 for more on beeswax and other types of wax), you have to melt your solid wax into liquid wax. You don't want to get your wax too hot, though, or it may combust, causing fire. (For more information on heating wax, see Chapter 2.)

Never leave your wax unattended as it melts. If you see smoke, you know you're in danger of a fire. Immediately turn off the heat.

When working with hot wax, don't be tempted to save time and melt your wax over direct heat or in a microwave. Using a double boiler slows the heating process and helps ensure your safety. However, you can't think you're safe just because you're using a double boiler. Just as when you're boiling eggs, you need to make sure that you have enough water to cover most of your top pot.

Be especially cautious when melting gel wax. Gel wax has a higher melting point than other waxes and is quicker to catch fire.

Treating spills

Whether you spill wax while you're making candles or while you're burning a finished one, cleaning wax spills is no treat. The best course of action is obviously prevention. Taking the time to prepare your workspace for candle making can save you valuable minutes of cleanup and maybe even articles of clothing. In addition, if you've properly matched your wick to your wax (see Chapter 4) and you haven't placed your finished, burning candle in a *draft* (a slight current of air, such as from a window), you won't have to cope with big accumulated pools of melted wax that can spill.

But alas, despite your best intentions, wax is now somewhere that it isn't intended to be. Perhaps the wax is on your floor, your carpet, your clothes, or yourself. Whatever your predicament, the following tips can help you clean up the mess.

- ✔ **No matter what type of wax you spill on you, the basic treatment is the same.** (If the burn causes blistering, definitely call your primary care physician or visit your local immediate care center.)

  - Immediately place your injured part in cool water. (Don't use cold water because extreme temperature shocks your skin.)

  - When the wax cools and hardens, gently peel it off and treat it like other any burn. (If your skin didn't blister, you can use calamine lotion or aloe vera. But, whatever you do, don't use butter!)

  - If you spill melted gel wax on you, the gel is hard to get off your skin. The longer it stays on, the more it continues to burn.

- ✔ **If the wax gets on something other than your body, wait until it hardens before you try to clean it up.** Otherwise, you are just spreading the goo and making a bigger mess. If you want to speed along the process, try rubbing an ice cube on the wax to help cool it. If the item is movable, such as clothing, you can even place it in the freezer.

- ✔ **After the wax hardens, try to scrape up what you can.** A wooden spatula works particularly well. But be careful not to scratch the surface if the wax is on something hard, such as flooring or countertops.

- ✔ **If your spill is on your carpet or clothing, scrape up what wax you can and then cover the area with paper towels or newspaper and iron over it.** You need to keep replacing the paper towels or newspapers and ironing the spot until the wax disappears (see Figure 1-4).

  If this method doesn't remove the wax from your clothes, try taking them to the dry cleaner. Their special chemicals can often remove wax from fabric. Just let them know what they're dealing with when you drop off the garments.

- ✔ **If your spill is on wood, scrape it off.** If you have any left, then use wax cleaner to mop it up.

You may not be able to remove wax from porous material, such as unfinished wood, unglazed tile, or concrete.

Extinguishing a fire

Unfortunately, mishaps occur. Hopefully, a fire won't be in your future — and it shouldn't be if you're checking your temperature — but just in case it is, I want you to be prepared.

Figure 1-4:
You can usually remove wax from your carpet by using a warm iron and paper towels or newspaper.

Turn off your heat source immediately if any of the following occurs:

- You check your wax's temperature, and it's dangerously high (anything over boiling point, which is 212°F).
- Your wax begins to smoke.
- You smell something burning.
- Your wax actually ignites and catches fire.

I can't stress enough that you may have no signs of an impending fire. You won't see bubbles, such as when you boil water.

If you think you're in danger of a fire, don't try to move your pan. A fire may occur at any minute, and you don't want to take the chance of spreading it or spilling dangerously hot wax everywhere.

Wax is actually oil, so never pour water on it in an attempt to put it out. If a fire occurs, you need to actually smother the flames. You can use a metal lid, damp cloth, fire blanket, baking soda, or an extinguisher — just not water!

After you've eliminated the fire, don't touch the pan right away. The pan is hot. When it's cooled down, you can clean up just as you would any other fire — air out the area, throw away the pan after it cools, and call a fire repair company if the damage is severe.

Chapter 2

Working with Wax

*W*ithout wax, your candle won't burn. If you look inside a burning candle, you see a pool of liquid. That liquid is the wax burning inside the flame. The wax is the wick's fuel. When you stop burning the candle and it cools, the wax returns to a solid.

But, making candles isn't as simple as heading to your local craft store to buy "candle wax" and then returning home to melt and mold it into a candle. Not only do you have to know what kind of wax you need, but you also need to know how to handle it. In this chapter, you discover the ins and outs of working with waxes, including what different kinds of wax you can choose and how to choose the type that's most appropriate for your candles.

Waxing On about the Types of Waxes

If you've ventured down the candle-making aisle of any craft store, you probably know that you can't just pick up a slab of wax and presto, be done with your candle. Well, technically, you can, and, sure, you may even luck out and choose the type that successfully forms your candle. But certain waxes are more appropriate for certain types of candles, and knowing what you're looking for ahead of time can save you much trial and tribulation.

The following sections walk you through common types of waxes and their uses. In addition, the projects throughout this book specify the type of waxes to use. Although most candles are made out of either paraffin or beeswax, you have other choices as well, especially if you shop online. The material in this chapter can help you determine which waxes are better suited to molding or dipping, for example, or adding scent or color. And just in case you're curious about what the different types of waxes actually look like, check out Figure 2-1. The figure shows you the different types of waxes you'll likely encounter during your candle-making adventures.

Figure 2-1:
The wax you choose depends on the type of candle you want to create.

Paraffin wax: The winner and still champion

Chances are, if you've tried candle making, you're familiar with *paraffin wax*. This petroleum-based wax is the most popular wax for making candles. If you're new to candle making, paraffin wax makes a great starting point. Paraffin wax is inexpensive, easy to color, and available practically anywhere. It has a colorless and odorless nature that enables you to easily add and reliably predict your end colors and aromas. (Crunched for time? You can buy paraffin wax that's already dyed.)

Paraffin wax is commonly available in chunks and large slabs. You can even find it prepared with the common additive *stearin* already included. (For more on this additive, which helps your candle burn more evenly, among other benefits, see the section "Venturing into New Ground: Using Wax Additives," later in this chapter.)

Bead wax: No muss, no fuss

If you're looking for a low-tech way to create a candle, bead wax (see related figure) may be just the ticket. *Bead wax* is actually just wax that's been shaped into small beads. This wax also goes by the names of granular wax, candle sand, prilled wax, or powdered wax.

To make a simple bead wax candle (see related figure), you don't even have to melt the wax. You just add your wick, pour the bead wax into your container, and you're ready to go. The wax even comes colored. The most difficult part of the process may just be choosing your container. (No sweat, though because Chapter 3 tells you all you need to know about that topic.)

Because you're not melting the wax, bead wax is a good candle-making material for children.

You may be thinking that you've found your answer in paraffin for a quick wax buy. Sorry! Paraffin wax comes in different melting points, ranging from 104°F to 160°F. The melting point you choose depends on the type of candle that you want to make. When you're in the store, make sure that you check the wax's label for both its melting point and the type of candle the wax is best used to create. For example, if you're creating a container candle, which burns in an actual container, choose paraffin wax with a low melting point. For other types of candles, such as ones you create and remove from molds, you can use paraffin wax with a higher melting point.

If you really and truly don't want to think about temperatures, go ahead and buy paraffin wax with a medium melting point, which is generally good for most types of candles. ***Note:*** Your candle may not burn as well or look as nice as if you'd matched the temperature to the specialized candle you wanted to make.

If you're just getting into making candles, you can experiment with easy candles created with paraffin wax. Take a look at the simple candle projects in Chapter 5.

Don't be tempted to do one-stop shopping and buy your paraffin wax at the grocery store. This wax isn't the type you use in candle making; instead, it's used for sealing food that you've jarred.

Beeswax: The benefits of honey, with no stings attached

A popular choice, *beeswax* is an all-natural product that has a pleasant honey aroma when burned. In addition to its natural golden shade, beeswax is available in white and other colors. You can buy beeswax in honeycomb sheets, blocks, or beads.

Beeswax is popular because it's easy to work with, especially when you're working with beeswax sheets. (For a recipe to try, see Chapter 5). Unlike most other waxes, you can melt beeswax with your hairdryer, if you want. (Just don't try to mousse it!) If you opt to heat beeswax on your stove, you want to remember that it, unlike paraffin, must be heated slowly. However, you do use a double boiler just as you do with other waxes.

Beeswax's low melting point (approximately 140°F) and strength (if you drop it, it dents, but doesn't shatter) makes beeswax a great wax to use when you're making container candles with children. On the downside, beeswax can be a little bit pricier than paraffin. However, because beeswax has a longer burning time than other waxes, you can use it most often in combination with other waxes to extend their burning time.

The wax sticks to your mold if the wax combination that you create uses more than 10 percent beeswax. To help with removal, lightly spray the mold with a *releasing agent* — such as vegetable oil — before you pour your wax. A releasing agent helps keep the beeswax from sticking to the mold. (For more on working with molds, see Chapter 3.)

Gel wax: Feels like jelly, but doesn't mix with peanut butter

A newer product on the market, *gel wax* is basically mineral oil combined with resin to create a mixture that's the consistency of jelly. (Okay, so gel wax isn't really a wax, but you can use it as one.) Gel wax is also called (surprise!) *jelly wax* and looks like a clear gel. You can find gel wax at most craft stores, usually in a round, bucketlike container. (For tips on getting the gel wax out of the container, see Chapter 8.)

If you've ever purchased a gel candle, then you're aware that gel wax doesn't set hard. (Touch a gel candle, and it actually feels like jelly.) As a result, you can't mold gel wax, but it's ideal for container candles.

Because gel wax is clear, it's popular for embedding nonflammable objects, such as shells or decorative glass objects. (For more on making an embedded gel candle, see Chapter 8.) Gel wax also burns longer than other types of wax candles.

Just because something looks pretty in a gel container candle doesn't mean that embedding the object is appropriate. Use common sense. If the item is flammable or will eventually rot, putting it inside a candle won't suddenly make it flameproof or enduring. (If it did, people may start putting their life savings in gel wax.) If you're unsure, read the item's labeling for warnings or err on the side of caution and don't embed it. In short, avoid plastic and food items, which give the candle a smell when being burnt, but it won't be the kind of fragrance you want.

If you're really set on using an object, think about using it outside the candle. One option is to attach the object to the side of the candle's container for a decorative effect.

You can buy gel wax at most craft stores. Depending on the manufacturer, gel wax is usually available in three different grades based on how much fragrance or how many embellishments you want to add. If you think you want to add several objects or fragrance to the clear gel, opt for high-polymer gel. No matter what type of gel wax you buy, it remains solid until heated.

Vegetable-based wax: Straight from the third rock from the sun

Believe it or not, waxes made from items such as soybeans, palm wax, and other vegetable bases, are available. (If you can't find these *vegetable-based waxes* in stores, just take a peek around the Internet. Appendix A gives you a list of suppliers and their Web sites.)

Fans of these waxes say they burn cleanly and are longer lasting than other chemical-based waxes, such as paraffin. But the main reason to opt for this type of wax is if you're a vegan. If you opt to use vegetable-based wax, your best bet is to make container candles because these waxes are more like lotions in consistency.

If the package doesn't specifically say that the wax is all vegetable, it probably isn't.

Appliqué wax: A few sheets will do ya

One type of wax that you'll probably see in a craft store aisle is *appliqué wax*. This wax comes in very thin sheets (complete with paper backing) and several color choices. You use the sheets to create shapes to decorate your finished candles. Cut your shape and press it onto the side of your candle (no glue required).

If you want to take the easy way out, you can even buy pre-cut shapes.

Figuring Out How Much Wax You Need

One of the nice things about candle making is that you can make a candle in almost any type of mold — that is, as long as you can remove the candle from the mold. But the more creative you are in your mold designs, the more math you need to do. The amount of wax that fills a votive candle mold perfectly won't be the same amount that tops off your favorite glass container.

I can give you several fancy mathematical ways to figure out how much wax you need, but I'm not big on making simple tasks difficult. The easiest way to come up with your magic wax number is to simply fill your mold with water and measure how much liquid you used.

Follow these steps:

1. **Block your mold's wick hole so that the water doesn't drain out as you add it.**

   If you don't want to get your mold wet, a plastic bag in the mold works nicely and blocks the hole at the same time.

2. **Fill your mold with water.**

3. **Pour the water into a measuring cup.**

4. **For every 3.5 fluid ounces of water, you need 3 ounces of unmelted wax.**

A 1-pound package of candle wax gives you approximately 19 to 20 fluid ounces (or 2⅓ cups) of melted wax.

If you make candles quite a bit and you have a dedicated container in which you melt your wax, try using a permanent marker to mark varying weights of wax, such as 1 pound, 2 pounds, 3 pounds, and so on. Just place a pound of wax in it, melt it, and then draw a line to mark the spot. Then, in Step 3 of the preceding list, pour the water into your container. Then read the line where it reaches, and that's how much wax you need.

Don't forget to melt a little extra wax so that you have enough wax to repour in the mold to make up for the wax shrinking as it cools.

Melting Wax

First, you need to decide what you're going to melt your wax in. (See Chapter 1 for tips on stocking up on basic candle-making equipment.) A double boiler is ideal, but you can use a couple of old pots that fit inside each other, if you want. No matter what kind of melting vessel you choose, remember that you're going to pour the wax from the container directly into your mold. A melting pot that has a spout, for example, is helpful.

Before you get started, make your kitchen a no-entry zone. When you're making candles, your kitchen is no place for your kids or pets. Find a sitter, have your partner entertain your children, or make candles while the kids nap. Let your dog outside for a break or move your cat to a different room. Depending on whether your home has an open-floor plan, you may be able to set up a safety gate to bar entry to your work area.

To melt the wax:

1. **Determine the amount of wax that you need**.

   If you're unsure about the amount, see the section "Figuring Out How Much Wax You Need," earlier in this chapter.

2. **Place your wax in the top part of your double boiler or in your smaller pot.**

   If you're using a slab of wax, don't forget to break it into smaller pieces so that it melts more quickly and evenly. Forget your hands; use stronger tools, such as a screwdriver.

   Choose your burner carefully. You don't want to heat your wax too close to the wall, or you may run into smoke damage if you overheat it. Also make sure that your double boiler is properly placed on the burner. You don't want to place it too far in one direction, or hot wax may tip all over you and your stove.

3. **Add water to the bottom section of the double boiler or to your larger pot.**

   If you're using the two-pot method, place the smaller pot inside the larger pot so that water reaches about halfway up the smaller pot's sides.

4. **Over medium heat, bring the water to a rolling boil.**

   You don't want to use high heat because the water boils too hard and may splash into your wax.

5. **Heat your wax until it has melted.**

   Boil your water for a while (the candle projects throughout this book give you approximate times), but don't forget to recheck the bottom pot occasionally to make sure that it still has enough water to cover at least two-thirds of the sides of the smaller pot.

   Don't be a messy cook in the kitchen. You don't want wax to get on your burner. If it does, clean it up after the wax cools or, better yet, move to another burner.

   Especially if you're using gel wax, make sure to clean up the wax. When you use the burner the next time, the gel wax may smoke or cause a fire.

6. **Using your thermometer, periodically check your wax's temperature.**

   Unlike food, wax doesn't look "done," and you can't test it with a fork. You need to constantly check your wax's temperature. As a rule, if you're registering temperatures in the 200°F range, you want to be careful. Most waxes combust if they're 400°F or more, and wax heats up quickly. Each wax's *flashpoint* — the temperature at which it combusts — is listed on its packaging.

   Place your thermometer directly in the wax and then immediately wipe off the wax (unless you enjoy trying to chip off hardened wax!). When it reaches the correct temperature, you're done.

   If your wax has a clip on it, attach it to the side of the pot and leave it there. That way, you don't have to keep inserting and cleaning it to monitor the temperature.

Gel wax is solid at room temperature and melts into a liquid quickly. So, use low heat and check its temperature frequently because it can explode easily. Again, don't forget to check the package's labeling for the correct temperature, because every manufacturer is different.

Pouring melted wax

If you're like the majority of candlemakers, you pour your melted wax into a mold. (For more on molds, see Chapter 3.) Hopefully, you use a melting pot that enables you to easily pour the wax into the mold. Either way, spilt wax isn't always easy to clean up. (Chapter 1 offers tips on cleaning up a waxy mess.)

Save yourself time and labor and cover your work surface before you start working. You can use an old tablecloth, sheets of aluminum foil, or anything else that you don't mind getting stained or throwing away. (See Chapter 1 for more on preparing your workspace.)

After you cover your work surface, you're ready to go. Here's what you do:

1. **Apply a releasing agent, such as vegetable oil or silicone spray, to your mold.**

   The releasing agent allows you to remove the candle from the mold much more easily.

2. **Place your wick in your mold and knot it on the outside of the mold.**

   For more on wicks, see Chapter 4.

3. **Seal the area around your knotted wick with a mold sealer and secure at top of mold by tying to a rod or skewer.**

   A mold sealer is a special putty that you use to close up your wick hole so that no wax leaks out.

4. **Carefully grab your melting container and begin pouring your wax smoothly into the mold.**

   Be careful when you pour your wax. Remember that the container is hot, so you want to use potholders and get a firm grip on the container's handle. Pour your wax into the mold until it's almost full. Stop about ½ inch before you reach the top of the mold. Pouring smoothly is key. Don't constantly change directions; you can wiggle the mold later to get it to set perfectly.

   Don't forget that your molds are hot. Although you didn't heat your molds, you poured hot wax into them, so they can get very hot. Aluminum molds in particular heat up more than others. Be careful!

   If you drip any wax down the side of the container, simply use a towel to wipe it up. Likewise, if water drips down the container's side, wipe it off. You don't want to get water into your wax. If you're using a metal handle, don't forget to use a potholder.

   Be especially careful if you're pouring melted gel wax into a container. Don't spill this liquid on you because the gel is extremely sticky and difficult to remove from your skin.

5. **Very gently tap the side of your mold to remove any air bubbles.**

   Don't be too aggressive when you tap — you don't want to dent your mold.

   The type of wax you're using determines what you do after you pour your wax. For example, if you're making a paraffin mold candle and want a smooth, shiny finish or simply want the candle to cool faster, you may want to place your mold into a cold water bath for a while. For details on making a paraffin mold candle, see Chapter 5.

If you have any leftover wax, you can store it for later use. See the following sections for information on how to do so.

The old shall become new again: Recycling and storing unused candle wax

It's better to err on the side of caution and melt too much wax when you're making a candle because you can just reuse old wax to make a new candle.

How you handle the wax you're recycling depends on where it came from. If you're using leftover candle wax that you used to create new candles, then simply label its scent, color, and wax type and store it for later use. Then, just make sure that you use this wax when you create another candle that requires the same type of wax. With this technique, you avoid mixing your waxes.

You can even recycle wax that you've scraped off from new candles that you're shaping or that you've collected from candle drippings or that other people have given you. Just strain out the large pieces of debris before melting. After melting, strain the wax again to remove small pieces that didn't melt. Just as you do with leftover wax, be sure to label the wax's scent, color, and type, if you can, because you want to avoid mixing waxes in the same candle.

Saying bye-bye to leftover wax — the right way

Never throw melted wax down the drain. After wax returns to a cool, hardened state, it clogs up your drain. Along those same lines, don't throw your boiling water down the drain, either. More than likely, it contains wax pieces as well. Pour the boiling water outside or let it cool so that you can remove the wax first.

If you're just going to discard the leftover wax, then just put it into a flexible container or half-gallon cardboard milk container and let it cool. Then you can take it out after it hardens and throw the hardened wax away.

If you'd like to reuse the wax, you also place it into a flexible container. Excess gel is the easiest to recycle. After it cools, just return it back to its original container. To store other types of waxes, just remove the hardened waxes and place them in plastic bags for later use. Don't forget to label the types of waxes you used.

If you're in a hurry, use small containers so that the wax cools more quickly.

If you're really in a hurry, don't think that you can save time by leaving the wax in your melting vessel and then trying to remelt it later. Although I know of several people who remelt way this way regularly, there's a potential risk involved: The top wax layer doesn't melt as quickly as the bottom, and the liquid wax underneath causes an unexpected explosion of hot wax. (For more on safety issues, see Chapter 1.)

Venturing into New Ground: Using Wax Additives

The more you make candles, the more you may decide to experiment with different wax additives (see Figure 2-2). These additives change the crystalline structure of the wax, which then affects attributes like the candle's appearance or burning time.

Figure 2-2:
A variety
of wax
additives
can improve
the quality
of your
candles.

 If you're having problems with your candles, such as mottling, cracking, or burning issues, wax additives may be just what you need to fine-tune them. (Chapter 10 covers common candle problems you may encounter, as well as potential solutions.) Keep in mind, though, that the more you add to your candle, the more opportunities you have for other problems.

Depending on the additive, you either add it directly to the melted wax, or you melt the additive separately with an equal amount of wax and then slowly stir it into the melted wax.

When working with wax additives, keep the following things in mind:

- Always use as small an amount as possible and then add more later if you need to.
- Measure as precisely as possible.
- Mix and blend well.
- Make notes of how much of the additive you used so that you can chart your results.

Use an additive only after you've determined that other factors — type of wax, wick, and temperature — aren't the problem. If you're sure those items weren't the problem, the next time you make your candle, try using an additive. For tips on troubleshooting your candle problems, see Chapter 10.

The following sections describe the most common additives.

Stearin: Your wax's no-stick assistant

Probably the most common candle-making additive is *stearin,* (also called stearic acid) although nowadays, candlemakers are using it more as a special effects additive and less as a corrective one. Stearin is simply a fat in flake or powder form. The majority of candles are paraffin, and you almost always add stearin to your paraffin creations. In general, you add 1½ ounces of stearin to every 1 pound of wax that you use.

You don't need to melt stearin separately. You can simply add it to the wax as it's melting.

Stearin has several benefits when it's added to wax. It

- Lengthens burning time.
- Shrinks the wax so that it's easier to remove from the mold.
- Makes your colors stand out more.
- Decreases the translucence of your candles.
- Gives your candles a glossy finish.
- Promotes mottling.
- Hardens candles so that they're less likely to bend or tilt.

Although stearin gives your candles many wonderful qualities, make sure that you don't use it when you're pouring your candles into a flexible rubber mold. The stearin can actually rot your mold. Instead, you want to use vybar in this instance. (I talk more about vybar later in this chapter.)

Because stearin does shrink the wax (a good thing when you're removing a candle from a mold), don't use it for container candles. Instead, opt for microcrystalline, which keeps the wax from shrinking away from the sides of your container.

Vybar: A qualified stand-in for stearin

Another popular candle additive is *vybar*. This additive is a great replacement for stearin when you're pouring your wax into flexible molds. (Stearin rots flexible molds.)

Sold in bead form, vybar comes in two types, based on the melting point of each form. Whenever you use vybar, simply choose the form that best matches your wax's melting point. You won't use much vybar — probably just 1 or 2 percent of the amount of wax you're using.

Vybar, like stearin, does many things for your candle. It

✔ Helps eliminate bubbles.

✔ Enables you to add more fragrance.

✔ Makes the candle harder so that it's less likely to bend or tilt.

✔ Gives you a smooth surface.

You don't need to melt vybar prior to adding it to your wax. You can simply melt it along with your candle wax.

Microcrystalline wax: A bit of a contradiction

Candlemakers use *microcrystalline* primarily as an additive to other waxes to make them stay softer longer and prolong their burning time. Ironically enough, microcrystalline, which is made of small crystals left over after paraffin has been processed out of crude oil, eventually makes the candle wax harder.

Most of the time, microcrystalline is already included in your wax, so you don't need to add it. Make sure that you read your package's label. If the wax already includes microcrystalline, don't add any more of this additive.

With microcrystalline wax, you have choices. More than 50 types are on the market today. Although that number sounds like a lot, in actuality only two basic types of microcrystalline wax exist.

- ✔ *Hard microcrystalline* wax lengthens burning time and improves the candle's finish. Like stearin, it also makes the candle stronger. More than likely, you can use hard microcrystalline when you want to dip your candles and create a pretty outside layer.

  Hard microcrystalline has a high melting point, and you use it only in minute qualities — 1 teaspoon of melted microcrystalline per 1 pound of wax. You want to melt the hard microcrystalline first and then add it directly to your wax.

- ✔ *Soft microcrystalline* has a low melting point and is what you use when you make container candles. Unlike stearin, soft microcrystalline enables the wax to stick to the side of containers better. (Stearin actually causes the wax to shrink.) Use approximately 10 percent soft microcrystalline for your container candles.

Microcrystalline thickens wax, and as a result, you may have problems with your wick. If you decide to use microcrystalline, you may need to choose a slightly larger wick. (For more on wicks, see Chapter 4. For troubleshooting tips, see Chapter 10.)

Other wax additives: Take your pick

You may wonder what some of the other additives are that you see in the candle-making aisle of your local craft store or, if you're a homebody, online. Keep in mind, though, that these additives are for more advanced users, and you may never need or want to use them — and that's okay. But just in case you're interested, the following list gives you the lowdown on other common additives on the market.

- ✔ *Wax glue* enables you to attach objects to the sides of your candles. You can use it just like regular glue or heat it and brush it on, if you prefer.

- ✔ *Luster crystals* have many of the same qualities as stearin, lengthening the candle's burning time as well and making the color more vivid. They also make the candle harder so that it's less likely to bend. You melt luster crystals separately from your wax and then add it. (The melting point is about 190°F.) Luster crystals also increase the gloss.

✔ You can use *mottling oil* (see Figure 2-3) if you want your candle to have a wintry, snowflake look. You don't need to melt the oil because it's already in liquid form; you just add it to your wax before you pour it into your mold or container.

Of course, the color and scents you add to your candles are considered additives as well. However, I devote an entire chapter to those topics — make sure that you check out Chapter 6.

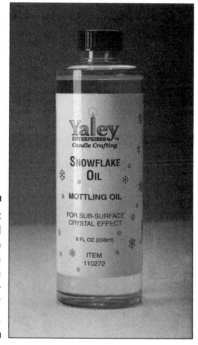

Figure 2-3:
Mottling oil can help you achieve a snowflake look on your candles' surface.

Chapter 3

Achieving the Look You Want for Your Candles Again and Again

....

....

A candle mold can help you create professional-looking candles, as well as creative works of art. Craft stores and Internet suppliers offer hundreds of molds to choose from, but your choices don't stop there. You can use common household items, as well as mold an object you like or create your own mold design. You can take your mold selection as far as you want to, limited only by your imagination. In this chapter, you discover the different types of candles you can create and what kinds of molds create each type.

Communicating in Candle Lingo

Before you even think about a mold, you first need to figure out the type of candle you want to create. The candle you decide on determines whether you even need a mold — or whether you can use your own two hands to shape the wax. Following is a list of the common candles you can create. You can see examples of these candles in Figure 3-1.

✔ **Taper:** *Taper candles* are long and slim and look elegant as centerpieces on your dining room table or on your fireplace mantel. Although taper molds are available, if you want to make these elegant creations, you can simply dip your wicks into melted wax.

Keep in mind that taper candles are usually a standard size at the base so that they fit into standard candle holders. Chapter 5 gives you a recipe for creating a basic taper candle.

✔ **Pillar:** *Pillar candles,* unlike tapers, are sturdy and thick. They can be short or tall and square or round. Some pillar candles are huge and contain multiple wicks. (Chapter 8 tells you how to create a classic multi-wick candle.) These candles are usually referred to by their diameter and height, as in a 3- by 5-inch pillar candle. You make pillar candles by using a mold, but it can be a readymade one or a homemade one, such as an empty yogurt container.

✔ **Container:** *Container candles* burn in the actual container that you pour them into. In essence, the container is your mold. Here's your chance to be creative. You can use a fish aquarium, shells, and gel wax to create an ocean-scene candle, or you can decorate an old jar to hold your wax. (Chapter 5 shows you how to make a container candle, while Chapter 8 contains instructions for creating a gel candle.)

One perk of container candles is that the container keeps the wax from dripping onto your carpet, counters, or tables.

✔ **Votives:** *Votive candles* are short, small candles that are only two to three inches high and ½-inch in diameter. Unlike pillar candles, votive candles are classified according to how long they burn. Most votives are 10-hour or 15-hour candles.

Candles use the melted wax as fuel for the wick. As a result, burn any type of candles, especially votives, in a holder as opposed to a flat surface so that the wick can use as much melted wax as possible.

✔ **Tealights:** *Tealight candles* are the same diameter as votives, but are just one inch high. You can place them in a tealight holder or place them under something, such as a pot of simmering potpourri or a lampshade.

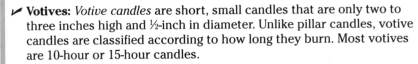

A real hands-on approach

Although most of the candles you make require a mold, some don't. Your perfect mold may even be something you carry around with you on a daily basis: your hands. For example, you can use your hands to roll beeswax or dip tapered candles. As one of your first projects, you may want to try making a beautiful, simple beeswax candle. The beeswax comes in sheets, and you simply separate the sheets, place the wick along the edge, and then roll the wax into a cylinder shape. Voilà — an instant candle.

Another option is to make hand-dipped tapered candles. You simply take a wick and dip it into melted wax. You continue dipping the wick, layering the wax each time, until your candle is as thick as you want it. Chapter 5 gives you detailed instructions on making both types of candles, as well as recipes for other simple projects that require you to use actual molds.

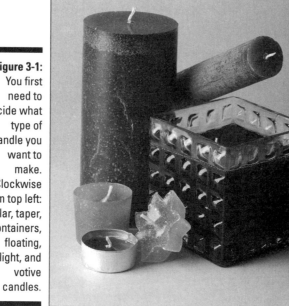

Figure 3-1:
You first need to decide what type of candle you want to make. Clockwise from top left: pillar, taper, containers, floating, tealight, and votive candles.

The Sky's the Limit: Knowing Your Mold Options

If you decide that the candle you want to make requires a *mold* — a hollow object to hold and shape your wax — you have endless options. You can buy molds for pillar candles and votive candles. In addition, you can buy molds that shape waxes in the forms of fruits and flowers. Just visit the craft store, and you'll see that readymade molds are available to make almost any type of candle.

If you can't find the mold you want in the store, take a peek around your home. Your trashcan and cupboards hold limitless possibilities for your candle-making adventures.

A key part in molding a successful candle is to spray a *mold release* on the inside of your mold prior to adding wax to it. You can buy mold release in a craft store or, once again, you can step into your kitchen and pull out some good old vegetable oil. It works just as well. Another option is to use silicone spray. Spray the inside of your mold before adding the wax, so your candle is much easier to remove.

In general, I suggest that you avoid using beeswax in molds. This wax is very sticky. If you decide that you want to try molding beeswax anyway, you'll definitely want to spray a mold release on the inside of your mold before adding it.

You also can't use gel wax in a mold. Gel wax doesn't hold its shape — remember, it's like jelly — so you can use this type of wax to make only container candles.

Taking the easy way out: Using readymade molds

Molds are very easy to use, and your results are almost guaranteed to be impressive and professional looking. If you're a first-timer, I highly recommend using readymade molds. What shape of mold you want is only the beginning of what you have to think about when purchasing your molds. Molds are made out of numerous materials and can be disposable or reusable. You can also buy flexible or rigid molds.

- *Rigid molds* are much easier to work with when you first start out in candle making. A rigid mold usually comes in hard materials such as plastic or metal. You're usually limited to basic shapes, such as cylinders, triangles, and rectangles.

- *Flexible molds* usually come in rubber or latex, and as a result, you can stretch and manipulate them. You have more design options with flexible molds. However, it can be harder to remove the finished candle from the mold because of the detail. Of course, when you're ready to move on to fancier designs, you may want to use flexible molds, which allow you to give more detail to your candle.

The following list describes the different materials used to create molds and gives the pros and cons of each one.

- **Plastic:** These popular, rigid molds come in a variety of shapes and are usually inexpensive. You can find them in both one-piece and two-piece designs. (Clamps hold the latter together.) Many plastic molds are transparent, which allows you to see what you're making. Transparent molds are especially nice when you're trying something new. Of course, if you use wax that's too hot, you risk melting the plastic. Don't use with wax hotter than 180°F.

- **Rubber or latex:** These flexible molds allow you to make candles with beautiful details. Because these molds are usually one piece, you need to actually turn them inside out to remove your candle. But because you're constantly stretching and manipulating the mold to remove candles whenever you use it, these types of molds don't last as long as other types.

You want to sprinkle talc powder on the outside — yes, the outside! — of your rubber or latex molds. That way, the latex has something to grab for traction as you turn it inside out to release your candle.

✔ **Metal:** If you're into buying items for the long term, then a metal mold may be just the material for you. These durable molds are more expensive than other types, but the old adage, "You get what you pay for," definitely applies here; they last much longer than their counterparts. Most metal molds are narrower at the bottom so that you can easily remove your candle.

Figure 3-2 shows you some of the molds you can find at your local craft store.

No matter what type of mold you opt for, you probably want to mix in *stearin* (a wax additive; see Chapter 2 for more details) with your wax so that you have an easier time removing the finished candle from the mold.

Figure 3-2:
If you're a beginner, start with readymade molds.

Recycling: Hunting around your house for molds and containers

Bored with the basic pillar, votive, and tealight candle molds you can buy or are you simply strapped for dough? Don't worry! You still have plenty of creative options available. For starters, open your kitchen cupboard. Unique jars, glasses, coffee cups, or salad bowls all make interesting candle containers, where you don't remove the finished candle from the item. Look inside your trashcan. Empty milk cartons cut in half, yogurt containers, and even empty tin cans provide fodder for your hobby. (Just keep in mind that if you're using a can, you may have trouble removing your candle.) Figure 3-3 shows you some potential molds you may find around your home.

Figure 3-3:
When
you're
comfortable
using molds,
you're
ready to
use existing
items as
your molds.

Here are a few more mold and container ideas:

- ✔ Pop cans with the tops removed
- ✔ Small aquariums
- ✔ Empty popcorn or candy tins
- ✔ Mixing bowls

- ✔ Aluminum foil that you've manipulated into a shape
- ✔ Gelatin molds
- ✔ Any hollow container

You can even use an object with two open ends. You just need to place it on something solid, such as cardboard, and then use mold sealer (a puttylike substance used to seal holes) so that the wax doesn't leak.

The only rules for choosing a mold are

- ✔ You must be able to remove the candle from the mold.
- ✔ The container itself must be able to withstand heat.
- ✔ The top of the container must be the same size or larger than the bottom of the candle.
- ✔ You need the candle to be somewhat cylindrical in shape if you want it to burn properly.

In some cases, you can use a glass jar to mold your candle because these jars are usually designed to hold food that you're canning. However, you should use them only as container candles (see the next section) and not as a mold because the neck at the top of the jar will cause you problems when you try to remove the candle. Don't be tempted to use a normal drinking glass, which doesn't have the neck, though, as a mold because they're usually not tempered like jars and probably won't be able to withstand the heat of the melted wax.

Going for looks: Decorative containers

One of my favorite things to do is to make decorative container candles (see Figure 3-4). Unique objects provide lovely settings for your candles and are inexpensive to create. You can even match the colors to your decor, as well as scent the wax with your favorite fragrance. (For more on aroma-therapy, see Chapter 19.)

Even when you're making container candles, you use a mold. The container is functioning as the mold, holding the wax in place; the only difference is that you don't remove your finished candle from your mold. It stays in the container as you burn it.

Figure 3-4:
Decorative containers make great container candles.

As long as your containers adhere to the basic rules of molds outlined in the section "The Sky's the Limit: Knowing Your Mold Options," earlier in this chapter, you can use just about anything. You just need to make sure that the mold you're using isn't flammable and that it's heat-resistant. My mom, for example, made a container candle inside a shell to match the beachy, seashell theme in my kids' bathroom.

If your kitchen is decorated in flowers or an outdoor gardening theme, why not use terracotta flowerpots as container candles? Hurricane vases, lantern-shape containers, or metal buckets can add a nice touch as well. You may even want to add a citronella scent outdoors to keep the bugs away.

If you're using terracotta flowerpots or metal containers, you may want to seal them with a silicone sealer before pouring wax into them to prevent fire hazards or leaks.

Have you ever wondered what to do with the old candy and popcorn tins that you buy from the neighborhood school kids? They make attractive containers for your candles as well. You can have a lot of fun with your containers. When I was a kid, I once had a candle shaped into an ice cream sundae, complete with a wax ball of cherry on top. Sundae holders, as well as unique dishes, make attractive container candles, too.

Sprucing up your containers

Not too thrilled about your boring old jar, but can't find anything else suitable for a container? Don't despair. You can spruce up your lackluster containers by decorating them with objects — nothing like a little sequin to add some spark to your life, right? And your container decorations don't have the same limitations as your candle embedments. In fact, if you want to use something embedded in your candle that may catch fire, it's more appropriate to place it on the outside of your container.

Try layering holders within each other by placing a small jar into a shorter, larger one. Then add shells or rocks in the large one. You can add fresh flowers, paint, or stickers — you name it. You can even punch holes in a tin can. I especially like the look of tin votive holders punched into the shape of a jack-o-lantern.

Short on ideas? Just go to a craft store and take a look around or thumb through your favorite magazine. You can come up with creations in no time.

Think about where you want to use the candle and what you're trying to accomplish. I love to take baths in my garden tub surrounded by burning candles, so I use a lot of lavender colored and scented candles. Not only does the color match my room, but the lavender is also very relaxing. Likewise, I love apple-cinnamon tealights in my kitchen. The aroma reminds me of a home-baked apple pie and gives a homey feel to guests when they enter the house.

Just remember the container you choose functions as your mold. As a result, you need to make sure that your container is appropriate for holding hot, burning wax. For example, a plastic or wood container is a definite no-no.

You don't want to use plastic containers with gel wax. Gel wax reaches a hotter temperature than other waxes and is more likely to melt plastic.

Working with Flexible Molds

If you're using a flexible mold made out of rubber or latex, you need to treat it differently than your normal rigid molds. Don't add the wax additive stearin. Stearin actually can eat through flexible molds, so you need to use vybar instead. Vybar is very similar to stearin, so you still achieve many of the same qualities — minus the mold eating, of course! (See Chapter 2 to find out what each of these wax additives can do for your candles.)

Because flexible molds are, well, flexible, they don't exactly stand up on their own. You want to make sure that you support the mold in some way before you pour your wax into the mold.

In addition, before adding your wax to a flexible mold, don't forget to spray your mold with a mold release. You apply mold release with rigid molds as well, but it's especially important with flexible molds because you actually peel away the mold. To help facilitate the process, try applying mold release or talc powder to the outside of the mold so the mold has something to grab as you peel it off. Finally, tapping a flexible mold to remove bubbles won't do anything for you; you need to pinch the sides of the mold instead.

Proper Care and Feeding (er, Cleaning) of Your Molds

Wax isn't something you just leave in your mold and keep making candles over it. You definitely want to keep your molds clean so that your future candles look like, well, what they're supposed to. You also want to make sure that you care properly for your molds. Otherwise, what's meant to be a multiple-use mold won't last as long as you want or may even become a mold that you can use only one time.

One of the most basic concepts to keep in mind when you're cleaning your molds is to avoid scraping them. Like with nonstick pans, scraping your mold not only removes what you want to remove (the wax or food), but it also removes part of what you don't want to remove (the mold itself or the Teflon coating on your pan).

If you really must scrape (and I can't stress enough how much you shouldn't!), at least use a wooden utensil. Better yet, why not just clean the wax using one of the following methods?

  ✔ **Use a wax cleaner.** Wax cleaners are available, and if you don't mind spending the money, by all means buy them. To use wax cleaner, you just squirt the remover on your equipment and wipe it away.

  ✔ **Bake it off.** Get out a baking pan (a cookie sheet works just fine), line it with wax paper or a paper towel, and place your mold on the pan. Place it in a 175°F oven for 7 to 8 minutes. The wax should just melt off, and because it's now liquid, you can wipe away any wax left in the mold. (You can clean your waxy tools this way, too.) Just don't get overzealous and heat your items for too long, or you risk damaging them.

Gel wax is easier to clean than other waxes. After it cools, you can usually just peel it off the bottom of your container. However, you probably still have gel remnants lying around; make sure that you pick them up right away because the oil stains whatever it's on.

You also want to be careful with how you handle your mold. Metal ones in particular are prone to denting. Toss it around too much, and your mold may have a new indentation that it shouldn't have.

Store your molds with care. Treat them as you treat your clean glasses. If you're not using them, store them upside down (to avoid attracting dust) somewhere safe, where your kids or pets can't get to them and where you won't step on them or place something on them.

Chapter 4

Finding the Perfect Wick

. . . .

In This Chapter

▶ Seeing how the wick functions within a candle

▶ Running down the various types of wicks

▶ Pairing your wick and your wax

▶ Watching out for lead

▶ Priming and inserting your own wick

▶ Checking your work

. . . .

The right wick can take your ordinary wax candle from basic to sublime. Although you can use almost any wick to make a candle, the best wick allows your candle to burn longer and cleaner. This chapter is about finding that perfect wick. You discover everything you need to know about choosing a wick, as well as how to prime, tab, and insert it into your candle.

Understanding How a Wick Works

Although almost any wick and wax combination will burn, correctly matching the wick to your candle determines not only how well but also how long your candle burns.

A *wick* is several pieces of cotton string that have been treated with boric acid and then braided together. These strings, or threads, are actually referred to as *plies*. But the wick's function is much more than what you may imagine for a simple piece of cotton string that you light.

The wick works more like the engine of a car. Just as the engine consumes gas to keep the car running, the wick uses the melted wax to continue burning. By lighting the candle, you allow heat to travel down to the wax, melting it along the way. The wick then sucks up the melted wax to keep the candle burning. If the melted wax isn't being used up at the right pace, the problem centers on the wick. You need to match the wick to the wax and candle size better. (For more on troubleshooting your candle's problems, see Chapter 10.)

Identifying the Types of Wicks

Although wicks come in many shapes and sizes, they all have plies that are braided. The spaces within the braided wick draw the liquefied wax up to the flame, providing a steady source of fuel. If the wick is correctly sized for the candle, it burns cleanly and all the wax is consumed.

In general, wicks come in three main types:

- ✔ *Flat-braided wicks* vary in the number of plies used. In general, the more plies in the wick, the thicker it is, which makes it more suitable for larger candles. A medium-sized candle probably uses a 24- or 30-ply wick (meaning that the wick consists of 24 or 30 plies). If you have a smaller candle, you want a smaller number of plies; larger candles require a higher number.

- ✔ *Square-braided wicks* are shaped just like they sound: square. How the wicks are named differ with each manufacturer. Unlike flat-braided wicks, however, the number of plies used isn't indicated in the wick's name. After you become accustomed to working with these wicks, you can figure out your particular manufacturer's numbering system. In the meantime, though, follow the manufacturer's recommendation or try eyeballing the size.

- ✔ *Cored wicks* consist of plies braided around a metal, cotton, or paper core. The core is designed to help the wick stand up straight when the candle is poured and as it burns. You usually find that these wicks are named in easy-to-understand language: small, medium, and large. These wicks are usually attached to a *tab,* or flat metal piece at the bottom of a candle, so they're great to place at the bottom of container candles. (For information on how to tab your wick, see the section "Attaching a Tab to Your Wick," later in this chapter.)

  If you're burning a paper core wick, don't panic if you see a little smoke. That's typical for this type of wick.

Some cored wicks can and do contain lead, which is a toxic metal. You need to make sure that the candles you have burning in your home aren't releasing this dangerous toxin. The one good thing, however, is that lead core wicks haven't been available in the United States for many years. For more information, see the section "Avoiding Lead-Cored Wicks," later in this chapter.

Matching Your Wick to Your Candle

Any wick you choose should cause your candle to burn. But a well-chosen wick consumes all the melted wax at just the right pace, so that the wax doesn't drip off the candle and so that there's enough wax to keep the flame going. Fortunately, choosing your wick doesn't have to be difficult.

Table 4-1 lists the types of wick and which candles they're most appropriate for. (If you aren't familiar with the different types of wick, read the preceding section, "Identifying the Types of Wicks." I talk more about the various types of candles in Chapter 3.)

Table 4-1	Types of Wicks and Their Uses
Type of Wick	*Best For*
Flat braided	Tapers
Square braided	Beeswax candles, pillars, and other large candles
Metal cored	Any type of candle, but especially container candles, gel candles, votives, and tealights
Paper cored	Votives, tealights, and container candles (but don't use in gel candles)

Sizing up your wick

After you decide on the type of wick, you need to figure out what size of wick you need. That decision depends mainly on your candle's diameter.

If you're not sure what the diameter is, simply measure the width of your candle at its widest point.

Table 4-2 gives you a general guide for choosing your wicks. Remember, square-braided wicks don't always have a uniform naming system. I can tell you generally what you're looking for, such as a small, medium, or large wick, and you can compare the wicks accordingly.

Table 4-2	Sizing Your Wick
If Your Diameter Is . . .	*You Probably Want a Wick That's . . .*
0–1 inch	Extra small, 20 ply
1–2 inches	Small, 24 ply
2–3 inches	Medium, 30 ply
3–4 inches	Large, 36 ply
4 inches or more	Extra large, 40-plus ply

If your candle is large — say, more than 5 inches — use multiple wicks. You can simply divide your diameter by three to come up with how many wicks you need for candles larger than 5 inches. For example, if your candle has a diameter of 9 inches, you want to use three medium or large wicks. You should never use more than 5 wicks in a candle, however.

If you have several wicks and discover that they're not big enough for your candle, try braiding them together and priming them (see the section, "Priming the Wick," later in this chapter" for details). The thicker wick should do the job for you.

All things considered

Of course, you can't just measure your diameter and go. You need to consider other factors as well, such as:

- **The wax's melting point.** You want your wick to use just the right amount of wax. If it uses too little wax, your candle may drip because excess liquid is still in the candle. If your wick uses too much wax, your candle won't last because it's burning too fast. If your candle is having problems with burning or the amount of wax, check out Chapter 10 for troubleshooting tips.

- **What kind of additives you included.** If you've used additives (see Chapter 2) in your candle, you probably need a larger wick to avoid the chance of clogging. You also want to use a larger wick (preferably metal-cored) for a gel candle.

Lengthy issues

Figuring out the right wick length for your candle is a lot more cut and dried than sizing your wick: Simply take your candle's height and add four to six inches for a pillar candle or ½ to inch extra for a votive candle. That extra length gives you ample room to knot it on the bottom, as well as secure the wick at the top of the mold.

If you don't know your candle's height, just measure it.

If yiou make candles a lot or you don't know exactly how long a wick you need, just buy your wicks in rolls. That way, you can measure what you need for each candle that you make and not worry about not having enough wick.

Avoiding Lead-Cored Wicks

You probably know that lead poses a significant health hazard, especially to young children. Lead can harm internal organs and cause brain damage or developmental and behavioral problems. Lead even affects adults, causing digestive, muscular, and nervous system issues, to name just a few.

The most widely known substance to contain lead, of course, is paint. Although lead-based paint was taken off the market more than 20 yeas ago, homes with old paint are still around. Even if you live in a newer home or have repainted, don't think you're off the hook when it comes to lead. In fact, a lesser-known carrier of this dangerous toxin is candles, or rather lead-cored wicks.

Manufacturers added lead to their wicks because it helped support the wicks and made them burn longer. Although lead-cored wicks are no longer manufactured in the United States, thanks to a voluntary ban by the National Candle Association members, companies outside the U.S. continue to import in their inexpensive candles made with lead-cored wicks. If you aren't aware of this problem, then you may even have problematic lead-cored wicks in your home.

The National Candle Association recommends the following test for checking for lead in wicks. All you need is a piece of plain white paper. Simply rub the tip of an unburned wick on the paper. (Be prepared — carry one in your purse or wallet.) If you see a light gray mark on the paper, don't buy the wick. It contains a lead core.

Not all metal core wicks contain lead. Zinc-cored wicks and metal core wicks manufactured in the United States are perfectly safe. You just need to be cautious when you purchase candles made elsewhere.

If you're concerned about possible lead poisoning, you can have your doctor test you or your children or contact the National Lead Information Center at 800-424-5323. The Center also has a Web site, www.epa.gov/opptintr/lead/nlic.htm.

Priming the Wick

A *primed wick* is one that you (or the wick manufacturer) have thoroughly soaked with wax. Priming does several things for your wick. It

✔ Jump-starts the combustion process by getting wax into the wick before you even light the candle.

✔ Helps keep water droplets or additives from clogging the wick.

✔ Makes the wick stronger, so you have an easier job threading it inside the candle.

✔ Eliminates air inside the wick so that you don't have unsightly bubbles.

✔ Makes the wick more likely to stand on its own so that when you thread it through the top of the candle, it actually protrudes upright and not all drooped over.

Most of the time, you use a primed wick, but two general exceptions apply. (Each individual project in this book specifies whether you need to prime your wick.) Those two exceptions are

✔ If you're making gel candles, for example, use an unprimed wick. (See the section on gel candles, later in this chapter.)

✔ If you're creating taper candles by dipping them in wax, the dipping process automatically primes the wicks for you. Why bother with an extra step? (See Chapter 5 for a project on creating taper candles.)

You can buy wicks primed or unprimed. Priming isn't tough to do, though, so more than likely, you want to prime your own wicks, especially if you purchased a roll of wick to use for both paraffin and gel candles. (Again, you're already priming your wicks when you dip your candles.)

Here's how to prime your wicks. Figure 4-1 also walks you through the steps.

1. **Just as you'd melt wax for your candle, place your wax for priming in your double boiler.**

2. **Melt your wax until it reaches 190°F.**

3. **Bend your wick in half and dip it into the melted wax for approximately 5 minutes.**

   You may see bubbles escaping from the wick. Don't remove the wick from the wax until the bubbles have disappeared.

   If you're the impatient type or you like to multitask, you can leave your wick soaking in the wax for five minutes while you do other things.

4. **Straighten your wick and place it somewhere to dry.**

   If you run the wick between your thumb and index finger as it cools, it makes it smoother and easier to thread into your mold. The wick also looks better in your container candle or votive.

   You can use waxed paper, aluminum foil, or a candle rack. When the wick cools, it stiffens. You're all done!

Figure 4-1:
To prime
your wick,
just melt
your wax,
dip your
wick, and
cool.

Attaching a Tab to Your Wick

A *tabbed* wick is a wick that has a metal base (or *tab*) attached at the bottom of it, as shown in Figure 4-2. You may also hear a tab referred to as a *sustainer*.

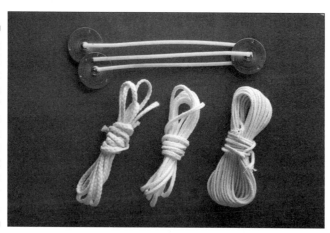

Figure 4-2:
A tabbed
wick
provides
support for
your wick so
it stands up
straight and
remains at
the bottom
of your
containers.

Tabs help your wicks stand upright and remain on the bottom of your container candles when you're pouring wax. Just as you can prime your wicks, you also can tab them.

You can purchase pretabbed wicks in the store. You can even purchase double-sided tabs that actually adhere to the bottom of the candle to ensure no movement.

High-collar tabs have a taller metal base and keep the wick from burning all the way down to the bottom of the candle. This extra height is especially important with gel candles, which have a higher melting point and are usually made in glass containers.

Make sure that your gel candle tabs are at least $\frac{7}{16}$ inches tall. Most tabs are shorter than this length, but you need to make sure that your tab extinguishes the flame well before the bottom of the container. (For more tips on working with gel candles, see the next section.)

To tab your wick, you need only a pair of pliers:

1. **Thread your wick into the open part of your tab (see Figure 4-3).**
2. **Close the tab around the wick using the pliers.**

   Gently squeeze on the metal. You now have a tabbed wick.

Figure 4-3:
To tab your wick, thread your wick into your tab and then squeeze it closed using your pliers.

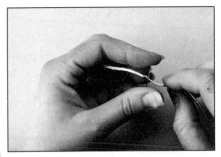 

Considering Gel Wicks

Although gel candles are a relatively new innovation, you can find wicks made especially for these container candles. If you can't find them, don't despair. You can use unprimed (not coated in wax) wicks.

Don't use primed wicks in your gel candles. When the paraffin wax melts, the cloudy mixture ruins your translucent gel candles.

If you're unsure if your wick is primed or unprimed, simply run your fingernail along it. If it's primed, you get wax on your fingernail. Of course, if you're not priming your wicks, then you're not removing the bubbles from them, either. In transparent gel candles, you notice the bubbles. As a result, if you're not using wicks formulated for gel candles, prime your wick to remove the air bubbles.

Gel candles are also better suited to high-collar tabbed wicks, which help the wick to stay on the bottom of the candle and to snuff out on its own. If you don't use a high-collar tab, the wick continues burning down to the bottom of the container, placing the flame in contact with the hot, melted gel, causing a likely fire hazard. (For more on tabs, see the section "Attaching a Tab to Your Wick," earlier in this chapter.)

Like everything else in life — think car, house, yard — gel candles require maintenance. In this case, I'm talking about wick maintenance. Keep your wicks less than ¼ inch tall. Otherwise, you may risk a fire. Because gel wax gets so hot, too much flame caused by an untrimmed wick may result in a fire — or simply spoil your candle's looks. (Remember, gel is translucent, and who wants to look at a sooty wick?) Fortunately, trimming a wick is easy. Just take your cooled gel candle (very important unless you want hot liquid gel everywhere!), turn it upside down so that the wick doesn't fall into your container, and, using scissors, trim the wick to ¼ inch or less.

Adding Your Wick

When you've settled on the perfect wick, you're ready to insert it into your candle mold. Most one-piece molds (see Chapter 3) have a hole at the bottom that allows you to thread your wick into your candle. Here's how it works:

1. **Thread your wick through the bottom of the mold, as shown in Figure 4-4.**

2. **Pull the wick to the top of the mold.**

3. **Reach to the bottom of your mold and pull the end of your wick tight.**

4. **When the wick gets to the top of the mold, simply tie it to a wick rod.**

   The rod lies across the top of your mold.

5. **Use mold sealer around the wick hole so that your wax doesn't leak out of your mold.**

   You're ready to add your wax.

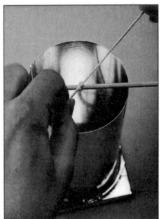
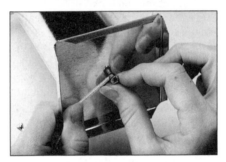
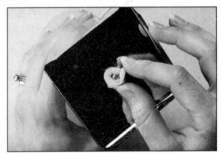

Figure 4-4:
Adding
your wick to
your mold.

Deciding Whether Your Wax and Wick Are a Match Made in Heaven

The real test to how well you matched your wick to your wax comes when you begin burning your candle. Does your candle smoke? Does the wick keep extinguishing? You can find solutions to those and other types of problems in Chapter 10. However, even if your candle burns and doesn't smoke, that doesn't mean that you've found wax and wick soul mates. You need to take a good, hard look at how your candle burns as well as figure out its burning rate before you give yourself a pat on the back.

Appearances count

You actually need to watch your candle's flame to figure out how well it burns. For starters, you want the flame to be steady (no flickering, please).

The following are a few other signs of a properly burning candle:

- ✔ Your burning wick should stand up straight or at a right angle.
- ✔ Your flame should be approximately an inch long.
- ✔ A small pool of wax should form around the wick; this pool should extend almost to the sides of the candle
- ✔ The candle should burn without a "tunnel" being formed along the sides of the wick.

Rate the burn

In addition to appearance, you also need to gauge your candle's *burn rate*, or how well your candle burns, to determine whether you've chosen the best wick.

To figure out your candle's burn rate per hour, do the following:

1. **Weigh your candle before you light it.**
2. **Burn your candle three hours.**
3. **Blow out your candle.**

4. **When the wax cools, reweigh all the wax that remains.**

If you have dripped wax, you need to go back and reformulate your candle or use a different wick.

5. **Subtract the new weight from the starting weight.**

For example, if your candle weighs 8 oz. when you start and 6 oz. when you finish, then the amount of wax it burned is 2 oz.

6. **Take the amount of wax burned and divide it by the number of hours burned to come up with your burn rate per hour.**

In this example, the new number is .66.

To find out how long your candle will burn, take your starting weight and divide that by your burn rate per hour. As you continue making candles, keep a log so that you know how well you're matching your wick to your candle. Your goal is to have a candle that burns as long as possible.

Changing your wick or wax can significantly alter your candle's performance. Take notes as you create your candles and if you're unsatisfied, try a different combination the next time around.

Chapter 5

Creating Simple Projects

· ·

In This Chapter

▶ Creating a molded candle

▶ Dipping tapers

▶ Working with beeswax

▶ Using containers as molds

▶ Jotting down notes about your recipes

· ·

*I*f you've read any part of this book, your creative juices are probably flowing. Whether you're digging through the trashcan in search of your empty yogurt cup from lunch (wash it, please!) or holding a freshly purchased pillar mold, this chapter is for you. You get to try your hand at what I call the basic projects: a molded candle, two dipped tapers, a rolled beeswax candle, and a container candle.

Always read through the project before you begin so that you can properly prepare your workspace and make sure that you have the necessary supplies. (For more on preparing your workspace and gathering appropriate supplies, see Chapter 1.)

Starting Simple: Basic Molded Candle

The type of candle you'll probably make the most is a basic molded candle. You can use this one basic technique to make many different types of candles. The type of mold you use doesn't matter; the steps are still pretty much the same. And if you're using a store-bought mold, professional-looking results are almost guaranteed (see Figure 5-1).

After you choose your mold, you need to figure out how much wax you need to melt. I give you the full details in Chapter 2, but basically you need to pour water into your mold and measure the amount you used. For every 3.5 fluid ounces of water, you need 3 ounces of unmelted wax.

Figure 5-1:
A basic
molded
candle
opens up a
realm of
possibilities.

Water can cause metal molds to rust so make sure that you thoroughly dry the mold after measuring or insert a plastic bag inside the mold before adding water. Also make sure that you record the mold's capacity so that you have the wax capacity for future reference.

Certain manufacturers label the mold with its wax capacity so that no measuring is necessary.

Don't have a kitchen scale? No sweat. For every 2 cups of water you use, you need approximately 1 pound of wax. As long as you're using wax that's prepackaged and weighed, you can just eyeball the required amount and break it off. (A hammer and screwdriver come in handy here.) Estimating is okay, as long as you err on the side of using too much, rather than too little, wax.

If you're using a metal mold, be warned that this method of measuring may cause it to rust if you don't dry it well. An alternative method of figuring out how much wax you need is to melt 2 pounds of wax, pour it into the mold you want to use, and then weight the finished product.

You then need to choose your wick. Chapter 4 gives you the scoop on matching your wick to your wax. After you chose your mold, determine the amount of wax you need, pick your wick, and follow these steps.

1. **Melt your wax to the package's specified temperature.**

   If you're recycling wax or you're unsure of the temperature, aim for 190°F and maintain that temperature for half an hour.

   Keep in mind that this number isn't the melting point of the wax, but quite a bit hotter because you need to pour the wax when it's about 190°F.

   In the future, label your recycled wax so that you know the proper melting point.

   If you're unsure of how to melt wax, see the detailed steps in Chapter 2.

2. **Spray your mold with a mold release, such as silicone or vegetable spray.**

   Using a releasing agent helps you remove the candle from the mold.

   If you make candles regularly, you may want to use commercial grade release spray instead of vegetable oil because over time, the vegetable oil can leave a film on your mold. However, if you make candles only on occasion, the vegetable oil spray works just fine.

3. **Cut your primed wick so that it's 2 inches longer than your finished candle's height and then insert it into your mold.**

   For instructions on inserting your wick, see Chapter 4.

   You can do Steps 2 and 3 prior to melting your wax, if you're worried about time or you prefer not to multitask.

4. **When your wax reaches the required temperature, add any additives, color, or scent.**

   Unless you're using a flexible mold (see Chapter 3), add stearin in proportion to 10 percent of your wax. (If you're using a flexible mold, use vybar.) Stearin has many benefits, as I describe in Chapter 2, but one in particular that is beneficial here is that it shrinks the wax. This shrinkage makes your candle easier to remove from the mold.

   When you add these ingredients, your wax's temperature will probably drop, so continue heating your wax a little longer until it reaches the proper temperature again.

   For information on choosing color and scent, as well as tips for using it, see Chapter 6.

5. **Remove your wax from the heat and slowly and smoothly pour it into your mold.**

   Be careful not to get any water into your wax. Chapter 2 offers tips on pouring your wax.

6. **Wait a few minutes and then gently tap the side of your mold to remove any air bubbles.**

7. **As your wax cools, poke holes in the wax around the wick to release tension.**

   If you don't, the wax pulls the wick off center and may create a concave section on the outside of the candle.

8. **After your wax has cooled quite a while, reheat the extra wax you saved and pour it into any holes that have occurred as the wax cools.**

   This step is called a *repour*.

9. **Let your wax cool almost completely and then do a second repour.**

   Don't rush this step, though. If you repour the wax while the candle is still hot and liquid, you're just adding more hot wax that has to shrink.

   After your candle has completely cooled, you're ready to remove it from the mold. You simply remove any mold sealer that you used, which should release the candle.

When you remove your candle from the mold, remember that the bottom of the mold now becomes the top of the candle.

If your candle isn't coming out of your mold, you may not have let it cool long enough. Wait a few hours and try again later.

After you've removed your candle from its mold, you're ready to make your candle look beautiful. Using a craft knife or other sharp object, level off the bottom of the candle. (The top of your mold is now the bottom of the candle.) Then, trim your candle's wick. Use a paper towel or cloth to wipe around your candle and remove any extra wax. Congratulations! Your candle is ready to burn.

Looking for Elegance: Basic Taper Candle

I vividly remember Pioneer Day in elementary school. During this annual day, parents volunteered to be pioneers and carried out their assigned tasks for the day — all so that their children could remember and tease them about it for years! Each parent handled a particular job. My mom made bread all day, and I also visited the soap-making and candle-making areas, of course. (How prophetic!)

The candle-making area was outside, and the "pioneers" melted wax over a huge cauldron. (Well, it was some type of big, black pot anyway.) Then they dipped wicks into the wax 20 or 30 times until they had created *tapers* — tall, slender, elegant-looking candles. They placed the candles over a clothesline or something like that until they dried. (I wasn't really paying attention to what it was hanging on at the time!) And that's all there was to it. When you're in fourth grade, it was all really quite impressive.

So okay, maybe you won't be able to create such a dramatic candle-production setup — or maybe you can if the neighborhood covenants aren't too restrictive about what you do in your yard! But you can make tapers pretty easily, and you don't even have to wear pioneer garb.

You can make basic taper candles (see the color section for an example of tapers) in two ways:

✔ Don your pioneer gear, pull out your cauldron, and start dipping. (Just don't let your bonnet or hat get in your eyes.)

✔ Buy a taper mold and follow the steps in the preceding section.

Because I tell you how to make a candle using a mold in the previous section, I focus only on how to dip a candle here.

Taking the dip with tapers

Dipping candles is a fairly easy process. The most difficult part of it for me is waiting for the wax to cool between each dip. If you're impatient like me, you may want to do what I do: I create several tapers at once so that I'm constantly dipping in rotation and don't have to wait.

The dipping process is pretty straightforward: You basically melt the wax, dip both ends of a wick in it, let it cool, and repeat 20 to 30 times or more until your candle is the desired width. (Most tapers are usually ½ inch in diameter, but don't feel like you need to follow the crowd. Just remember that if you make the candle too thick, you're creating a funny-looking pillar instead of a slim taper!) Fortunately, you don't have to do anything special to create the tapered look; it just naturally happens.

Here's how the process works:

1. **Figure out how tall you want each taper, add a couple of extra inches so that your wick protrudes, double that amount, and then add 4 inches for space.**

   When you make tapers, you usually dip in pairs, but you use only one wick. If you want to create a 6-inch taper, for example, then you take 6 inches plus 2 inches to get 8 inches. You multiply that number by 2 to get 16 inches (enough wick for two candles) and then add 4 inches to the total so that you have space in between the candle. (You don't want the ends of your wick to touch each other when you dip.) So to make two 6-inch tapers, you need to cut your wick to 20 inches.

2. **Tie a weight to each end of the wick so that it stays submerged and straight while you dip.**

   Rocks work just fine as weights. You remove these weights later when the wick is strong enough to stay straight.

3. **Melt your wax.**

   When you dip candles, you usually use paraffin wax or a mixture of beeswax and paraffin. Either way, you probably need to add the usual 10 percent stearin. (For more on stearin, see Chapter 2.) Melt twice the wax you think you need. You need to have plenty left over so that you have enough wax to dip in.

   Dipping works best when your wax is approximately 160°F to 170°F. For details on melting wax, see Chapter 2.

4. **Fill your dipping can with wax.**

   You need to make sure that your dipping can is tall enough to accommodate the size of the candle you want to make. Also fill the dipping can fairly full so that you can dip almost all the way up the wick. You have to keep adding wax to the dipping can throughout the process to keep it full.

5. **Dip your wick into your melted wax (see Figure 5-2).**

   You want to dip your wick deep enough so that you have only a couple of inches of undipped wick remaining. Don't linger too long on this dip, though. You want your wick in the wax only for a second. Plunge it in and then remove it smoothly so that the wax doesn't blob.

Figure 5-2:
To dip a taper, dip your trimmed wick into the melted wax, allow it to cool, and then redip your wick repeatedly until you reach your desired diameter.

The first time you dip your wick, you're actually priming it, so you can submerge it longer in the wax. (See Chapter 4 for details on priming your wick.)

I give you troubleshooting tips in Chapter 10, but basically, here's what you need to know at this point:

- If your taper looks bumpy, your wax isn't warm enough.

- If your wax isn't building up on your wick, your wax is too hot.

- If the wax isn't firming up enough between dips, you need to let it cool longer in between dips.

Make sure that the ends of your wick don't touch each other, or you end up with a wax glob. You can use your hands to keep the ends apart, or you may want to use a straw, dowel rod, or piece of cardboard. (Refer to Figure 5-2.)

6. Place your wicks over a rack or dowel rod until they cool.

The cooling process takes approximately 3 minutes. Basically, the wax should feel cool to your touch.

7. Repeat Steps 5 and 6 until your candle is the diameter you want.

When I said you needed patience, I wasn't kidding. You may have to dip your candles 20 or 30 times or even more. Every time you dip, more wax builds up on your wick. Eventually, your wick becomes two tapers.

If you want your surface to be glossy, then dip it immediately into cool water after your last dip.

8. Let your tapers cool a few hours before handling them and trimming your wick to ¼ inch.

Sizing the base

In general, taper candles are ⅞ inch in diameter at the bottom so that they can fit into most candleholders. If you're not using a mold, you probably need to cut the base of the candle down to that size.

Of course, if you already know which candle holders you'll be using, you can cut your candle's base down to that particular holder's size. To do so, use a craft knife to score around the base of your cooled candle. Then simply remove the strips of wax until your taper fits perfectly into the holder.

Sweetening Things Up: Beeswax Candle

A simple beeswax candle (see the color section) can create quite a buzz and may just be the perfect first candle for beginners. You don't need to melt any wax or use a lot of fancy equipment. You simply roll sheets of beeswax into a round candle. (You can easily make other shapes as well.)

This project in particular is ideal for young children. I made a beeswax candle with the help of my three-year-old daughter, Katie, and I didn't have to worry about her getting harmed by hot wax or making a mess.

The only downside is that beeswax is sticky at any temperature, and it gets even stickier when it's warm. (So don't let your child touch her hair when messing with this stuff!) But it's not so sticky that you and your youngster can't work with it. You just need to make sure that you don't pick up any extra fuzz. That stickiness can actually work in your favor because the beeswax sheets adhere to each other as you roll them.

When you roll your candle, you want your beeswax sheet to be at room temperature. Ideally, it's been at this temperature for at least a few days.

To roll a beeswax candle, you need two sheets of beeswax and a primed wick. Here's what you want to do:

1. **Cut your primed wick so that it's ¾ inch longer than the height of your finished candle.**

   If you're using a normal beeswax sheet, which measures 8 inches x 16 inches, your candle will be about 8 inches tall, so you want your wick to be approximately 8¾ inches. If you want to make two 8-inch tapers instead, just cut the sheet in half long ways and roll two candles.

   When you're working with beeswax, you want to use a wick that's one size larger than you would normally use. See Chapter 4 for details on choosing the correct size wick and for information about what to do if your wick isn't already primed.

2. **Lay your beeswax sheet on a hard surface and place your wick along the edge, as shown in Figure 5-3.**

3. **Apply pressure, smoothly but firmly rolling the edge of the sheet around the wick and continue rolling the beeswax into a cylinder shape.**

   You want to make sure that you're rolling straight; otherwise, your edges won't align. You also want to roll tightly enough so that you don't trap air between the layers, which can affect how well your candle burns.

   If you want to make a square candle, just flatten each side with a hard object as you roll. If you want to make a shorter candle, cut the short side of the beeswax sheet in half prior to rolling it.

Figure 5-3:
Making a
beeswax
candle is as
simple as
adding a
wick and
gently, but
tightly,
rolling it into
a candle.
Make sure
that you
apply
pressure
so the
beeswax
adheres
to itself.

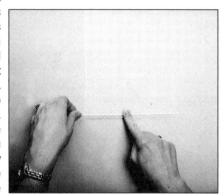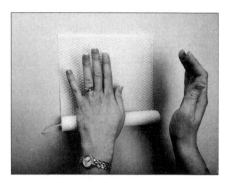

4. **When you reach the end of the first sheet, attach your second sheet of beeswax by firmly pinching the edges of each sheet together and then continue rolling.**

   For a larger candle, you can use as many sheets of beeswax consecutively until you reach your desired diameter.

5. **Trim your wick.**

   Wait at least a day, preferably longer, before lighting.

You want your beeswax to be at least room temperature or warmer, or it will break. If you're having trouble, try using a hairdryer to heat the sheets. But don't go too warm, or the wax may begin to melt and become a sticky mess.

Using Everyday Objects: Container Candle

If you're the creative type, you may find yourself gravitating toward container candles (see color section). In fact, they're one of my personal favorites. I love searching for different containers to hold my candles, and I also don't have to worry about the wax melting onto my carpet.

The technique for making a container candle is very similar to making a molded candle. The container, in essence, acts as your mold. The only difference is that you don't use stearin because you want the wax to adhere to the sides of your container. (Remember, you're not removing the candle from the mold.) Instead, you'll probably opt for 2 percent soft microcrystalline, which has the opposite effect of stearin. (See Chapter 2 for more on these additives.)

After you choose your container, determine the amount of wax you need, select the best wick, and follow these steps.

1. **Melt your wax to the package's specified pouring temperature.**

   If you're recycling wax or you're unsure about the temperature you want, heat the wax to 190°F. (If you're unsure of how to melt wax, see Chapter 2.)

2. **Cut your primed, tabbed wick so that it's 1 inch longer than your container.**

   You want your wick primed so that it's strong enough to stand up when you pour the wax. The tab helps your wick stay in place at the bottom of your container.

3. **When your wax reaches the required temperature, add any additives, color, or scent you want.**

   To find out about additives, see Chapter 2. For information on choosing color and scent, as well as tips for using both, see Chapter 6.

   If you add anything to your wax, your wax's temperature will probably drop, so heat it a little longer until it reaches the proper temperature again.

4. **Remove your wax from the heat and slowly and smoothly add a ½-inch layer of wax to your container.**

   Chapter 2 offers tips on pouring your wax.

5. **Rest your tabbed wick in the center of your candle.**

   You want the wick to rest on the bottom of the container, so it needs to be tabbed. If your wick isn't tabbed, you can easily do it yourself, as long as you have the supplies. (See Chapter 4 for more on wicks.)

6. **After the wax cools, add another ½-inch layer of wax.**

   You want only about an inch at the top of your container that's uncovered by wax.

7. **As the wax begins to harden, poke holes around the wick.**

8. **Pour another ½-inch layer of wax to fill in the holes you pricked.**

   This step reduces the temperature of the wax so that your candle doesn't shrink as much. It also helps you avoid the nasty center hole that sometimes develops as the wax burns. If you see this concave in a container candle, you know the person probably skipped Step 6.

9. **Repeat Steps 7 and 8 until the container is full and the surface remains level.**

10. **Allow the candle to cool completely.**

11. **Trim your wick to ¼ inch.**

Glass tends to break if it comes into contact with a flame for a long time, so trimming your wick is especially important when working with this type of container. I experienced this surprise in my first apartment when a candle I was burning in a beautifully shaped glass holder suddenly shattered — and scared the living daylights out of me. If you're using glass and you think that the length of the wick may cause the wick to touch the sides of your container or candle holder, by all means shorten the wick's length. Other ways to help avoid this problem include making sure that your wick is centered when you pour your wax and that you're using a good quality glass container that can withstand heat.

Gel candles are a whole different ballgame. Although the technique you use when making a gel candle is similar, candle gel is highly combustible, so you need to take extra precautions. Don't try using the preceding steps to create a gel candle. Instead, head to Chapter 8 for detailed instructions.

Broadcasting Your Successes — and Remembering Your Failures

You did it! Whether you're silently thinking it or loudly running around the house screaming and clutching your perfect candle, you finally mastered the perfect wax creation. You can't wait to make one for Aunt Lois for Christmas, your candle-loving sister for her birthday, and your hard-to-buy-for brother-in-law just because. (Yeah, he sure could use a scented lavender candle to lighten up, you laugh to yourself!)

No bubbles this time, you smile to yourself when you calm down from your sprint. A perfectly centered wick, you think with a grin. As you twirl the candle around, eyeing it from every angle, you allow your grin to turn into a pleased chuckle. "This guy may just be the perfect candle," you think gleefully.

Unfortunately, if you don't write down what you did to create that masterpiece — worthy of a magazine cover, really, you continue to preen — you won't be laughing for long. Taking notes as you work not only helps you duplicate your successes, but also it helps you remember what doesn't work so that you *don't* duplicate your failures.

I can't stress enough the importance of taking notes on every candle you make. Maybe the candle doesn't burn great, but you love the scent. Or maybe you finally found the exact size wick for your wax. Whatever you've done — good and bad — you need a record.

Recording information about your candle-making process enables you to repeat your successes and problem solve your failures. If you don't know what you did right, you can't do it again. If you don't know what you did wrong, you can't avoid repeating your mistake. Why waste time and energy making a candle that doesn't work? I bet you have a great memory. I used to have great memory. Well, I think I did anyway. I can't really remember. My point here is to not rely on your memory. It may not be as great as you remember.

If you're trying to correct a candle problem, try changing one variable — and only one — the next time you make the candle. Don't change everything at once. You won't be able to pinpoint what works and doesn't work.

When you're taking notes during your project, record some basic information (see Figure 5-4 for a form you can copy and use):

- ✔ **The type and amount of wax you're using.** Also make sure that you write down whether you had too much or — woe is me — not enough wax for your project. Remember that you can re-use extra wax, but if you didn't melt enough — well, let's just say you can start over and remelt the wax.

- ✔ **The amount, if any, of additives, you're using.** You may not have used any additives, and maybe adding 10 percent stearin can solve your problems. Or maybe you used way too much vybar — or even used stearin in a container candle, which is a definite no-no. If you don't know what you did, you can't fix it. (For more on additives, see Chapter 2.)

- ✔ **The temperature you melted the wax to.** If you don't melt the wax to the right temperature, you're in for trouble, particularly if you're dipping tapers. The easiest way to solve this problem is to read your wax's packaging to find the specified temperature and then use a thermometer to ensure that you're melting it to the correct degree.

Too hot can be too much of a good thing. You may have a flame, all right, but it won't be one that's in the shape of a candle. (Okay, so I'm exaggerating a little bit, but gel wax really can catch on fire!)

✔ **The type and amounts of color and scent you used, if any.** This record is especially important when you're combining different colors and fragrances to create a certain shade or aroma. In this chapter, you don't add color or scent, but Chapter 6 gives you all the details you need to give your candles this wonderful accent.

✔ **The size of wick you used.** The key to a great-burning candle is to match the wick to the wax. When you finally master it, you'll want to refer to your notes. For more on choosing a wick, see Chapter 4.

✔ **Your daydreams.** Write down how you feel about traveling to xxx (insert tropical location of your choice), sitting on the beach, drinking margaritas all day, and having a bronzed xxx (insert stud or beauty, depending on your orientation) wait on you hand and foot. Okay, now it's time to wake up and get back to reality (and your candle making).

When you're finally ready to burn your candle, think of it as a science experiment. Take a good, hard look at it and observe how it burns. What do you like? What would you like to correct next time? Take a peek at Chapter 10 to find out how to fix what you don't like. Remember, a little time up front minding the details can save you time and effort in the long run.

Writing It All Down

Wax

The type of wax: _____

The amount of wax: _____

What I thought of the results: _____

How I'd like to improve this project next time: _____

_____

Additives

The type of additives: _____

The amount of additives: _____

What I thought of the results: _____

How I'd like to improve this project next time: _____

_____

Temperatures

Temperature poured at: _____

Color and scent

Color or color combination used: _____

Scent or scent combination used: _____

What I thought of the results: _____

How I'd like to improve this project next time: _____

_____

Figure 5-4:
Use this
form to take
pertinent
notes during
your candle
project.

Wick

Size of wick used: _____

How the candle burned: _____

Miscellaneous _____

Part II
Jazzing Up Your Candles

The 5th Wave
By Rich Tennant

©RICHTENNANT

"Please hand me that mallet and a box of chocolate chip cookies. The kids want to make scented candles for their bedrooms."

In this part . . .

*I*f you're a pro at making candles or you're just eager to take your candles up another notch, then this part is for you. Not only do you find out how to experiment with color and scent, but you also discover how to add decorative touches, such as embellishments, stamps, and stencils. You also can experiment with some more advanced projects, such as gel candles, floating candles, layered candles, and multiwick candles. You also find out the secrets of caring for and displaying your wax. Lastly, Chapter 10 clues you in to common candle challenges. Not only do you find out how to solve appearance, color, and scent problems, but you also discover how to fix many technique issues as well.

Chapter 6

Adding Color and Scent

• •

• •

A candle doesn't seem quite finished until it has a little color and scent. Whether you're dyeing your candle to match your room or adding fragrance to match your mood, this chapter guides you through the must-dos and the must-don'ts.

Coloring Your Candles

Coloring candles is like coloring a page. You have a blank canvas on which to create your magic, and you're in charge. No one can tell you that the sky has to be blue or the grass green; the perfect picture and candle are what you want at that moment.

Whether your day is yellow, blue, or a one-of-a-kind shade day, coloring candles is fun. In fact, when you combine color with scent, it can be mood enhancing. Fortunately, coloring candles isn't difficult; it's just one extra step in the candle-making process.

If you want to add decorative finishes, such as paint, wait until the overdipping process. For more on overdipping, see Chapter 8.

Coloring with dye

You'll most likely use dye to add color to your candles. More often than not, you want to use solid wax dye disks or liquid dyes. Both are oil-soluble, which is the key when adding color. (Alcohol-based coloring agents evaporate as you melt the wax, whereas water-based agents, such as food coloring, separate and end up at the bottom of the melting pot under the wax because wax and water don't mix.)

No matter what type of wax you use, be careful. Dye colors (or stains) what it comes in contact with, and that includes your clothes and plastic molds. Consider wearing plastic gloves, especially if you're going out that evening!

You don't have to worry about coloring beeswax, which you roll and don't melt. Just buy it in precolored sheets.

Although you can buy special dyes designed specifically for gel wax, you don't need to. You can use the same types of dyes that you use to color paraffin wax. Whenever possible, though, go with liquid dyes as opposed to wax-based dyes because the latter can cloud the gel.

Solid or liquid wax dye

Also called candle dye, the solid version of this dye comes in either disks, chips, or squares (see Figure 6-1). The dye is basically wax and concentrated color and melts in plain heated wax. Liquid dyes come in small bottles, and you just squeeze a few drops of dye into your melted wax.

Solid or liquid dyes are the easiest to use, although powder dyes stand up better to the test of time. (See the following section for more on powder dyes.)

Figure 6-1:
Solid wax dye disks are an easy way to add color to your candles.

Color me beautiful

Although pure wax crayons can color your candles, you shouldn't use them unless you absolutely have to — and I can't imagine when that would be the case. From a purely aesthetic point, your crayon's color, although true on coloring paper, doesn't look the same when your wax hardens. Second, and most important, crayons can clog your wick and affect how your candles burn. If you truly think you need to use crayons or you just want to give them a try, use them on the wax you overdip with. (For more on the overdipping process, see Chapter 8.)

How much wax the disk colors varies from manufacturer, so check the instructions; generally, one disk colors about 4½ pounds of wax. Most of the time, you dice the disk because you aren't melting that much wax at once. If, for example, you tint half that amount, then you want to use half the disk, and so on. If you want to acquire a pastel shade, determine how much you'd normally use, and then use a little bit less of the disk.

Powder dye

Professional candlemakers usually opt for powder dyes because the colors they render last longer. These strong dyes require only a small amount to tint large amounts of wax, which is one reason the general public shies away from them. You also risk inhaling the ground powder. In addition, you have to be willing to order and purchase huge quantities of the wax at once. Because of the downsides of powder dye, if you're not selling your candles, I advise sticking with solid wax dye (see preceding section).

If you do opt to use powder dye and you're having trouble dissolving your powder, then add stearin and premelt a small batch of wax with the dye prior to adding it to your wax.

Blending your colors

The hardest part of dyeing your wax may be getting the shade of color you want, and that takes practice. In general, you'll have no trouble finding primary colors (red, yellow, and blue) and, depending on where you're shopping, even other colors.

If you don't find the color you want, though, don't hesitate to blend colors to try to come up with the color that works for you. But don't get too carried away as you're combining colors — too much dye can affect how your candle burns, and too many colors tends to end up as a funky reddish-brown shade. (See Chapter 10 for more information on burning problems you may encounter.)

Coloring candles isn't black and white

You'd think if you added only black dye to your candle, it would be black, and that white would be white. Unfortunately, coloring candles isn't a black-and-white issue.

First, with black, if you use an opaque wax, you end up with more of a gray than a black. So if you want to make a black candle, melt leftover pre-colored wax to make your candle and then add black to it. White also poses a problem, but for different reasons. For some reason, chalky white dye doesn't burn well, so if you really want this color, use it as an overdip layer. (See Chapter 8 for more on overdipping.)

Don't think you can be sneaky and get away with pearly white, either. It doesn't melt very well, so you have to break it into small chips and melt it separately with a small amount of wax at a higher temperature. Why go to all the trouble for plain-Jane colors, though? I say if you're going to use color, have fun with it and use a dye that shouts color instead.

If you want a darker shade of any color, just add a dab of black dye. If you want a lighter shade, just add less dye.

Keep in mind that the wax type you use affects how the color appears. Gel wax, for example, is clear and needs less color than an opaque wax, such as paraffin, requires. However, even opaque waxes vary in how they take color, so the best thing you can do is to experiment.

Along those same lines, the color of your cooled wax won't resemble the perfect color you created in hot wax. If the color is important to you, then melt a small batch of wax, reduce the amount of color you're adding in proportion to the amount of wax, and then make a votive candle or just drop a few drops on wax paper. When it cools, you'll know what color you'll really end up with.

Dyeing your candle wax

Coloring your candle literally requires just one extra step — adding the color to your wax. To add color to your molded candles or your gel candles:

1. **Melt your wax as usual.**

   See Chapter 5 for instructions on how to make a basic candle.

2. **When the wax reaches 190°F, stir your dye into the wax, as shown in Figure 6-2.**

   Keep stirring until you don't see any streaks. Don't overstir, though, because stirring too much incorporates air bubbles into your wax. (See Chapter 10 for more on avoiding air bubbles.)

3. **Pour your wax into the mold and finish your candle as usual.**

Figure 6-2:
Thoroughly
stir your
dye into
melted
wax and
then pour
it into
your mold.

Here are a few tips to consider during the process:

- ✔ **Stearin makes your colors more vibrant, but at the same time, it can affect your candle's burning ability.** If you decide to add stearin, melt the wax and stearin together and then add your dye to your melted wax. (For more on stearin, see Chapter 2.)

- ✔ **If you don't want to worry about adding color, then consider buying predyed wax.** It comes in many colors, and all you have to do is melt it as you would any wax.

- ✔ **If you want to color your dipped candles, just add the dye to your melted wax.** Then dip your wicks as usual. (See Chapter 5 for detailed instructions.)

- ✔ **If you didn't add color to your candle when you made it, it's not too late.** You can give your candle an outer layer of color by overdipping it in dyed wax. (For more information, see Chapter 8.)

- ✔ **Don't waste your leftover colored wax.** You can use it in layered candles, as well as when you make black candles. In case you forgot your elementary art class days, when you combine different colors, you get black. (For more on layered candles, see Chapter 8.)

When you color your candles, make sure that you write down what form of color you used, as well as how much dye and wax. That way, you can repeat your triumphs and avoid your failures. (For more on what to write, see Chapter 5.)

Playing with Fragrance

Whenever I work, I can't stop myself from lighting a lemon-scented candle. I close the door to the office, and before long the fragrance fills the room. Not only is the smell soothing and relaxing, but also it helps me think more clearly and focus on the job at hand.

If, like me, you're a fan of scented candles, then you'll like the idea of adding your favorite scents to your wax creations. Although you can find scented candles in almost any department, craft, or candle store, the scent you want may not always come in a candle design that you like or can use.

Plain paraffin wax doesn't emit a fragrance as it burns, although other waxes, like beeswax and bayberry, have their own beautiful aroma and don't require a fragrance. For more on waxes, see Chapter 2.

Choosing your form

You can add fragrance to your candles in many ways, but you must use an oil-based form of scent. Water-based and alcohol-based fragrances, such as perfumes, simply evaporate or don't mix when you add them to the hot wax. The following sections describe the most common ways to scent your candle.

Candle fragrances

Candle fragrances are basically synthetic scents made solely for the purpose of scenting wax (see Figure 6-3). These fragrances go by many names, such as candle perfume or fragrance oils, and come in several forms: liquid, and solid. All are synthetic and pre-scented. The type you buy doesn't matter.

Many people don't want to use synthetic scents in their candles. If you're into aromatherapy — which involves using natural scents to affect your everyday moods — then you may want to add scents by using essential oils, which I describe in the next section. (See Chapter 19 for more information about aromatherapy.)

Figure 6-3:
You can use
synthetic
fragrances
formulated
especially
for candles
to add scent
to your
candles.

You can scent your gel candles by using fragrances designed for candles, but you're better off not venturing into the land of essential oils. Because gel wax has a higher *melting point* (the temperature at which the wax liquefies) than other waxes, you're in danger of starting a fire because most fragrances' *flash points* (the temperatures when they catch fire) are much lower (140°F to 220°F) than gel wax's melting point. If your scent's flash point manages to stand up to the gel's high melting temperature, you then have to make sure that the scent works in mineral oil. To do so, place 1 drop of scent into 3 drops of mineral or baby oil and let it stand 5 minutes. You don't want to see any separation. If you notice a separation, then the fragrance won't break down in the gel wax, and your wax will cloud. You can also sometimes find scent specially formulated for gel candles. If you can find it, your best bet is to go this route because you know it's been tested for these two concerns.

Essential oils

Although an aromatherapy candle sounds wonderful in theory, unfortunately, in practice, the results aren't good. Very few essential oils work well in candles. Often times, the oils clog the wick, making it difficult for the candle to burn. Other times, the scent simply doesn't survive the process.

Keeping Father Time at bay

Blame it on the sun or growing old — your hair color fades to gray or lightens. Candles are no different. Before you know it, old age creeps up on your candles and fades their once vibrant colors. (At least candles don't wrinkle!) Age is particularly hard on pinks and purples. You also may notice more of a color change on your overdipped candles (see Chapter 8) because the wax is a thinner layer. Unfortunately, you can't do much about these changes. (No such thing as plastic surgery for candles.) But, the biggest prevention, of course, is storing your candles out of direct light — sunlight bleaches your candles. Furthermore, make sure that you use your candles as quickly as possible.

If you want your color to last a little longer because you're using your candles for decoration, then you can consider purchasing an *ultraviolet inhibitor*. Available in craft stores, this additive limits the fading, but doesn't entirely prevent it. If you decide to give a UV inhibitor a try, then add the amount specifically recommended by the manufacturer.

Despite these warnings, if you still want to try to scent your candles with essential oils, then check out Chapter 19. I give you the lowdown — as well as the caveats — on scenting your candle with essential oils.

Adding scents

Adding scent isn't difficult; like adding color, it really is just one extra step in the process. But make sure that you remember two important points:

- ✔ **Don't add too much scent.** If you add too much scent to your wax, you'll have *mottling* (white splotches within the candle), oil coming out of your candle, smoke, or soot — not good things. In general, use approximately ½ teaspoon scent per pound of wax.

- ✔ **Add your scent at the last possible moment.** If you add it to your wax too early, you risk losing the scent to evaporation.

If you're working with gel candles, add your scent at approximately 210°F. That way, you don't have to stir as much because the gel is more liquid. The less you stir, the less chance you have of incorporating bubbles.

You can add scent to your candles in two ways:

- ✔ **Add scent to your candle wax just before you pour it into its mold or container.** Don't use this method with plastic molds because the oils can damage your mold.

✔ **Soak your candle's wick in your fragrance before you prime it.** This way works best with essential oils and helps their fragrance last longer as well. Use this method if you're working with plastic molds.

Remember, though, that soaking your wick before priming may affect your candle's burning qualities.

Don't think that you can just add a few drops of scent onto an existing candle and light it. The oils, not the wax, burn first, and you won't have any smell. Rather, the burning oil produces smoke.

How you add your scent to the melted wax depends on the form of your fragrance:

✔ Just stir *liquid* scent into your melted wax. In general, you need approximately one ounce of fragrance oil to one pound of wax.

✔ If you're using *powder* scent, dissolve it in melted stearin and then mix it into your melted wax.

✔ *Solid* scent usually comes in wax squares or blocks. Just break them off as necessary and add to your melted wax as usual.

The biggest complaint when it comes to adding scent is that the fragrance doesn't last the life of the candle. Your best bet is to use a candle fragrance that's specifically designed for candles.

Although candle additives help your candles retain scent, they also affect your candle's burning quality. Try to find a balance or switch to a stronger scent.

Chapter 7

Decorating Your Candles with Flair

*I*f you enjoy visiting craft stores and are always looking to incorporate other techniques into your hobbies, then you'll love this chapter. Not only do you get to enjoy making candles, but you also get to try your hand at several popular craft techniques, including painting, embossing, stamping, stenciling, and decoupaging.

Venturing into Appliqué

The word *appliqué* describes a technique with a name that's harder to pronounce than it is to actually do. Appliqué is simply the process of attaching shaped wax to the outside of your candle (see Figure 7-1). You can apply simple shapes, such as circles, or you can intricately create designs, such as flowers. If you're a creative type, then you're probably thinking of a zillion things you can attach to create a look that personalizes your candle.

Figure 7-1:
Appliqué candles are easy to create. The hardest part may just be choosing which wax shape to attach.

What you need to remember

If you're the type of person who doesn't like to rush, then appliqué probably isn't for you. Those cute little wax shapes dry quickly, which means you have to work fast.

Use these following tips when you're working with appliqué:

- ✔ Buy yourself more time by using dip-and-carve wax or paraffin wax with a low melting point.

- ✔ You'll have an easier time if the candle and the wax are both a little warm, so consider setting them in warm water or using a hairdryer on a low setting to warm them up a bit.

  If you're opting for the hairdryer, don't overheat your wax. You risk damaging the appliqué.

How you do it

First, you need to choose and create the wax shapes that you want to attach to the candle. The easiest, although arguably less creative, approach is to purchase precut wax. You then remove the paper from the back of the wax and simply attach the pieces to your candle. (If you can't find the precut wax sheets in your local craft store, then check out Appendix A for a list of suppliers.)

To make your own wax shapes:

1. **Pour your melted wax on an oiled board or old cookie sheet (see Figure 7-2) and then let the wax cool until it's firm but still soft enough to work with.**

   The idea is to create a surface on which you can cut out shapes.

2. **Cut out your shape.**

   For the best results, try using a cookie cutter. You can also use a small cake-decorating cutter.

3. **Quickly and gently press the shape onto your candle.**

   When you get the shape in just the right position, apply firm pressure. Try to press somewhere where it isn't obvious, such as the base of the appliqué, to avoid fingerprints. If you do get fingerprints, gently smooth them out with a craft knife or spoon.

Figure 7-2: To appliqué, form a sheet of melted wax, cut out your design, and apply the shape to your candle.

4. **Continue cutting and applying shapes until you have the design you want.**

   You may need to reheat the wax with a hairdryer or remelt it again in your melting pot, depending on your work speed.

You can easily break hardened wax, so be careful during the project, as well as when the candle is finished. If you can, purchase appliqué wax, which is specially formulated for this type of work. Beeswax also works well.

Embedding Items in Your Candle

Chances are that you've seen a candle that actually has some object lodged inside it, such as shells or wax chunks (see Figure 7-3). Gel candles, in particular, are known for their seascape and fruit effects. But paraffin wax can spotlight objects like shells, marbles, and flowers just as well as gel can. Fortunately, this classy little embellishment is an easy effect to achieve.

What you need to remember

Although you have creative license when embedding objects, don't embed just anything. Follow these tips when choosing and embedding items:

- ✔ If an item burns outside a candle, it will burn inside your candle as well; nonflammable items are best.

- ✔ Objects can cause bubbles in your candles, so if you want to avoid bubbles, consider warming your container prior to pouring and then pour your wax as slowly as possible.

- ✔ You can see your gel candle embedments clearly; paraffin wax gives you a little more room for error.

- ✔ Always clean your embedments.

- ✔ Don't place an object too close to the wick, which may extinguish when it reaches that point.

If you're making a gel seascape candle, don't use dried sea life, such as a starfish. Beautiful as it looks, the sea life will eventually bloat and look awful. (Shells, on the other hand, are okay to use.) For more tips on making gel candles, see Chapter 8.

Figure 7-3:
You can
embed wax
chunks into
your candle.

How you do it

Depending on what you're adding and where you want it to end up in your candle, you can embed items in one of two ways:

- ✔ **Place your embedment at the bottom of your container and then add your wax:** Use this technique mostly for gel candles (see Figure 7-4). After you add your wax, make the candle as you normally would, taking care to remove bubbles. If you're using a heavy embedment, you don't need to glue it down. Otherwise, if you're making a container candle, you can use fast-setting epoxy glue, available at most stores, which also helps place items at various heights. Just place a little glue on the bottom of your object, and then press it down on the bottom of your container.

- ✔ **Add your wax and then add your embedment:** Make your candle, but instead of allowing it to cool completely, wait until you see a ½-inch thick film on top, which takes about 10 minutes. Cut a hole in the wax. Using a spoon, return the soft wax in the center to your melting pot, and then add your embedments where you want them — for example, place them into the soft wax on the sides on the candle. Remelt the wax and pour it back into the hole. Your embedment appears to float within the candle.

Figure 7-4:
To make a
gel candle,
add your
embed-
ments first,
add glue if
necessary,
and then
pour your
wax.

- You can also embed objects by making a core candle. You then place that candle into a larger mold and fill the perimeter with your items. You then pour wax into the mold. Dried flowers, spices, and other typically flammable materials are fine to use with this method because the wick is sized for the diameter of the core candle and, ideally, shouldn't extend out to the objects.

Painting Designs on Your Candles

Trust me, I'm not an artist, but I love the look of decorative paint designs on candles (see color section) — even mine! You can make your designs as simple or exotic as you want, depending on your artistic talent. Your candle's surface is the ideal canvas for your creativity.

Painted snowflakes, a pumpkin, or a festive "Ho, Ho, Ho" add simple seasonal touches to your candles and don't require you to be Monet.

Even if you don't want to spend the time or clean up the mess from making a candle, you can still have fun by decorating store-purchased candles. Buy a plain white or red candle and paint something festive on it to spice it up.

What you need to remember

Most of the time, your weapons of choice are acrylic paints. You can buy these water-based paints at most craft stores. Acrylic paints make a good first painting choice because they're easy to use.

If you want, you can even use basic hobby paints. They're not very expensive, but, of course, you get what you pay for. Your coverage isn't as good as when you splurge for acrylic paints (which are still cheap, even though they cost a little bit more than hobby paints; you can buy a two-ounce bottle of acrylic paint for less than a $1 at most stores).

You can buy special candle paint at craft stores.

You also can "paint" with hot colored wax or beeswax, although their quick cool-down time means that you have to brush quickly and maintain the wax temperature often by remelting or constantly heating. (See Figure 7-5 for examples of paint that you can use.)

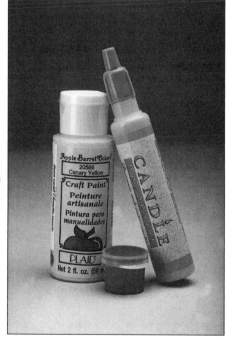

Figure 7-5: Both wax paint and acrylic paint add a decorative flair to a plain candle.

Anyone can paint and have a great time, but your results depend on a few factors. Keep these few tips in mind:

- ✔ **Add a little dish detergent to your acrylic paint.** The detergent makes the paint stick better to the candle.

- ✔ **Concentrate your painting on the sides of the candle, not its top.** Otherwise, the paint may get on your wick and affect your candle's burning quality.

- ✔ **Don't use too much acrylic paint.** Paint isn't wax, so it doesn't burn as well. Use too much, and you may end up affecting your candle's burning qualities.

- ✔ **Paint smudges, so watch your fingers as you work around the candle.** Consider placing your candle in a candleholder and rotating the holder as you paint each side. Just make sure that you cover the holder with plastic to protect it.

- ✔ **Pay attention to dirt.** Not only do you want a clean work surface, but you also need to wipe down your candle as well. Use a damp cloth, but make sure that you completely dry the candle before you begin painting.

- ✔ **Start with a simple design.** You'll have a much easier time making large brush strokes with a large brush than doing a lot of detail work. Don't be too detailed in your plans the first few times you attempt to paint. Start simple.

How you do it

Painting your candle's surface isn't difficult. In my eyes, the hardest part is choosing your design and paint colors. I actually love to paint my candles because it helps me connect to my preschooler, who enjoys painting as well. (Of course, I'm using acrylic paints to enhance my candles, and she's using watercolor paints to color her coloring books!)

If you have an extra candle, why not give it your child to paint? You can also allow your child to paint candles to decorate his or her bedroom. (Just don't allow them to burn them.)

After you choose your design, clean your candle, and prepare your workspace and paints, you're ready to start painting:

1. **(Optional) Using your paintbrush, place dots on the candle where you want each design to end up.**

   This step (see Figure 7-6) ensures that you're spacing your designs evenly around the candle. If you're painting only one design on your candle, then you don't have to do this step.

Figure 7-6:
Place dots where you want to paint your design and then start painting.

If you're painting on only one side of the candle, choose the most attractive side as the front of your candle.

2. **Paint your design on the candle.**

   If you're layering colors or designs, allow each coat to dry before adding another layer or color.

3. **After each coat of paint dries, continue painting your next layer or color.**

4. **When you're done painting, let your candle dry at least four hours before burning.**

   To be safe, wait 24 hours before lighting.

Trying Sponge Painting

You've probably heard about using a sponge to give your painted walls a textured effect, but you may not be aware that you can sponge paint your candles as well (see color section). Because the sponge has an irregular surface, it gives your item's surface an interesting look and softens the item at the same time.

Choosing the correct brush

I was amazed at the number of brush options available at craft stores. They were as cheap as a dollar or two and went all the way up to $15 or so. You can buy individual brushes or entire sets. Sometimes the individual brushes cost as much as an entire set of cheaper brushes.

So what's a painter to do? You'll enjoy yourself more and be happier with the results if you use a quality artist brush. Sure, you can paint with cheaper brushes, but your hard work and effort won't get the same results.

I do have one caveat, though: If you're painting with wax, don't use a nice brush. You'll probably end up throwing the brush away anyway because wax is extremely difficult to remove from bristles. And speaking of bristles, if you're working with actual paint and not wax, go with manmade fibers, which can stand up to acrylic paints. Choose a small brush for detailed work, such as painting small letters or shapes, and a larger brush for more coverage. If you paint a lot, you'll probably develop quite a collection of brushes.

What you need to remember

Because you're using paint, many of the tips in the "Painting Designs on Your Candles" section, earlier in this chapter, apply. In general, you probably want to use acrylic paint with a little added dish detergent. Make sure that your candle's surface is clean. Fortunately, you don't have to worry about smudges as much because the overall look of the candle is a blended one.

How you do it

Sponge painting is even easier than normal painting, especially because you're not striving to achieve a certain design but instead an overall look. In effect, your sponge functions as your brush.

To sponge paint:

1. **Squeeze your acrylic paint onto a foam plate.**

   A quarter-sized portion is plenty.

2. **Dip a damp sponge into the paint.**

3. **Dab the sponge over your candle until the entire surface is covered.**

4. **If you want to add another color, wait for the paint to dry and then repeat Steps 1 through 3.**

5. **Wait for the paint to dry before burning.**

Leaving Your Mark: Embossing

Embossing is a popular craft these days. Basically, *embossing* is where you make an outdent, or raised pattern, on a surface. My first encounter with embossing came when I embossed copper leaves to place on my scrapbook pages. I used a special tool to draw lines on the bottom surface of my leaves. When I flipped over the leaves, I had veins on the leaves' surfaces. Cool, huh? And the best part was that it was so easy to do. Soon I started embossing my candles (see Figure 7-7).

What you need to remember

You can emboss your candles in several ways.

- Purchase a mold that already has the lines premade inside of it (see Figure 7-8).

Figure 7-7:
Embossing
your
candles
gives them a
raised look.

Figure 7-8:
The easiest
way to
make an
embossed
candle is to
use a mold.

✔ Using everyday, waterproof glue to attach your design along the wall of your mold before you pour the wax. (Don't forget to spray a release agent on the mold and design.)

✔ Scoring lines on the inside of your mold. (Keep in mind any alteration to the inside of your mold is permanent and also many cause problems removing the candle.)

✔ Using corrugated cardboard as an insert in your mold.

✔ Using a glue gun to draw on your candles. (The glue is nonflammable and nontoxic, so you don't have to worry about a fire or health hazard.)

If you use a glue gun, try to use glue that matches the color of your wax. If not, you can paint over the glue so that it matches your wax.

If you like the look of embossing but don't want to go to all the trouble, you can buy embossed votive holders for your candles.

How you do it

The easiest way to emboss your candle is to use a storebought mold and form your candle in the usual way. However, you're limited in your selection, so you may want to go a more labor-intensive route to achieve your special look.

If you're using a cardboard piece inside your mold, make your candle as usual. When you remove the mold, the vertical lines from the corrugated mold stand out on your candle's surface.

I personally prefer to use a glue gun (see Figure 7-9) when I emboss my candles. I like to see what I'm working with; I feel more in control if I can watch the design come to life. To emboss with your glue gun, use your heated glue gun to draw lines of glue on your candle. You want the glue to touch the candle's surface before you move to another part of the design.

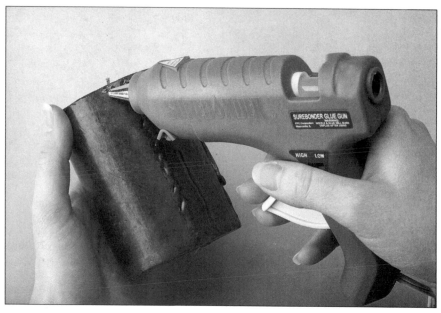

Figure 7-9:
A glue gun enables you to emboss your finished candles from the outside instead of from inside the mold.

If glue threads followed your glue gun when you pulled it away, let them **dry** and then just cut them off.

Working with Stamps

If you want the same pattern to appear on your candle over and over again, then stamping it with paint may be the perfect option for you. You can find a stamp for just about anything (see Figure 7-10). General craft stores offer hundreds of stamps, so you can imagine what specialized stamping stores and Web sites offer.

Figure 7-10:
When it
comes to
stamps, you
have many
choices.

What you need to remember

Try practicing on paper before you start stamping on your candles. Unlike paper, however, if you mess up on your candle's surface, you simply wipe away your mistake as long as the paint is still wet.

A candle's surface is curved, not flat, so you need to roll your stamp from side to side to get the complete image on the candle's surface. Don't press too hard, or you may smudge your stamp.

Because you're working with paint, you may want to read the section on "Painting Designs on Your Candles," earlier in this chapter.

How you do it

To add stamps to your candle's surface:

1. **"Paint" some paint onto your stamp (see Figure 7-11).**

   You can use a brush to apply your paint to your stamp. Don't apply too much paint, though, or you won't be able to see the lines in your stamp.

Painting with beeswax

You may want to try painting with melted beeswax for a change of pace. Although sticky, beeswax is less likely to flake off than paraffin wax or paint, but that stickiness means you have to work fast. You can paint beeswax on any type of candle.

The key to painting with beeswax (or any other wax, for that matter) is to keep it warm: If it hardens, you can't stick your brush in it, so you need to keep it as liquid as possible. I find the easiest way to accomplish this task is to use clean baby food jars as double boilers. Because they're under constant heat, the beeswax is

constantly warm. Place a little beeswax — no more than a third the height of the jar — in each jar (one for each color) and just melt the wax in a double boiler, just as you normally would. Instead of one small pan at the top of your boiler, though, you have several jars. You want the water to cover about half of the jar, so you may want to prop up the jars with a large trivet. If you're not using precolored beeswax, just add a few drops of color and stir. You're ready to paint. You'll need to "reload" with hot wax after each stroke.

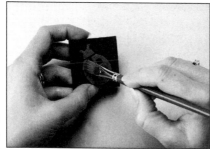

Figure 7-11:
Add paint to your stamp and then gently stamp your candle's surface.

2. **Stamp your candle, making sure to get both edges of the stamp on the candle.**

3. **Continue stamping around your candle.**

4. **Allow your candle to dry.**

Punching Up Your Candles with Stencils

A few years back, my friend told me she was stenciling all the rooms in her house. I remember thinking she was crazy. Something like that just had to be too much work. Then I visited her house and saw the results. Her rooms looked finished and attractive, especially if you like the country decor look. (Of course, the country look depends on the stencil design you choose.)

A *stencil* is simply a cutout shape that you trace inside and paint. Although I'm not up to stenciling my walls, I do stencil my candles (see Figure 7-12). The small surface area of a candle doesn't scare me. Plus, you can always melt the candle and start all over, but who wants to repaint an entire room?

Figure 7-12:
Stencils add
pizzazz to
any candle.

My daughter Katie loves butterflies, but I didn't want to add stencils to the walls. Instead, I bought a few butterfly wall plaques and coat hooks, hung some butterflies from the ceiling, and made her candles with butterflies stenciled on them. Not only did I not have the stress of stenciling her walls, but also now, when she wants to redecorate in a few years, I don't have to repaint — unless, of course, she hates her current favorite color, pink!

Another benefit with stenciling is that you can mass-produce candles with the same design. (For information on starting your own business, see Chapter 20.)

What you need to remember

Stencils, like stamps, are a popular craft item right now, so you have many options. The one downside is that if you're stenciling smaller candles, you may have trouble locating a stencil small enough. One option is to buy dollhouse stencils. (Hey, dollhouses have walls that need decorating, too!)

If you can't find pint-sized stencils at your local craft store, then visit a dollhouse shop.

Your stencils need to be flexible so that you can wrap them around your candle's curved surface. When you evaluate a stencil, remember that you have to attach it tightly around your candle.

You can use acrylic paint, stencil paint, spray paint, or wax paste to fill in your stencils. If you opt for the spray paint, remember that you want to fill in only the inside of the stencil, so you need to protect the rest of the candle's surface by wrapping paper around the uncovered portions.

To add shine to your dry, stenciled candle, rub it with a soft cloth.

Don't forget to protect the candlewick. If you get paint on the wick, your candle may not burn.

How you do it

The key to stenciling: Wrap the stencil as tightly as possible around your candle's surface. Otherwise, the design doesn't look right. You can use either masking tape (it works just like it would on any other surface) or spray adhesive to accomplish this task.

Follow these steps to stencil your candle with acrylic paint, stencil paint, or wax paste:

1. **Attach your stencil tightly to your candle (see Figure 7-13).** Don't forget to make sure that your design isn't crooked.

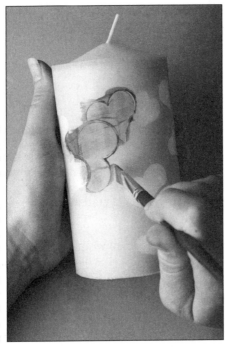

Figure 7-13:
Stencil your candle by attaching the stencil, painting the open areas, recleaning the stencil, and then repositioning the stencil.

2. **Paint the cutout sections of your stencil.** You can use a brush for this task. For tips on choosing a brush, see the sidebar "Choosing the correct brush," in this chapter.

   Make sure that your brush doesn't go underneath the edges of the stencil, or your design won't look right.

3. **Remove the stencil and clean the paint off.**

4. **Retape the stencil at its next location.**

   Make sure that you're not attaching the stencil over your wet stencil design.

5. **Continue moving, retaping, and painting the stencil as necessary.**

6. **Add any details, such as a face, and touch up paint as necessary.**

7. **If you have any paint buildup, gently scrape away the paint.**

8. **Allow the candle to dry completely before burning.**

Constructing your own stencil: No heavy-duty machinery needed

Just as you can make your own candle molds, you can create your own stencils. You can use lace material or doilies as your stencils to create a lacy effect, or you can choose any other design with cutouts.

To actually design your own stencil, you need to complete the following steps:

1. **Measure your candle's circumference and height.**

2. **Draw your design on waxed stencil paper, posterboard, or polyester acetate.**

   Don't forget to make sure that the design fits into your candle's measurements.

3. **Cut out around your candle, leaving an extra inch around your stencil.**

4. **Cut out the interior of your stencil.**

If you're working with spray paint, choose a well-ventilated area (preferably your garage with the door open) out of the way of drafts to avoid the wind blowing your paint. Attach your stencil tightly to your candle, protect any exposed surfaces, and lightly spray your paint onto the cutout area of your stencil. Spray in several squirts instead of one long one.

Spray your paint onto paper to make sure it works properly and to see how the can works.

Embellishing Your Wick

Why not go the extra mile when it comes to your candle? Whether you want to add something that highlights your candle's decorative finish or you prefer to keep the candle itself plain, an *embellished wick* — a wick that has something attached to it — gives your candles a simple and sophisticated touch (see the color section). Better yet, you can easily do it!

What you need to remember

No matter what type of item you choose to attach to your wick, you or your gift recipient will remove it before burning the candle. But you want to put some thought into this decision so that it gives the candle a personal touch. Try to choose something that has meaning to you or the recipient and that ties in with the candle.

A candle with an embellished wick is a great gift idea. For more great gift suggestions, see Chapter 22.

How to do it

All you're doing when you embellish your wick is attaching an object to the end of the wick.

If you plan to embellish your wick now or possibly later, don't trim the wick. You need it to be at least a couple of inches longer than usual so that you have enough room to attach the object.

1. **If the object that you want to attach doesn't already have a hole in it, then make one.**

   Beads, buttons, and many other decorative items already come with a hole, but if you're thinking out of the box, you may need to use a needle or drill to make a hole large enough to accommodate your wick.

2. **Thread your wick through the hole.**

3. **Tie your wick so that the object doesn't fall off.**

You need to remove the item from your wick, as well as trim the wick, before lighting your candle.

Chapter 8

Making More Advanced Projects

*I*n this chapter, I guide you through a handful of popular advanced techniques. You find out how to create cracked candles, floating candles, frosted candles, and gel candles. You also play with stripes, multiple wicks, and wax chunks. (If you want to add decorative finishes, such as paint, see Chapter 7.) Although the results look extraordinary, I can let you in on a little secret about these advanced techniques: They're really not that hard!

Mastering an Advanced Technique: Overdipping

Many of the projects in this chapter ask you to overdip your candles. *Overdipping* is merely the process of adding another coat of hard wax to both your dipped and molded candle. This common candle technique is popular because not only does it help you add many decorative finishes (see Chapter 7), but you can use it to change your candle's color as well.

In fact, you may opt to use overdipping on simple candles that you don't plan to embellish. That's because overdipping or adding an extra coat of wax:

- **Allows you to hide errors.** If you don't like your candle's appearance but know it won't affect your candle's burning capabilities, just overdip your candle for a new and improved surface. (For information on solving appearance problems, see Chapter 10.)

- **Helps ensure a dripless candle.** Because the outer layer of wax is harder, the inside layers melt first, so the wick consumes that wax first.

- **Lets you add color to a candle.** If you didn't add color originally or you just don't like the current shade, just overdip the candle in a different color.

- **Makes your candle appear "finished."** An overdipped candle is shinier and more formal than one that hasn't been overdipped.

- **Protects your candle.** When you overdip, you usually add microcrystalline to your paraffin wax, which creates a harder surface that stands up better to wear and tear. (For more on wax additives, see Chapter 2.)

- **Works like glue (when warm), enabling you to attach many decorative effects.** Many of the advanced projects in this chapter and in Chapter 7 require you to overdip your candle before attaching your embellishments.

To overdip your candle, you need to use paraffin wax with 10 percent microcrystalline. You can also use the additive Poly 400 in place of the microcrystalline. (Poly 400 is a hardener, and you need 1 teaspoon per pound of wax.) Take the following steps when overdipping your candle:

1. **Figure out how much wax you need by placing your candle in a dipping can or other tall can, adding water until the candle is covered, drawing a line to mark the spot, and then measuring the amount of water you used.**

   Because wax floats, make sure that you press down on the candle to keep it submerged.

2. **Completely dry off your candle and dipping can.**

3. **Melt enough wax to fill the can to that line.**

   You can just melt the wax as you usually would. (See Chapter 2 if you need more details.)

   If you want to change or enhance your candle's hue, then don't forget to add color as you melt the wax. Add more color than usual to get the same color as you would in a candle that hasn't been overdipped. (For more on adding color, see Chapter 6.)

Add 10 percent microcrystalline to give your overdipped surface added strength and protection.

4. **Warm your candle by placing it in a warm spot, such as on top of an in-use stove or oven or in the sunlight.**

   The warmth helps the next layer of wax stick better to the candle's surface.

5. **If your melting vessel isn't your dipping can, transfer the melted wax to the can.**

6. **Dip your candle into the can, slowly and steadily.**

   You can hold your candle by the wick with either your fingers or a tool, such as pliers.

7. **If you want a thicker layer, let your candle cool and then dip it again.**

   You can even dip it a third time, after it cools, if you want an even thicker layer.

8. **Dip your candle into cold water.**

   This last step helps ensure that you get a nice, shiny finish.

Achieving an Old-World Look: Cracked Candle

Have you ever seen a decorative look where the candle's exterior is actually cracked (see Figure 8-1)? No, the candle wasn't dropped, although cracks do happen by accident. (See Chapter 10 if you have one and don't want one.) You can acquire these intentional cracks by taking your finished candle and alternating between overdipping and freezing it. (The previous section covers overdipping.) The cracks add interest to an otherwise plain candle.

Take the following steps to crack your candle:

1. **Freeze your finished candle for two hours.**

   Sometimes, however, freezing can fracture your candle all the way through, so keep an eye on your candle during this time.

2. **Overdip your candle by plunging it in a dipping can full of hot wax.**

   If you're not familiar with this process, see the previous section on overdipping.

3. **Repeat Step 2 one to two more times, until your candle is completely covered.**

Figure 8-1:
You can create cracks in your candle by overdipping and freezing it several times.

4. **Place your dipped candle on wax paper and return it to the freezer for an additional two hours.**

   If you want fewer cracks, leave your candle in less time; if you want more cracks, leave it in the freezer longer.

5. **When you have the number of cracks you want, remove the candle from the freezer.**

6. **When the candle reaches room temperature, find and push out any air bubbles that you see on the candle's surface.**

Relaxing on Water: Floating Candles

Floating candles are simply small candles with a wider top than base that float in water (see photo in color section). Ironically, all candles float because wax itself floats. The key, though, is the candle's shape. Think back to your swim lesson days. Didn't you float better if you held yourself prone and perfectly straight, with arms and legs outstretched in front of and beyond you? Likewise, a candle floats best if its top is wider than its base, which is usually the opposite of a typical candle. If your base is wider than the top of the candle, its floating days may be over.

Really, the only difference about making a floating candle is the oddball-inverted shape of your mold. You can go to your craft store and find molds specially designed for floating candles, or you can use soap or candy molds or anything small and shaped appropriately. If you see something that you think may work, go ahead and experiment. If the candle doesn't float, then you know to cross it off your mold list. No matter what type of mold you use, you need to use some type of mold release, which you can purchase at a local craft store, or use vegetable oil.

Definitely use a primed wick for your floating candles. If your wick gets wet, your candle won't burn. A well-primed wick helps protect your candle's burning capabilities in case it gets splashed. (See Chapter 4 for more on priming.)

To make a floating candle:

1. **Spray your mold with vegetable oil or some other type of mold release.**

2. **Pour your melted wax into your mold.**

3. **Tap your mold to remove any air bubbles.**

4. **When the candle is partially set, insert your wick into the wax.**

   Your wick should be pretabbed, primed, and cored. (For more on these techniques, see Chapter 4.)

   The wax should be soft enough to accept the wick but set enough to support the wick. If the wick moves, you can reposition it later.

   If your mold has a hole in it for the wick, by all means insert and secure your wick prior to pouring your wax.

   You probably won't have to top off your mold with wax because floating candles are so shallow.

5. **When your candle has cooled completely, remove it from the mold.**

   Floating candles don't burn for very long, so you may want to make several at once. Most store-bought molds have room for you to make six candles at once.

Looking for Elegance: Frosted Candle

If you want your candle to appear as if it's been out in the cold — known as a *frosted effect* — then you're in luck. You can gain this mottled appearance (see color section) by stirring your wax as you make your candle and allowing the wax to cool a little bit before pouring it. Try not to incorporate too much air into the candle, however, or it won't burn well.

Let it snow — on your candle

Although a frosted candle has an all-over lightened look, a snowflake effect gives your candle, well, a snowy look with spots of white on its surface. You don't have to put in as much elbow power when you make a snowflake candle. Just add snowflake oil to your melted wax and prepare your candle as you usually would. You can find the oil, also called mottling oil, in the candle-making aisle of your local craft store. (See Chapter 5 for instructions on making a basic candle.)

Keep the following pointers in mind:

- Mottling oil doesn't work with waxes that already contain additives, such as vybar.

- You can substitute mineral oil, available at grocery stores, for mottling oil to achieve the same effect at a cheaper price.

- If you're adding fragrance oil, use less mottling oil so that the oil doesn't seep out of the wax.

To create a frosted look:

1. **Choose a mold that's taller than the candle you want to make.**

   You want to be able to move the mold around without spilling the wax, and the extra height enables you to do so.

2. **Prepare your wick.**

   For more on working with wicks, see Chapter 4.

3. **Melt your wax, as well as any additives.**

   For details on melting wax, see Chapter 2.

   If you're adding color to your candle, remember that stirring the wax lightens the color, so you may need to add more dye than you would for a normal candle. (For more information on color, see Chapter 6.)

4. **When your wax reaches 190°F, remove it from the heat.**

5. **As your wax cools, make sure that you stir it constantly.**

   A buildup on the surface should appear soon, which is the sign that you're ready to start adding your wax to the mold.

   If you want your candle to look really light in color, use a whisk.

6. **Pour a little wax into your mold, gently swishing it around the mold so that the sides become covered in wax.**

7. **Return the wax to the pan and resume stirring until bubbly.**

8. **Pour your wax into the mold, saving some to top off your candle later.**

9. **Place your mold in a water bath to cool.**

10. **When you notice a well around the wick, add the rest of the melted wax.**

    You may have to reheat the melted wax before adding it.

11. **Let the candle finish cooling and then remove it from the mold.**

    Don't forget to trim your wick, unless you plan to add an embellishment. (See Chapter 7 for more on wick embellishments.)

Having Fun: Gel Candles

Gel candles are extremely popular, and you may even already have a few store-bought ones around your house (see the color section). You use gel wax to make them, and the transparent nature of the wax makes it a perfect medium for container candles, with or without embedments.

You won't ever make a gel candle without a container; gel wax isn't strong enough to stand on its own when cooled.

Gel candles are really simple to make, especially when you create them without embedments. However, the reason I include gel candles in a chapter on more advanced projects is because gel wax is highly combustible and you have to take a few different steps than when you're creating a paraffin candle.

Gel is sticky, which makes it difficult to remove from fabric. Be careful and wear an apron.

Standing tall: Making a simple gel candle

Making a gel candle is similar to making a basic wax candle in the sense that you melt and pour your wax. But the similarities end there. Gel candles require a hotter melting temperature and the wax is more combustible, so you must use a thermometer to constantly monitor your temperature. (For more on gel wax, see Chapter 2.)

Wicks have different rules, too. In general, gel candles require a wick one size larger than the wick you use in a standard paraffin candle. You also want a wick that hasn't been primed with paraffin because paraffin wax leaves a cloudy residue in your transparent gel, which doesn't exactly add beauty to your translucent gel candle.

You can buys wicks specifically made for gel candles. They are primed with a very high-temperature paraffin, which helps keep your gel wax from clouding.

You also need to use a tabbed wick so that your wick is supported at the bottom of the candle. But don't use just any tabbed wick. You need the tabbed part to be at least $\frac{7}{16}$-inch tall so that the wick snuffs out well before it gets to the base of your candle.

If you can't find that tall of a tabbed wick in your local craft store, then add glass beads or marbles to your wick to extend the tab's length (see Figure 8-2). If you use glass that matches your candle's color (or clear glass if you have no color), then you don't even notice the beads or marbles when you look at the candle. (For more on wicks, check out Chapter 4.)

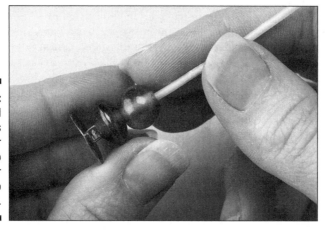

Figure 8-2:
Just thread some beads onto your wick to extend your tab to $\frac{7}{16}$ inch.

To make a simple gel candle without any embedments:

1. **Melt your gel wax to 200°F or to the manufacturer's recommended temperature.**

   Just as you would when melting paraffin wax, make sure that you don't get any water in your wax.

   Definitely keep an eye on the temperature. You don't want to overheat gel wax because it's highly combustible.

2. **As the wax melts, prepare your container by placing your tabbed wick at the bottom.**

   You can either use fast-drying epoxy glue or a little melted gel to attach the tab to the bottom of your container, or just let it stay loose and reposition it in Step 3. (I usually prefer the latter method.)

3. **Add a little wax to your container and then reposition your wick.**

Hold your container sideways as you pour the wax to reduce bubbles. To avoid the wax cooling too quickly, causing bubbles to form, you may want to place your container on a baking sheet and warm it in a 200°F oven for a few minutes.

4. **When the gel sets, pour the rest of your wax into the candle.**

5. **Let your candle cool completely.**

For tips on avoiding bubbles in your gel candles, see Chapter 10.

Looking pretty: Embedding objects in your gel candle

Because of its translucent nature, gel wax is ideal for embedding objects (see photo in color section). You can create a seascape by adding shells, give a warm, homey touch to your kitchen by embedding fruit, or add a romantic aura to your bedroom by including dried flowers. You can even embed shapes molded from paraffin wax, but remember, when it melts (no fire danger here), the paraffin will cloud your gel.

Almost anything is fair game as an embedment, as long as it doesn't melt or burn when you light the candle and as long as it doesn't react with the wax. (See Chapter 7 for more on embedment options.)

To make a gel candle with embedments:

1. **Melt your gel wax to 200°F or to the manufacturer's recommended temperature.**

2. **As the wax melts, prepare your container by placing your tabbed wick and embedments along the bottom.**

You can use fast-drying epoxy glue or a little melted gel to hold your embedments in place, if you want.

You don't want your embedments to be near the wick (place more than an inch or two away, please), or they may cause your wick to snuff out.

3. **Pour a little melted gel into your container and then reposition your wick and any embedments, if necessary.**

4. **When the gel sets, add the rest of your wax.**

If you're including embedments at different levels throughout the candle, then you can add the embedments now as well.

Remember to check your wax's temperature. If it's too cool, you need to reheat it so that your embedments stay in place.

5. Let your candle cool completely, and you're all finished.

Maximizing the Look: Layered Candle

If you like the looks of stripes, then try making a layered candle (see Figure 8-3). To make a layered candle, you simply pour layers of different colored wax into a mold. You can make as many layers as you like, as well as control the thickness of the stripes.

If you want a striped candle, but don't want to go through the trouble of coloring different waxes, then you're in luck. You can use masking tape to create stripes on your candle. Then melt just one batch of wax, add color to it, and overdip your candle. (For more on overdipping, see the section "Mastering an Advanced Technique: Overdipping," earlier in this chapter.) When the wax cools, just remove your tape, and voilà! Instant stripes!

Figure 8-3:
A layered candle is basically a candle with stripes.

To create a layered candle without overdipping, follow these steps:

1. **Divide your wax into separate melting vessels, depending on the number of layers your candle will have.**

   For example, if your candle is to have three layers, then you need to have three different colors of wax.

2. **Melt your wax, along with any additives, such as color.**

   For more on color, see Chapter 6.

3. **As your wax melts, prepare your wick and mold.**

   See Chapters 2 and 4 for more on these two items.

4. **Pour your first layer of wax into your mold.**

   Because wax bleeds, pour your darkest color first.

5. **When the first layer cools, add your second layer of wax.**

6. **Repeat Step 5 as necessary until you've completely added your layers.**

7. **When you reach the last color you'll be adding, save a little bit of wax so that you can top off the candle later.**

8. **As the candle sets, if a hole begins to develop, top off your candle with the remaining wax.**

9. **When cool, remove the candle from the mold.**

A layered candle is a great way to use leftover colored wax.

You can also use gel wax to create layered candles. However, you need to skip Steps 7 through 9.

Going for a Classic: Multiple-Wick Candle

A large candle with several wicks scattered throughout, a *multiwick candle* is a timeless addition to any home (see Figure 8-4). Fortunately, you can achieve this classic by making a large basic candle and just adding multiple wicks.

Never use more than five wicks in your candle.

Figure 8-4:
A multiwick candle is classic, beautiful, and simple to make.

To make a multiwick candle:

1. **Prepare your mold and melt your wax as you normally would.**

   See Chapter 5 for details on creating a basic candle.

2. **Place your main wick in the center of the mold.**

   In general, you want to use smaller wicks (than if you were using only one) for this size of candle.

3. **Space your additional wicks between the center of the mold and the outside edge of the candle.**

   To figure out how many wicks you need, see Chapter 4.

4. **Pour your wax as usual and let your multiwick candle cool.**

You can make multiwick gel container candles as well following the same steps.

Getting a Little Chilly: Ice Candle

I didn't know what an *ice candle* was until I saw one — and giving you a visual is really the best way to describe this candle, which looks more like Swiss cheese than a candle that actually burns (see Figure 8-5). Although the candle looks a bit worse for wear, that's actually its style. And the effect is astounding, especially when you choose glorious shades of color, such as an ice blue or vivid purple.

The great thing about an ice candle is that you can easily achieve these lustrous results by following a few simple steps. Here's what you do:

1. **Melt your wax to the package's specified temperature.**

   If you're recycling wax or you're unsure of the temperature, aim for 190°F and maintain that temperature for half an hour.

2. **As your wax melts, prepare your mold by spraying it with mold release.**

3. **Add your wick to your mold.**

   Although fabulous looking, an ice candle isn't suitable for burning, because the wick doesn't have a continuous supply of wax. If you want to have an ice candle that burns, place a taper candle in the middle of the mold, instead of your wick, before you put in the ice cubes.

4. **Fill your mold with ice cubes.**

   Yes, ice cubes! Keep in mind, though, that the water can harm a metal mold, so you may want to use another type of mold. If you do opt for metal, make sure that you dry your mold immediately after making this candle, or your mold may rust.

Figure 8-5:
An ice candle looks like Swiss cheese and looks stunning whether you burn it or not.

5. **When your wax reaches the required temperature, add any additives, such as color or scent.**

6. **Remove your wax from the heat and slowly and smoothly pour it into your mold, reserving 1 cup for a repour.**

7. **Immediately use your reserved wax to fill in any indentation around the wick.**

Don't wait too long for this step. If you do, when you repour, you'll actually be filling in the holes created by your ice cubes, which defeats the purpose of adding the ice.

8. **Periodically drain the water out of your candle by tilting it over your sink.**

9. **When your candle cools, remove it from the mold as usual.**

Don't be surprised, however, if some extra water pours out when you remove the candle.

Adding on the Pounds: Chunk Candle

If you want your candle to have an interesting look, try creating a *chunk candle* (see Figure 8-6). No, the candle isn't overweight, but it is carrying around something extra — extra chunks of wax embedded inside it. These wax chunks are a different color than the candle itself, so they stand out quite a bit, especially if you choose high-contrast colors.

You can always make your own wax chunks. (See the sidebar "Making your own wax chunks.") But the easiest thing to do is to purchase premade and precolored wax chunks. You can find them in many shades in the candle-making aisle of your local craft store.

Making your own wax chunks

To make your own wax chunks, melt your wax and add your color. (Remember to choose a color that's very different from the shade of your candle.) Instead of pouring your wax in a mold, however, pour a ½-inch layer of wax onto a cookie sheet or jelly roll pan. Or, you can even make instant chunks by pouring the wax into a plastic ice cube tray.

When the wax cools to the point that it's solid but still pliable, you're ready to cut the wax into the size of chunks you want. You can even cut shapes out of the wax using a cookie cutter.

Here's a tip: Whenever you have leftover wax, consider making wax chunks and then storing them. That way, you'll always have them on hand when you're ready to make a chunk candle.

Figure 8-6:
Wax chunks embedded within a candle add interest to your candle, as well as provide a nice change of pace to the typical candle.

To make a chunk candle, follow these steps:

1. **Melt your wax to the package's specified temperature.**

   If you're recycling wax or you're unsure of the temperature, aim for 190°F and maintain that temperature for half an hour.

2. **As your wax melts, prepare your mold by spraying it with mold release.**

3. **Add your wick to the mold.**

4. **Fill your mold with wax chunks.**

   Pack the mold tightly so that the chunks are pressing on the sides of the mold. That way, you see the chunks on the surface of the candle.

   You want the wax chunks to be within 1 inch of where you want your candle's finished height to be.

5. **When your wax reaches the required temperature, add any additives, such as color or scent.**

   Remember, you want to be able to see your chunks, so don't use too dark or too similar a color for your candle.

6. **Remove your wax from the heat and slowly and smoothly pour it into your mold, reserving 1 cup for a repour.**

   To avoid air bubbles, try tilting your mold, just as you would when pouring a beer.

7. **Wait a few minutes and then gently tap the side of your mold to remove any air bubbles.**

8. **Wait approximately 45 minutes and then use the 1 cup of reserved wax to fill in any indentation around the wick.**

   Of course, you need to reheat this wax.

9. **When your candle cools, remove it from the mold as usual.**

Chapter 9

Displaying Your Handiwork

*I*f you're like me, you don't like hiding your candles in a drawer (stored properly, of course!). I love to have my handiwork on display, but I hate clutter. That means the candles I make serve a purpose: They decorate my home, add wonderful scents, and are meant to be burned.

This chapter is all about what to do with (and how to show off) your handiwork. You discover how to properly burn your finished candles, as well as how to use them to decorate and enhance your home. And if you have too many candles (is that possible?!), no problem — you also find out about giving candles to your family and friends as presents, as well as how to properly store them.

Burning Your Candles the Right Way

Burning a candle includes more than lighting it with a match, letting it burn, and then blowing it out. (In fact, you don't ever blow out your candles — see the upcoming section on extinguishing your candles.) How long the wick is, how long you let the candle burn, and then how you extinguish it all play a role in the quality of your candle's life.

Before you light your candle, you need to trim its wick. You want it to be no more than ¼-inch long. Trimming your wick keeps the wick from bending, which gets soot in the wax and on your candleholders and causes the candle to burn unevenly. Trimming the wick also keeps the candle's flame the proper size.

To remove soot from your candleholders, clean them with rubbing alcohol —
when the candle is unlit, of course!

Even lighting your candle isn't as straightforward as using a match. Although
you can use a match, you risk dropping carbon onto the candle, which may
end up in the wax pool. Even lighting your candle with another candle can
drip wax onto the candle being lit — or even catch fire! Instead, use a good
butane lighter to light your candles.

Burning issues

After you light the candle, monitor how long you burn it. Burn your candle
for only one hour per inch of diameter. In other words, if you have a six-inch
candle, you should only burn it six hours. If you burn the candles longer than
that, you're weakening the wall of wax that retains the wax pool, which can
result in a spill.

You also don't want your candle to burn all the way down to the bottom of its
holder. The heat may harm your candleholder.

Never, ever leave your candle unattended. Don't leave your home while a
candle is burning and certainly don't fall asleep. I can't tell you how many
fires I've heard about that have been caused by these situations. Stay in the
same room with your burning candle at all times.

When your candle is burning, don't try to move it. The melted pool of wax
can easily splash or spill. Don't move it until the wax has cooled and hardened again.

If you're using scented candles, make sure that you put a lid on them after
they cool so that the scent won't dissipate in the air.

Putting candles out to pasture

When it's time to extinguish your candle, don't blow it out. If you haven't discovered this downfall already, blowing out your candle causes the liquid wax
to scatter. Unfortunately, my three-year-old daughter discovered the scatter
factor when she decided to "help" me by blowing out our candles around our
house. Talk about new wall décor! In addition, blowing out the flame actually
moves the wick, which can cause it to burn unevenly.

To extinguish your candle, use a snuffer (see Figure 9-1). A snuffer covers the
flame and deprives it of oxygen so that it can no longer burn.

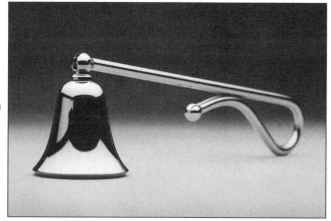

Figure 9-1:
Use a
snuffer to
extinguish
your
candles.

Don't pour water on the candle to extinguish the flame. It doesn't work, and the water only causes the wax to splatter.

If you've a brave soul, you can always wet your thumb and forefinger and extinguish the flame between them. I don't recommend this technique, though, because if you don't get your digits wet enough, you'll feel the burn. And who wants to discover the right amount of wetness through trial and error?

Decorating with Candles

Candles are great decorating tools because of their elegant shape and beauty. How you place the candles and what you set them in determines whether they look formal or informal. The serene flicker of a candle flame adds undeniable warmth to any home.

Even more than the shape, the candle's color helps decorate your home. If you have a harsh purple multiwick candle in a soft lavender room, the effect won't be quite what you want. You may hear a muffled "Ugh" instead of an awed "Ahh" when your guests come in.

I have candles in every single room of my home. Not only do they look nice and provide inexpensive decor, but they also make me feel good when I see them burn and smell their aroma. (Try lighting a couple scented candles in your bathroom. You won't have to buy any fragrant spray again.)

When you're making candles, try matching your colors to your rooms.

Placing your candles

Most of the time, you want to place your candles near a focal point in each room. If you have a fireplace, its mantel makes a wonderful spot for all types of candles. You can place your candles symmetrically on each end of the fireplace, or you can line up candles of varying height in the middle of the mantel. You can also try placing candles inside the fireplace.

If you do decide to place candles on your fireplace, when you light the fire in your fireplace, make sure that the candles aren't getting too hot or they'll melt.

Grouping your candles around your home lends a more informal feel to a room.

When you place your candles, you need to ask yourself the following questions:

✔ **Are my candles out of the way of drafts?** If not, the draft can affect how your candles burn and cause problems. If your candle is flickering, it may be in a draft. (For other causes, see Chapter 10.)

✔ **Is the placement practical?** If you have to move your huge dining room candle centerpiece every time you eat dinner, then it probably isn't a good location.

Kitchens usually have a lot of hustle and bustle with people cooking, eating, and cleaning up. You want to make sure that this room in particular uses common-sense placement of candles. A lighted candle in a spot where you or some absent-minded cook can easily knock it over is definitely a bad idea. And if you have to remove a group of candles from your stove every time you preheat your oven or cook dinner, you won't enjoy it. (However, if you don't cook at home and takeout is your thing, go ahead and leave the candles on the stovetop!)

✔ **Are my candles easy to move, if necessary?** If you'll be moving group settings of candles a lot, consider placing them on a tray for easy transportation.

✔ **Are my candles on a flat surface?** An uneven surface increases the likelihood of an unintentional fire.

✔ **Are my candles far enough away from the wall or any shelves above it?** A candle placed too close to the wall can cause soot build-up — not exactly a nice decorating touch (unless you want your white walls to have uneven black highlights)! And anything on a "too-close" shelf will become fair game as fire starter. Check out what's around your candle. If something is getting warm, move it or move the candle.

✔ **Are my candles away from anything flammable?** Some things may catch you by surprise. For example, does your curtain blow in the breeze and possibly into the candle?

✔ **Are my candles out of sunlight?** Light from a window can cause the color to fade. If you're going to burn your candles regularly, this factor probably won't be an issue.

✔ **Are my candles out of the way of my little ones' — or furry pals' — reach?** Kids and pets are curious, so don't tempt them by placing a burning candle on an end table. For that matter, if your kids are like my son, Carter, don't place candles on anything that they can reach by climbing or moving chairs!

I love using tealights and votives in my bathrooms, bedrooms, and kitchen. Not only do they take up a small amount of space, but you can also find decorative holders that add to your room's charm. For example, sunflower candleholders in my kitchen complement my summery theme, while seashell-shaped tealight holders in my kids' bathroom emphasize the seashell motif.

If you don't have a lot of space for candles, you still have options. Think about chandeliers or, my personal favorite, wall-mounted candleholders. Not only do they not take up much space, but also my young kids and dog can't reach them!

If you take a lot of baths, try placing candles around the tub for a relaxing effect.

Where you position candles vertically in the room also has an effect on the room's mood. If you're into drama, place your candles down low. For a brighter room, place your candles up high.

If you notice an off odor in your house, why not burn a scented candle? Like your decor, the scent of your house can provide a warm welcome to guests. That's the reason that realtors suggest baking bread or pies before potential buyers come for a tour.

Using candleholders and containers

When you're decorating, you're not limited to just the candle itself. You have its container and holder to use as accessories as well. When you're making a container candle, think about where you want to use it and how it can complement your room. For example, if you want to use the candle outside, why not use a metal bucket or clay pot? (Bug-repelling citronella is sounding good here!) If you're going to use the candle in the kitchen, you can have a lot of fun creating a food-based container candle.

Another option is to find candleholders you like and then make the perfect candles for them if you don't have any already on hand. You can use something as simple as an old wine bottle or something as elaborate as a wrought iron stand. Or see what you can find at garage sales. If you take it home and don't like the look, you haven't spent much.

You can even use old lanterns as a holder for your candles or a candleholder with a shade, which provides a nice, light-like touch (see Figure 9-2). You can even use wooden candleholders, but snuff out the candle at least 2 inches from the base of the candle.

Figure 9-2:
Your choice
of candle-
holders is
almost
endless.

No matter what type of candleholder you opt for, always make sure that your candle fits snugly into it. You certainly don't want an unsecured, flaming candle to tip over.

When my husband complained of dripping wax from taper candles, my mother-in-law came to the rescue with round, plastic concave holders that you thread your candles through. Called *wax shields* or *bobeches,* these disks are designed to protect your surfaces, carpets, and, yes, your candleholders from errant wax drops. (For more on treating spills, see Chapter 1.)

To keep your votive candleholders clean, place a drop or two of water inside it before you insert the candle. The water creates a barrier between the holder and the melted wax. You can also use a drop of dish soap as well.

Giving Candles as Presents

If you enjoy making candles, chances are you'll soon have an abundance of them. Your extra candles can make wonderful gifts for families and friends. According to the National Candle Association, seven out of ten U.S. households burn candles, and retail sales of candles top $2.3 billion annually, which excludes candle accessories. What better gift to give to a family member or friend than a handmade, personalized candle?

I don't know about you, but I always struggle with unique gift ideas for my daughter's preschool teachers. A candle shaped in the form of a thick pencil or apple immediately comes to mind as an option.

Cleaning your candleholders

My husband's grandparents gave us a beautiful set of brass candleholders. I placed them on each end of my fireplace mantel, added matching taper candles, and then enjoyed their glow for a while. Unfortunately, the candles dripped onto the beautiful holders. (In hindsight, I probably burnt the candles too long.) However, I cleaned them up good as new by using the following tips:

✔ **Remove the wax first.** You can either run hot water over the wax to melt it, or you can freeze the candleholder, which causes the wax to shrink. I found the latter method particularly effective.

✔ **Drop that knife!** You don't want to mar or break your candleholder. As tempting as it may be to scrape off the wax, it's also the most common method of damaging candleholders.

You don't know what kind of candle to give your friend or family member? Think about your recipient's wants and needs. Choose a candle mold or container that fits his or her personality. Match the scent and color to his or her home.

How you present the gift isn't as important as the thought you put into making it. You can give it away in a basket wrapped in cellophane tied with a ribbon, in a plain gift bag, or as is with a simple ribbon wrapped around its base. For some great gift ideas, see Chapter 22.

Storing Your Finished Candles

If you're going to put hard work into making candles, then you need to make sure that you take care of them. Because you probably won't be burning all the candles you made simultaneously — for example, when you make a batch of votives or tealights — you need somewhere to store them. What you do to your candles after you finish making them and how you store them affects not only how well they burn but also how attractive they are as well.

You need to let your candle *cure,* or rest, for at least 24 hours after removing it from the mold. Some candles can actually take months to cure.

Picking a storage spot

If you find that you have too many candles to display around your home, you need to find somewhere to store them. I store my candles in a corner cabinet in my living room. Not only is the cabinet in a room where my kids don't often go, but also it fits the requirements of proper storage: a cool, dry, dark place. If you decide to store your candles in a drawer, just make sure that it's dedicated to candles only — no other junk on top, please, unless you absolutely have no choice.

Don't store your candles in a spot that gets more than 70°F on a regular basis. Wax is designed to melt so that it can serve as fuel for your wick. If it gets too warm, well, it does what wax is designed to do — melts. If the wax occasionally gets warm, you're probably okay, but if you're one of those people who uses windows in 90°F summer heat, be careful.

You can get too much of a good thing. Never store your candles in the freezer because they may crack.

If you're storing taper candles, then make sure that you store them flat. Otherwise, they'll bend. Unfortunately, I discovered this fact the hard way — but at least it happened with store-bought candles before I had started this hobby!

Wrapping your candles

Before you store your candles, you want to wrap them in undyed tissue paper or cloth so that they don't rub against each other and mar the candle surface. You also want to wrap any candles that you've added scent to in cellophane first so that the scent doesn't dissipate while you're storing it.

Stay away from plastic wrap or baggies because they tend to absorb the fragrance, which takes the scent out of the candle.

As an added precaution, try placing your candles in boxes. If the box has a lid, it serves as double protection because the box counts as a dark place. So does a drawer or a cabinet. (Darkness protects against color fading.)

Fixing your candle's surface mars

If you were a little careless in how you stored your candles or you caught the dog barreling down the hall with a taper hanging from his mouth, don't panic. Yes, candles are fragile, but you can take some steps to minimize the damage:

- ✔ If you see scratches and other marring on your candle's surface, try rubbing them away with nylon hose. This little trick works wonders!

- ✔ If your candle is a little dusty, get out the nylon hose again or a cloth and rub it down. Better yet, bring on the bath — that is, wash your candle in lukewarm soapy water.

- ✔ If the candle is beyond repair, recycle the wax.

Chapter 10

Handling Common Candle Problems

*E*ven candle-making "pros" encounter problems and less-than-welcome results at one time or another. Some problems . . . err, challenges . . . are more common than others. If all goes well, your candles not only look attractive, but also burn properly, meaning that they have a nice, steady flame and don't produce smoke.

In this chapter, I share with you the solutions to some common candle-making challenges. Whether it's a simple solution, such as moving your candle out of a draft, or a more complex one requiring that you remelt your candle and begin again, this chapter has many answers to common woes.

When Your Candle Doesn't Look Its Best: Appearance Problems

You've probably been at a potluck dinner or party where something on the table just didn't look quite right. Maybe the ham looked a little too dark or the cookies resembled Frisbees. Chances are, if the food didn't look good, you didn't plop it on your plate. And although food can be the exception — it may still taste great even if it looks overdone — can you imagine trying to sell an unattractive candle in a store? Even if you're not marketing your wares — and my guess is that you're probably not — you probably won't be inspired to put your unattractive wax creations on display.

Fortunately, you can easily fix most appearance problems. And even if you can't fix it, you can usually pinpoint the root of the problem so that you can avoid repeating your mistake. The following sections address specific appearance issues that new candlemakers commonly encounter.

Timber! When a bend isn't cool

A leaning tower may look cool in Pisa, but it probably doesn't work too well on your fireplace mantel. Pillars that end up leaning or bending may be the result of one of several faux pas:

- ✔ **You didn't store your candles flat.** Obviously, this problem is a relatively easy one to solve in the future. In the meantime, try warming your bent candles and then rolling them again on an even surface.

- ✔ **Your wick is actually what's bent.** If so, you need to make sure that you straighten the wick between each dip.

- ✔ **You didn't add enough stearin.** Be sure to add more of the additive stearin next time. For more on additives, see Chapter 2.

A "chip" off the old block

If you notice tiny nicks or chips on your candle's surface, more than likely you weren't too careful when you stored or moved the candles. Candles are wax, so they do chip if they bump against other candles or other wax. Wrap in tissue paper next time and make sure that you follow proper storage guidelines. For more on storage, see Chapter 1.

If you're sure that you were careful, then another possibility is that you added way too much stearin to your wax. Added in large quantities, stearin makes the wax brittle. Next time you make this type of candle, try reducing the amount of stearin that you add.

A little bubbly, anyone?

Air bubbles can be good — for example, when you're using gel wax to make a seascape candle and want bubbles — but for the most part, you want to avoid them. Bubbles are actually pockets of air trapped inside the candle. Most of the time, they occur when you pour your wax too quickly or when you don't tap the side of the mold to gently release the trapped air. Next time, pour your wax more slowly and make sure that you take the proper steps to release trapped air. (For more on the basic technique, see Chapter 5.)

If the bubbles appear only at the bottom of your candle, then the water level in your water bath wasn't high enough to completely cover your entire candle mold. As a result, the bottom of your candle (which, remember, was the top of your mold) wasn't completely immersed and thus didn't cool as quickly.

If you're noticing the bubbles between layers of a dipped candle, try heating your wax more next time or taking less time between each dip.

Being overly generous with your mold release or essential oils can also cause bubbles in your candles. (See Chapter 3 for more on mold release and Chapter 19 for more on essential oils.)

If water drips into your gel candles, you get the same effect as if you had air in your candle, thanks to evaporation. When you melt your wax, be careful if you use a lid, which can create steam and condensation.

Remember, the best offense is the best defense. If you're careful about avoiding the bubbles in the first place, then you won't have as much of a problem removing them. If you do get air bubbles in your candle, you need to take the time to help the air escape.

To minimize the amount of air bubbles:

- ✓ Slowly stir your wax.
- ✓ Dip your embedments in gel wax prior to embedding to fill up any air pockets. (To embed an object in a gel candle, see Chapter 8.)
- ✓ Prime your wick to avoid trapped air. (See Chapter 4 to find out how to prime your wicks.)
- ✓ When you pour your wax, tip your mold or container.
- ✓ Pour your wax slowly.
- ✓ Tap the sides of your mold to encourage bubbles to escape.
- ✓ Don't allow your candles to cool too quickly — for example, by placing them in the freezer — or the bubbles that do exist won't have time to escape.
- ✓ If you're pouring multiple candles, check your candle's temperature between each pour.

Avalanche! When your candle caves in

If your candle collapses on one side, you more than likely didn't poke relief holes in the candle as it cooled. The wax contracts as the candle cools, which makes the candle appear to pull inward. Next time, try poking holes in the top of your candle or wiggling the wick to release it from the wax so that the wax, as it shrinks, pulls away from the wick instead of from the outside wall of the candle.

You "crack" me up!

If your candle cracks, review your wax's temperature during the process. Here are some potential causes of cracks in a candle's surface:

- **The candle was cooled too quickly.** Next time, use warmer water in the water bath.
- **The candle wax was too cold when the candle was redipped.** The hot wax on the cooler wax resulted in the crack.

In either case, I usually recommend remelting the wax and starting over again, paying particular attention to the wax's temperature.

When your containers have a hang-up

You know how some people have hang-ups about certain things. Maybe they don't like cats, or maybe they don't like kids in restaurants. Whatever the issue, hang-ups occur in container candles, too. Actually, though, in candle-speak, a *hang-up* is simply excess wax that remains on the side of your container candles. Hang-ups are always frustrating because you have a beautiful candle and all this wax that wasn't used. You don't get half the life out of your candle as you wanted, and it looks funky, too.

Ironically, hang-up seems to happen more with candles I purchase at local festivals than the ones I create. My guess is that my purchased candles' wicks are too small for the candles, and the wax wasn't melted properly. Ideally, your container candle consumes all the wax evenly. But if you're getting hang-up, your candle is probably drowning in the excess wax.

Next time you make your candles, try using a larger wick. (For more on choosing the proper wick, see Chapter 4.)

If you're not burning your container candles at least one hour per inch in diameter after you light them, you may have just found your culprit. Not burning your container candles long enough also causes *hang-up* or a "tunnel" to form down the center of the candle.

Bubbles be gone!

Gel wax is particularly prone to bubbles. Sometimes, you want them, and sometimes you don't, but even when you do want them, you need to control them. In addition to following the tips in the, "A little bubbly, anyone?" section, keep these pointers in mind:

✔ The hotter your candle gel, the fewer bubbles you'll have. As the gel liquefies, the bubbles can escape.

✔ Certain types of gel wax, such as HP gel, are more prone to bubbles than other types.

✔ Prime your wicks in gel wax to eliminate trapped air bubbles.

✔ Preheat your container so that it doesn't cause your gel to cool too quickly.

✔ Stay away from embedments that contain glue, which causes air bubbles when mixed with gel wax.

✔ Test your embedments by placing them in gel prior to using them. If you see bubbles, you may want to choose another item.

When age takes its toll

If your candle looks like it's been around the block a few times, you may need to clean it to see its true condition. Try wiping the candle with a nylon stocking or cloth. If you're feeling more adventurous, you can try overdipping the candle in fresh wax. (For more on overdipping, see Chapter 8.)

Lumps and bumps

If your dipped candle isn't nice and smooth and is instead sporting a few bumps, then more than likely your wax was too cold by the time you did your subsequent dip. You can solve the problem by warming the candle, gently re-rolling it on a smooth, hard surface, and then redipping it in hot wax. (Sometimes, you can avoid the redipping step; use your own judgment as to how well you've ironed out the lumps.) The next time you make this type of candle, you want to recheck your wax's temperature every few dips or so.

If you're absolutely sure that the wax was the correct temperature when you dipped the candle, then you may not have primed the wick long enough, resulting in lumps and bumps. Remember, your first dip is basically priming the wick, so it needs to last a little longer than the other dips — aim for at least 30 seconds.

If your molded candle is a bit bumpy, then the most likely problem is that the layers of wax separated as your candle cooled.

Overcompensating by heating the wax too hot won't solve your problems. If the wax is too hot when you're dipping a candle, it simply slides off your wick.

Watch out for the sink hole!

Don't panic if you see an indentation around your candle's wick, known as a *sink hole,* in your paraffin candles. This common occurrence results as your wax cools because most types of wax normally shrink as they cool. Keep an eye on your candle as it cools and simply fill in the hole with wax after the candle has shrunk quite a bit. You may have to add wax several times as the candle cools.

Don't just pour the wax over the top of the candle. You want to center your efforts on the well. Otherwise, you have a strange line toward the top of your candle where you added the wax.

Sink holes typically develop at the bottom of your candle because that part is what served as the top of your mold. To counteract the sink hole, you can just trim off the bottom of the candle with a sharp knife. You have a candle that's a little shorter than you intended, but you won't have the sink hole.

The shrinkage that resulted in the sink hole can also cause the wax to come away from the sides of the mold as it cools. A little bit of shrinkage is actually desirable so that you can easily remove your candle from the mold. However, if you notice too much shrinkage, you can again top off the candle with hot wax. Just make sure that you don't add too much wax, though, or the excess will flow down the sides of the mold and lock your candle in place.

A frosty reception: Mottling

If you notice *mottling,* or frost marks resembling snowflakes, on the surface of your candle, then excess oils in the wax may be at play. Most additives, except stearin (which actually increases the mottling effect in candles when used with essential oils or mottling oil), can help eliminate mottling. The additive vybar is a good bet to reduce mottling in your candles if you're faced with this problem.

Help! My candle's stuck, and I can't get it out of the mold!

If your candle won't budge in your mold, consider how much mold release you applied. If you didn't use a mold release at all, that's probably your problem. Even if you did use a mold release, you may not have used enough.

That knowledge probably doesn't help you now, however. Your best bet is to pour the wax at the highest temperature permitted and then not to attempt to remove the candle until it's fairly cured (about 24 hours). You can try to place the candle in your refrigerator, wait five minutes or so, and then attempt to remove it. If that doesn't work or you're really frustrated, you can run hot water over it, although it may ruin the candle and the mold.

Beeswax is naturally sticky, so if you're using it in a wax mixture, that's probably the problem. Next time, use less beeswax.

Take into consideration these other possibilities:

✔ A damaged mold may result in difficulty removing candles, as well as a damaged candle. If you see that your mold is damaged, don't use it, unless you don't mind possibly wasting your time or having a disfigured candle.

✔ If you pour too much wax into a shrink well and the wax overflows, it can cause difficulty.

✔ Perhaps your wax was too cool when you poured it. The hotter the wax is, the more it shrinks, making it easier to remove.

✔ You used stearin in a flexible mold. Stearin eats rubber molds. See Chapter 2, which talks about additives.

It's sprung a leak!

Sometimes something you do earlier comes back to haunt you. If you weren't careful when you sealed your mold's wick hole, wax can seep out. Next time, you know what you need to pay special attention to.

Burning Issues

Almost any wick will burn in your candle. But how well the wick consumes the wax is the key point. If you choose a wick that's too small for your candle's size, wax pools form and either drip down the sides of the candles or extinguish your burning wick. If your wick is too large, it doesn't have enough wax to use as fuel and thus smokes and flickers.

The following sections tackle common burning problems.

My candle burns straight down the middle

If you find yourself with a hole because your candle is burning straight down the middle, you're probably using too small of a wick for the melting point of your wax. Next time, use wax with a lower melting point or a larger wick.

One potential cause of this problem may have nothing to do with your candle-making abilities. If you're not burning the candle long enough each time, a hole around the wick develops. The general rule is to burn your candle at least one hour per inch in diameter.

Drip, drop, drip, drop

A dripping candle isn't good. Not only is your candle not burning correctly, but you also may be ruining your furnishings or carpet at the same time.

The easiest problem to fix is when your candle is in a draft. If you notice that one side of the candle seems to have most of the dripping, try moving your candle to another location. If a change of scenery doesn't help your candle, then your wick may be too small for your candle's size. If that's the case, then the wick can't use all the melting wax, which then has nowhere to go but down the candle's side.

Another possibility is that the wax has too low of a melting point for the type of candle you made. As a result, it's melting prematurely and dripping. In all those cases, I prefer to remelt the wax and begin again. If your wax has too low of a melting point, the candle quickly melts and you have a problem with excess wax — think of it oozing out of your candleholder! Removing wax from places it's not supposed to be isn't a job I relish.

Or, consider this possibility. Your wick may simply be off center, which is causing the drip down one side. While the wax is warm, try centering the wick.

This little flame of mine . . .

When your candle isn't burning as big and bright as you like, you may have a number of problems on your hands:

- Your wick is too small, too short, or too loose. Try a different wick size. (See Chapter 4 for more on choosing wicks.)
- Coloring agents have clogged your wick. Be careful not to get anything on your wick next time you make candles.

- ✔ You didn't inspire your candle with a moving rendition of *This Little Light of Mine.* Grab a glass of water, clear your throat, warn the neighbors, and let loose.

- ✔ Your wax has too high of a melting point. Try a wax with a lower melting point next time.

- ✔ You used too much stearin or other additives. Decrease the amount of additives when you make this type of candle again.

This big flame of mine . . .

When your flame is burning too big and bright, you pretty much have the opposite causes as in the preceding section. The solution is simple enough: Use a smaller wick next time.

Smokin'!

If your candle is sending smoke signals, more than likely it's trying to tell you that your wick is too large for your candle. First try trimming your candle's wick. If that doesn't work, use a smaller wick when you make the candle next time.

Candle placement can result in a smoking candle. If your candle is in a draft, it can smoke as well.

Sputter, sputter, sputter . . .

If your flame isn't steady and is instead flickering, you probably have a damp wick. Give the wick time to dry completely — say, a couple of days — and your problem should dissipate.

If your candle still flickers after your wait, then water may still be the culprit. If you dripped water into the wax when you poured it into the mold or if water seeped in from an improperly sealed wick hole, your flame may sputter.

Other culprits may be an air pocket inside the candle, or even an oil pocket resulting from adding too much essential oil. In those cases, you need to make sure that you take the necessary steps to allow bubbles to escape when you make the candle and also add less fragrance on your next go-around. (To avoid bubbles next time, pour your wax more slowly and make sure that you take the proper steps to release trapped air — for more on the basic technique, see Chapter 5.)

What is all this black stuff?

If you've ever seen a black residue on your wall or candleholder and wondered what you're looking at, wonder no more. It's *soot*. Soot results when a fuel isn't broken down completely. If a candle isn't made correctly, it can create excess soot. If you see a candle that's producing soot, stop burning it. Something's not right, and it's not worth polluting your air and lungs.

If you live in a newer home, be especially cautious because your well-sealed windows not only trap in the heat but also soot.

Soot problems can occur when the wick and wax aren't a good match or you added too much of an additive.

Is a candle really a candle if no one sees the flame?

Candles are made to burn, but even if they don't, they can still be useful as decoration. But most people prefer to burn their candles instead of placing them around the house for decorating sake alone. Nothing is more frustrating than a candle that doesn't burn. At least candles that look bad can still burn!

A number of factors may be at play. Of course, if your wick isn't large enough for your candle, you have a problem. And if you don't prime your wick, you have another count against you. (In the latter case, you can just light your candle upside down and allow the wax to drip down the wick.) Or perhaps a clogged wick from too many additives is the problem.

Fragrant Blues: Color and Scent Concerns

Sometimes a little color and fragrance is just what you need to make a simple candle divine. But the more you fiddle with a simple candle, the more opportunity you have to introduce problems. (For more on adding colors and fragrance, see Chapter 6.)

Color me . . . what?

You've found the perfect blue, but somehow it's coming out more of a, well, pinkish-purple. What's going on? Coloring in candles behaves differently from one wax to another and from one additive to another. The most important factor to consider is the curing process. Color can go through a considerable change as the wax cures. Some colors may appear light and pastel after a few hours of cooling, but don't reach their true dark richness until weeks after the candle has been finished.

If the color change happens right after you make the candle instead of after the curing process, you can rest assured that your wax was too hot when you added the color. Pink, in particular, poses a problem when your wax is too hot. Another possibility is that your mold or wax wasn't clean.

If the color change occurs over a period of time, make sure that your candle isn't in sunlight or fluorescent lighting. (If so, add UV inhibitor next time.) Just as sunlight fades your carpet and furniture, it also fades candles. Certain colors, such as purple, are more susceptible to this fading.

Store your candles in a dark place, and if you don't want them to fade when on display, don't set them in front of a window or other source of direct sunlight.

When you color a gel candle, be careful not to add too much color. Gel is transparent, not opaque like paraffin wax, so you don't want to use as much color when making a gel candle.

When layering colors goes awry

When you're making a layered candle and all your layers are mixing together, don't despair. Instead, try waiting a little longer between each pour so that the layers have time to set. You want the layer to look semi-congealed, or to look like it's starting to form a skin, before you pour another one.

However, the layers inevitably blend together some; that's just the nature of layered candles. The key is, though, to start with the darker colors first, so that the blending isn't as obvious.

If your candle's layers are separating, you erred too much the other way and waited too long between layers. The best thing to do in this scenario is to start all over.

For more on making layered candles, see Chapter 8.

Really, it has a fragrance

You added what you thought was the perfect amount and blend of fragrance, waited anxiously for the candle to set, and then lit it to smell . . . nothing. The good news is that it takes at least an hour of burning for a candle's true scent to be determined. Remember, the wax and not the wick contains the scent, so the wick needs time to melt that wax.

If you still think the scent is too light, then maybe it is. If the wick is too small, the pool of melted wax may not be hot enough to release the scent fully. If you added fragrance when the wax was too hot, then that may be the problem. Or maybe you just didn't add enough fragrance. Next time, increase the amount. (And don't forget to take notes so that you can pinpoint just the right amount when you get it.)

Another possibility is that the candle didn't cure long enough. After you make your candle, cover or wrap it so that its surface doesn't lose its scent and then set the candle aside for at least a few days before burning. Some fragrances don't need this curing stage, but most scents get better with time. A candle also burns better after curing.

Part III
Tackling Soap-Making Basics

The 5th Wave   By Rich Tennant

@RICHTENNANT

"I wanted to make oatmeal soap but all I could find were Cocoa Puffs."

In this part . . .

In this part, you find out everything you need to know about making soap for the first time, including what equipment and materials you need. I go over techniques for both hand milling and melting and pouring, as well as how to work with molds and additives.

Chapter 11

Preparing to Make Soap

. . . .

In This Chapter

▶ Figuring out what you need to get started

▶ Organizing your work area

▶ Cleaning up your workspace when you're finished

. . . .

*I*f you're thinking about making soap, then this chapter is for you! You find out which supplies you need to get started and discover how to organize a top-notch workspace.

Stocking Up on Equipment

My husband is the type of person who loves technology. When he starts a new hobby, he researches all the equipment he needs and then starts acquiring it. He's worked his way through woodworking, photography, and cycling. He loves the thrill of acquiring new specialized gadgets. Granted, he uses his tools and has fun with them — but sometimes I wish he'd opt for some less expensive hobbies.

If you're like my husband, I have some bad news for you: Soap making isn't a hobby where you get to go out and buy tons of new gadgets and supplies. Sure, you may have to buy *some* items, but nothing too fancy.

Now, if you're a person more like me who likes to dabble in a hobby a little bit before pouring money into it, I probably just gave you some good news. What's even better is that the equipment that you do need is probably already in your kitchen. (So if nothing else, maybe you can get some new kitchenware out of this adventure!)

The following list describes the equipment you need to make soap (see Figure 11-1) using the techniques discussed in this book. (For descriptions of the various techniques, see Chapter 12.)

Figure 11-1:
You need
this
equipment.

Here is what you'll need for making the soaps in this book:

- ✓ **A double boiler or microwave:** You need a heat source to melt your soap, so a double boiler is ideal. If you're making melt-and-pour soap, you can even use a microwave. If you don't have a double boiler, you can improvise one. If you're not familiar with a double boiler, see Chapter 1.

- ✓ **Glass or heat-resistant plastic bowls:** Use these bowls to melt your soap. Having bowls that you can see through is an added bonus so that you can monitor the soap as it progresses to the melting stage.

- ✓ **Smaller bowls:** These bowls contain premeasured items, such as your additives, as well as soap scraps.

- ✓ **Spoons:** As the soap melts, stir it. Opt for stainless steel or wooden spoons. Although wooden spoons don't last forever, they're cheap to replace.

- ✓ **Stainless steel measuring spoons:** If you use too much essential oil to fragrance your soap, you'll ruin your soap quality, so you need precise measurements. You can also use glass droppers. For more on adding fragrance and color, see Chapter 15.

For larger batches you can weigh your fragrance on a postal scale in a stainless steel cup. Pour it in after setting the tare button on the scale to cancel out the weight of the measuring cup. If you don't have a tare feature on your scale, note the weight of the measuring cup and keep track of the additional ounces as you pour in your scent.

Essential oils eat through plastic, so make sure to avoid plastic utensils or containers when working with them.

✔ **Flexible molds:** You don't have to buy soap molds, although you can if you want. You can use candy molds, candle molds, or any flexible item as a mold. (Don't use ceramic or glass molds, which aren't flexible.) Make sure the mold is flexible enough so that you can remove the soap without breaking it. (For more on molds, see Chapter 12.)

✔ **Parchment, freezer paper, or wax paper:** You can cover your molded soap with these papers, as well as line your work area. For more on organizing your work area, see the section "Preparing Your Workspace," later in this chapter.

If you're making hand-milled soap, you also need a hand grater, preferably stainless steel, to grate your soap. You can also use a food processor.

Many kitchen utensils can be used for both soap making and food preparation, but avoid using any soap-making equipment for cooking that may have retained fragrances, such as plastic spatulas or wooden spoons. You don't want your brownies to taste like patchouli!

Investing in Materials

Just like equipment (see the previous section), you don't need to buy tons of materials to make soap, and what you do need is relatively inexpensive.

Evaluating soap bases

Because all soap bases are different, try a variety to see which you like best. Obviously, you have your personal preferences as far as lather, but ask yourself the following questions as you experiment with different soap bases:

✔ **How transparent is the soap?** You should be able to see through it. (If it's a real soap base instead of a detergent base, it's likely going to be an amber color, but still transparent if it's for melt and pour.)

✔ **What does the base smell like?** You don't want it to smell like ammonia. Also, if you plan to add fragrance, you want the base to have little or no scent.

✔ **How does the soap feel on your skin?** You want the base you are using to feel mild on the skin and not drying when you wash with it.

TIP

If you're willing to spend a little more money for the convenience, you can buy a melt-and-mold soap-making kit, which includes all your supplies. Depending on the kit, you receive soap base, molds, colors, and fragrances. You can buy these kits at craft stores or through online retailers. (See Appendix A for a list of resources.)

Use the following materials when making melt-and-pour soap, which is the easiest and quickest technique for first-timers (see Figure 11-2).

✔ A releasing agent, such as vegetable oil or nonstick cooking spray

✔ Rubbing alcohol, to lightly spray over the molded soap to eliminate bubbles and also to spritz embedded objects before pouring around them

✔ Any additives you want to add, such as color or scent (see Chapter 15)

✔ Melt-and-pour soap base

If you're just getting started making soap, then try your hand at making melt-and-pour soap. (See Chapter 12 for a description of the basic technique.) Simply melt the base and then mold it. You can be as creative with your design, scent, and colors as you want.

Figure 11-2:
You need just a few materials to craft melt-and-pour soap.

Unlike cold-process soap making (which is for more advanced soapmakers and not covered in this book), crafting melt-and-pour soap doesn't require the handling of lye. A melt-and-pour base never contains active or excess lye. But that's where the generalization ends. Different manufacturers make various melt-and-pour bases, and most contain detergents. The packaging doesn't tell you what the base is made of. You can try asking the manufacturer, although it may not want to reveal its "secret recipe."

If you can, try a pure soap base from your local craft store or online retailer. They contain few additives and have a high glycerin content. Pure soap bars tend to *sweat* (moisture beads appear due to exposure to air), but they lather better and longer.

For more information on the melt-and-pour technique, see Chapter 12.

Preparing Your Workspace

Just as with candle making, your kitchen is probably the best spot to set up shop for your soap-making endeavors. That's because you need a heat source, such as your stove or microwave, good lighting, water, and room to spread out.

At least when you work with soap, you know that it's clean. Even if you get it on your counter, you can easily wipe up the mess. However, to make your cleaning job even easier, you may want to line your counters with freezer paper or wax paper. You may use newspapers if you have them, but be aware that they can sometimes leave a black residue on your countertops.

Cleaning Your Workspace and Equipment

Even if you won't be eating off your soap-making tools (and I hope you won't be!), you need to spend time cleaning them. Not only will your tools last longer, but you also won't affect the quality of your future soap batches.

After the soap cools, scrape as much of the soap as possible off your equipment before you clean it. In the case of melt and pour, you can save your scrapings for future use. Otherwise, toss them in the trash or rinse the excess soap down the drain.

You don't need any special supplies to clean your equipment. Just use dish soap and warm water. Don't use the dishwasher, though, because the soap you made isn't the same as dishwasher detergent, and it could cause a suds catastrophe that you won't soon forget. Anyone who has accidentally used liquid dishwashing soap in his dishwasher by mistake has learned this the hard way!

Also make sure that you completely dry your tools. Some metals can develop discoloration if put away wet. If you notice a problem, you may want to try coating your metal tools with oil after you clean and dry them.

Chapter 12

Grasping Soap-Making's Basic Techniques

....

....

The technique you use to make your soaps determines the amount of time you invest in your hobby, as well as any risk factors involved. In this book, I cover two basic soap-making techniques: hand milling and melting and pouring. (You can also make soap from scratch using lye, but the cold process, as it's called, is more complex and requires care in handling sodium hydroxide, which is a caustic substance. I don't cover that in this book.)

Hand milling and melting and pouring may not meet diehard soapmakers' definitions of soap making (because someone else already made the soap). But the truth is, you're taking an existing soap or commercial soap base and molding and transforming it into your own design. The melt-and-pour method is the one taught at most craft stores, and many people — myself included — believe that the melting-and-pouring technique qualifies as real soap making.

If you're just getting started with soap making, then this chapter is for you. Here, I describe the hand-milling and melt-and-pour processes and discuss each method's pros and cons. I also talk about working with molds.

Everything Old Is New Again: Hand-Milled Soap

If you don't like the idea of working with chemicals, you may want to try making hand-milled soap. All you do is take an existing bar of commercial soap, grate it, and then remelt it with water. You can then color, scent, and mold it as you please. (For more on color and scent, see Chapter 15.)

Many diehard soapmakers scoff at this technique. They say that you're technically not making the soap because you're using commercial soap, which *may* be soap but more than likely is a synthetic detergent bar. (If you have a preference for "real" soap, be sure to read the label and buy soap that has ingredients such as sodium cocoate, sodium palmate, sodium olivate, and so on.) But if you want to exercise a little creativity, you can still do so when you hand-mill soap. You can craft soap that looks and smells the way you want it to — something you can't always find at the store.

If you plan to scent your soap, then make sure that you start with an unscented bar of commercial soap.

Advantages and disadvantages

The advantages of hand-milling soap are many:

- ✔ You don't have to work with lye.
- ✔ You can buy a bar of your favorite commercial soap at your local grocery store.
- ✔ You don't have to invest much time.
- ✔ You can still color and scent the soap as you please.
- ✔ You can choose any mold design that you like.
- ✔ You're still exercising your creativity.

The con, however, is a big one: You're using a prefabricated product so you have no control over the ingredients.

Basic steps

If you think you want to make soap, then why not try hand-milling soap that you already have? The only special tool that you really need is a hand grater.

Here are the basic steps.

1. **Grate your soap (see Figure 12-1).**

    The smaller you grate your pieces, the quicker the melting time.

Figure 12-1:
When you hand-mill soap, you grate an existing bar of commercial soap into smaller pieces, melt it, and then remold it.

2. **Melt your pieces in water in the top pot of a double boiler or in a microwave.**

   In general, use approximately 1 cup of water for every 2 cups of soap gratings. If you're unfamiliar with a double boiler, see Chapter 1. If using the microwave, take care not to get the soap too hot. Heat the shavings and water in short bursts and check often, stirring as needed. Some people set their microwaves at 50 percent power when melting clear glycerin soap base or shavings. Experiment with what works best for you and your microwave.

3. **Stir your soap as it melts.**

4. **After the soap has melted, stir in your color.**

   For more on color, see Chapter 15.

5. **Continue stirring until the soap is thick and creamy and then remove it from the heat.**

6. **Add any other additives, such as essential oils.**

   For more on adding scent, see Chapter 15.

7. **Pour your soap into the mold.**

   For more on molds, see the section "Working with Molds," later in this chapter.

8. **Let the soap cool overnight before removing it from the mold.**

Your soap isn't finished just because it's out of the mold. Allow it to solidify for three to seven days.

A Step Ahead of the Game: Making Melt-and-Pour Soap

If making hand-milled soap (see the previous section) sounds like cheating to you, then making melt-and-pour soap may be right up your alley. Instead of using commercial soap, you actually use a melt-and-pour soap base that you purchase in a craft store. The base comes in blocks, chunks, or nuggets, and you simply melt the amount you need and then mold it.

Advantages and disadvantages

The advantages of melt-and-pour soap are plentiful:

✔ You don't have to work with chemicals.

✔ It takes less than an hour to make.

✔ You can still color and scent the soap as you please.

✔ You can choose any mold design that you like.

✔ You're still exercising your creativity.

✔ As long as you supervise the cutting and melting, melt-and-pour soap making is a great craft for kids.

On the downside, if you want to make soap so that you have control over the ingredients, you don't really have much of a say with this technique. However, different manufacturers use different ingredients to make their bases, so you can experiment until you find one you like.

Basic steps

Probably more than any other soap-making technique, melt-and-pour soap making resembles the steps involved in making candles. Like candle making, you use premade material, melt it, and mold it. If you love to make candles, chances are you'll enjoy making melt-and-pour soaps.

Here's how melt-and-pour soap making works:

1. **Melt your soap chunks in a double boiler over medium heat or melt them in a heat-resistant bowl in the microwave (see Figure 12-2).**

   You can also cut 1- or 2-inch chunks off a large 1-pound or 5-pound block of soap if you're not using precut chunks.

Figure 12-2: You can use a microwave to melt your soap chunks. Then you just need to pour your melted soap into a mold.

If you're melting your soap in the microwave, melt your soap at 50 percent heat for approximately 1 minute. Stir your soap. Continue melting it at 20-second intervals until the soap is completely melted.

2. **Remove your melted soap from the heat and stir in any additives, such as color.**

3. **Pour your melted soap into the mold.**

   Most melt-and-pour soaps shrink as they set, so you probably don't need to spray your mold with a releasing agent.

   For more on molds, see the section "Working with Molds," later in this chapter.

4. **Allow your soap to cool for approximately 1 hour.**

Although melt-and-pour soap is immediately safe for the skin, let it dry out and harden for a few days before use, so that it will last longer.

Working with Molds

If you want to make soap that's in a shape other than a ball or a puddle, use a mold. Just as in candle making, your mold options are endless. The only caveat is that you must use a flexible mold — not glass or ceramic — so that you can remove your hardened soap without breaking anything.

You can use traditional soap molds, but your options don't end there (see Figure 12-3). In fact, if you make candles, many of your molds may be appropriate for making soaps as well. (See Chapter 3 for more on candle molds.) You can also use candy molds or other household items, such as mini muffin tins, cake pans, or even ice cube trays. Some people have found plastic cat food containers, round Pringles chips containers, or other packaging items to be wonderful molds after being thoroughly cleaned. Or try raiding the hardware store for PVC pipe, just making sure to seal one end so that the soap doesn't leak out. You can even make a sheet of soap and then use cookie cutters to create your designs.

Preparing your molds

You want your molds to be clean and dry before you use them. Depending on your past experience using a particular mold and recipe, you may decide to spray it with a releasing agent, such as vegetable oil, so that the soap is easier to remove. If you're making melt-and-pour soap, however, it typically shrinks, so you probably don't need to use a releasing agent.

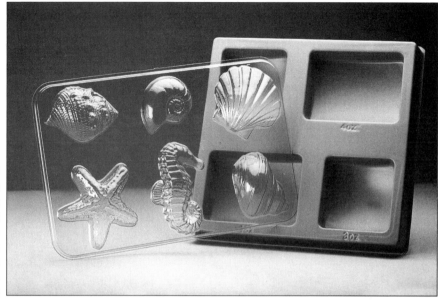

Figure 12-3:
Be creative
when it
comes to
choosing
your soap
molds.

If you don't want to worry about cleaning your mold, then consider lining it with a plastic bag. Just make sure that you smooth the bag down to avoid creases, which will show up in your finished soap. For molds with straight sides, freezer paper is nicer because it lays out smooth. Be sure to put the plastic-coated side of the freezer paper toward the soap.

After you pour your soap, keep it in the mold at least one day.

Cleaning your molds

Unlike candle wax, soap is easy to wash off your molds. As long as you stick to the hand-milling or melting-and-pouring methods described in this book, you don't have to worry about wearing gloves, and you can rinse the excess soap down your kitchen-sink drain. What could be easier than that?

Chapter 13

Delving into Additives

In This Chapter

▶ Experimenting with additives to improve your soap

▶ Making your soaps last

No matter what soap-making technique you use, you will likely want to include additives in your products. That's much of the fun of crafting your own soaps at home! In this chapter, I include descriptions and guidelines to help you along in your decision.

Using Additives

Additives are generally anything you add to your soap base to enhance its color, scent, texture, skin-care benefits, or overall aesthetic value.

Hands-on help

You stir in the additives as the last step before pouring your soap into the mold — after the soap has been melted.

If you're adding a solid additive to melt-and-pour soap, be aware that it may *separate,* or sink to the bottom of your mold. To avoid this occurrence, let your soap cool more than you usually would, stirring the additive into the soap the entire time. You want the soap mixture to thicken in your bowl before you pour it into the mold, much like thickening gelatin. Waiting longer than usual can help the solid additive stay suspended in the soap.

Keep these tips in mind when working with additives:

✔ As a general rule, if you think something may irritate your skin, refrain from adding it.

✔ If you add mashed fruit or other items that may go rancid, consider adding a preservative, such as Vitamin E or carrot seed oil.

✔ Unless specified, add no more than 1 tablespoon of an additive per pound of soap. Too much of an additive can cloud your soap.

✔ When working with butter and oil additives, don't add too much because they may separate, as well as decrease your soap's lathering ability.

Your additive options

The additives I describe in this section work wonderfully with melt-and-pour soaps. Table 13-1 describes popular additives.

Table 13-1	Common Soap-Making Additives
Additive	*Description*
Almond oil	Soothes irritated, itchy skin. Also used as base. Has slight odor.
Aloe vera	Relieves dry and burned skin. Can use in plant or gel form.
Apricot	Softens skin. A popular bath additive. To use, place dried apricots in water for several hours and then liquefy.
Apricot kernel oil	Softens skin. Especially good for sensitive skin.
Beeswax	Hardens soap and contributes scent. Need to melt before adding to soap. Don't use more than 1 ounce per pound of soap.
Clay	Helps dry out oily skin. Choose finely powdered French clay.
Cocoa butter	Hardens soap and moisturizes. Looks and smells like white chocolate, but can be purchased in a deodorized form if you want its qualities without the chocolate smell.
Cucumber	Acts as astringent. Use grated skin or liquefied.
Glycerin	Moisturizes skin.

Additive	Description
Herbs	Contribute texture and color.
Honey	Moisturizes skin and makes soap softer.
Lanolin	Hardens soap. Moisturizes and softens skin. Can cloud soap. Don't use if allergic to wool.
Lemon	Adds texture and speckling, as well as antibacterial qualities. Use grated peel.
Oatmeal	Softens and exfoliates skin. Adds texture. Use ground rolled oats. Limit to a maximum of ½ cup rolled or ¼ cup ground or pulverized oats per pound of soap. A blender works very well for making oat flour.
Pumice	Removes tough dirt, but can be harsh. Adds texture.
Vitamin E oil	Use as a preservative when you add fresh fruit or other additive at risk of spoiling.
Wheat germ	Exfoliates skin, as well as adding bulk and texture. Shows up in soap as light speckling. Use no more than 3 tablespoons per pound of soap.

Storing Your Soap

If your soap contains glycerin, as most melt-and-pour soaps do, then over time, it will *sweat,* or develop little beads of water on it, as the water in the air is drawn to the soap's surface. This sweating doesn't actually harm the soap, but it does detract from its appearance.

To avoid sweating, make sure that the air doesn't come into contact with the soap's surface. The easiest way is to wrap the soap in protective plastic wrap if you won't be using it right away. Wrapping your soap in plastic wrap also protects its surface from fingerprints.

If you're feeling a little creative, you can even wrap your prewrapped plastic soap in transparent cellophane in various colors. That way, you're not only protecting it from air exposure, you have a decorative item or a premade gift ready to give away at any time.

Chapter 14

Creating Basic Soap Projects

· ·

· ·

*T*he microwave is a wonderful appliance, and its usefulness isn't limited to heating and cooking foods. In fact, most of this chapter's recipes take advantage of your microwave so that you can make quick work of your soap projects. (If you don't have a microwave, you can use a double boiler.)

In this chapter, I offer you simple melt-and-pour and hand-milled soap projects well suited to the novice soapmaker. (You can find overviews of the basic techniques in Chapter 12.)

Starting Small . . . or Not

If you're just getting starting in soap making, I suggest beginning with the basic melt-and-pour recipes in this chapter. Don't worry about adding color or scent yet if you'd rather have a lower-cost practice run. The melt-and-pour technique is easily mastered, and you can tackle those additives on your next go-round when you think you are ready.

Hand-milled soaps are also good starters. Like your melt-and-pour soaps, you can quickly melt them in your microwave and then pour the liquid into your mold. A few hours later, you have beautiful, molded soaps.

The true test for how well your soap turns out isn't whether it looks like those perfect bars you see at the market; the true test is how happy you are with the results when you wash with the soap.

Making Melt-And-Pour Magic

Melt-and-pour soap is so easy to make, you really don't need a recipe, but I'm going to give you some anyway. You simply cut off the amount of soap base — the big block or chunks of translucent melt-and-pour soap available at your local craft store — you need, chop it into cubes, and melt them in the microwave. (You can even buy the base precut, if you want.)

You don't even need to measure how much soap your mold requires. You can eyeball it, and just include a little extra soap. If you melt too much soap, no problem — you can reuse it next time. (For more on molds, see Chapter 12.)

If you really prefer to measure how much soap base you need, choose your mold and fill it with water. Transfer the water to the bowl your melted soap will end up in and mark a line with a pen or masking tape. Melt your soap, pour it into the bowl, and note where it reaches. If you're short on soap, just add some unmelted soap cubes. The heat of the melted soap will cause them to melt.

The following sections offer basic melt-and-pour recipes; don't limit yourself to these options, though. Create your own recipes!

Going for clear: Translucent melt-and-pour soap

Melt-and-pour soap is naturally translucent, so you can easily create a clear bar of soap. Try this basic recipe:

1. **Using a knife, cut 1 pound of melt-and-pour soap base into 1-inch cubes or smaller, place them in a microwave-safe bowl, and cover.**

   If your bowl doesn't hold that much soap, feel free to melt just half the base. Even doing the lesser amount, you still end up with several small bars of soap, depending on your mold's size.

   If you don't want to cut your soap, then buy your soap precubed. (You can usually buy it precolored as well.) You can easily break it off with your hands.

2. **Place your soap in the microwave and heat for 45 seconds.**

3. **Stir your soap.**

4. **Continue melting your soap in 15-second intervals, stirring in between each time, until your soap base is completely melted.**

   Keep an eye on your mixture. You don't want it to boil over or become frothy. Just like food, you can burn your soap. (It even looks burnt because it turns a brownish-yellow color.)

5. **Add in any other additives you want to use.**

   Keep in mind that solid additives may fall to the bottom of your mold unless you let the soap gel a bit before adding. (For more on additives and this technique, see Chapter 13.)

6. **Pour your soap into your mold.**

   You don't have to, but you can lightly spray your mold with a releasing agent, such as vegetable oil, if you like, so that the soap is easier to remove. When you pour, try to aim for the middle of the mold so that the mold doesn't overflow before it's completely filled.

7. **Lightly spray your soap with rubbing alcohol (optional).**

   This step can help eliminate bubbles that form on the surface of your soap.

8. **Remove your soap from the mold after it solidifies.**

   You usually need to keep your soap in the mold anywhere from one to three hours. The soap doesn't completely harden, but it does get hard enough to remove from the mold. If you're a more patient person, you can leave the soaps in the mold overnight so they're totally firm before removal. This ensures that they keep a sharp outline if they have an intricate pattern.

   To remove your soap from the mold, invert it and press gently on the bottom of the mold. If your soap doesn't pop out, it may need to cool longer. If you're still having problems, you can pour some warm water on the bottom of the mold or freeze it for a few minutes.

9. **If you're not going to use your soap right away, wrap it in plastic to store.**

Changing your look: Basic soaps

Glycerin soap, avocado cucumber soap, coconut soap — they all sound like a nice change of pace, don't they? Fortunately, you can make them all as easily as you do the basic translucent soap in the section "Going for clear: Translucent melt-and-pour soap," earlier in this chapter.

When you're using a double boiler

If you don't have a microwave, you can use a double boiler to melt your melt-and-pour soap base. (See Chapter 1 for a description of a double boiler.) Place your soap base in the top part of the double boiler and add water to the bottom part. Then gently heat your soap until it's mostly melted. Turn off the burner and cover your double boiler to trap the heat in, and continue to melt the soap. After your soap is melted, you're ready to stir in additives and mold your soap.

Here's the secret. Follow the same steps, but just change your soap base. You don't even need to alter the recipe. Go to your local craft store aisle and buy some white glycerin soap base, avocado cucumber soap base, and clear glycerin soap base. And don't forget to explore precolored soap bases as well. Who would have thought so many different soaps could be obtained so easily?!

Pouring it on: Layered soap

Layered soaps alternate colors and sometimes scent, all in the same bar. Although they look like you spent a lot of time making them, these visually appealing soaps are a snap! To make layered soap:

1. **Melt your melt-and-pour soap base in a covered microwave-safe bowl for 45 seconds; stir.**

   Don't forget to cut your soap into 1-inch cubes to make the melting go faster.

2. **Continue melting your soap at 15-second intervals, stirring in between each time, until your soap base is completely melted.**

3. **Working quickly, divide your soap into bowls based on the number of colors you want.**

   For example, if you want a layered soap featuring three colors, you divide your melted soap base among three bowls.

4. **Stir a different color into each bowl.**

5. **Add any scent; stir well.**

    This soap is particularly nice when each layer features a scent that corresponds to the color. (For more on color and scent, see Chapter 15.)

6. **Pour your first layer of soap into the mold; let cool until it thickens.**

   Your soap usually takes five to ten minutes to cool. You're looking for a thin skin to form.

Make sure that you keep an eye on your soap. If your soap isn't cool enough, the second layer of color will bleed through the first layer so that the colors run together. If you wait too long and allow the first layer to become too solid, the layers won't stick together.

7. **After your first layer cools, lightly spritz it with rubbing alcohol.**

   The alcohol helps the layers adhere to each other.

8. **Pour your second layer of color.**

   This layer should be no more than 120°F, or it may melt your first layer.

9. **Repeat Steps 6 through 8 as many times as necessary to complete your layers.**

10. **Remove your soap from the mold after it cools completely.**

    Don't rush this step. If you remove the soap too soon, your layers may separate.

11. **If you're not going to use your soap right away, wrap it in plastic to store.**

Mixing things up: Marbled soap

If you want to make your soap look like you've gone to a lot of trouble, do I have a technique for you! One easy step pays big appearance dividends, and the result is *marbled soap,* which is also known as swirled soap. (See the photo in the color section.)

Marbled soap is just two or more colors mixed together to achieve a marbled effect. To make marbled soap:

1. **Melt your soap base.**

2. **Separate a small amount of melted base into another bowl.**

3. **Add your main color to the bowl that contains the majority of the soap.**

   Don't choose too dark of a base color because you want your contrasting swirl to be visible.

4. **Add a darker color to the small amount of base.**

5. **Pour your main color of soap into the mold.**

6. **Take the smaller portion of swirl color and pour it evenly over the top of your base soap in a zigzag fashion, trying to evenly pour over the top so all parts of the soap will have both colors.**

Using a toothpick, knife, or other utensil, marble the combined soaps much like you would when making a marbled cake. Put your knife or toothpick down through the soap and gently drag it back and forth from side to side, from one end of the mold to the other. Some people like to repeat that step from the opposite direction, but if you're working with a small mold, this may overmix your two colors. Use your discretion. A bit of practice will help you know how much is enough.

7. Remove your soap from the mold after it hardens.

This step can take anywhere from one to three hours.

Reshaping Your Home: Basic Hand-Milled Soap

You can take a bar of everyday household soap and transform it into shapes, colors, and scents of your choice by hand-milling soap. The process is very similar to melt-and-pour soap. The main differences are that you're using commercial soap instead of a soap base and you're adding liquid to your soap chunks before melting. Use this basic recipe.

1. Take an unscented bar of soap and grate it with a hand grater.

As you're grating, occasionally rotate your soap so that you're grating the sharper corners. This step helps you avoid cutting your hands.

2. For every 1 cup of grated soap, add ½ cup of water.

When I grate a 4½-ounce bar of soap, I end up with 1½ cups of soap, so I add ¾ cup of water.

3. Place your soap in a microwave-safe, covered bowl and melt it in the microwave for 45 seconds; stir.

4. When your soap has melted, add your color and then scent (optional).

5. Add any additives you want (optional).

6. Pour into your mold and let it set at room temperature overnight.

Hand-milled soaps need to stay in the mold longer than melt-and-pour soaps, due to the higher water content at the time of pour.

7. Remove from mold.

8. Let the soap dry at room temperature for about a week before using.

Don't hesitate to have fun with this soap. You can include additives just as you would with soap you make using any other technique. Take a look at Chapter 13 for a list of additives.

Part IV
Fancying Up
Your Soap

The 5th Wave   By Rich Tennant

"I'm making my own scents with celery seed, almond oil, and rosemary. What we don't use in the homemade soaps I'll toss with lettuce and save it for dinner."

In this part . . .

You can make all good things great, and soap is no exception. Add a little color and fragrance, and boom, ordinary, everyday soap transforms into a work of art. In this part, you find out how to go beyond basic soap and make colored soaps, scented soaps, decorative soaps, and more. You also discover how to make home-spa items, such as bath salts, body lotion, and bubble bath. Lastly, if you encounter problems, you can check out Chapter 18, which helps you figure out what went wrong.

Chapter 15

Creating Scent-sations: Adding Color and Scent

In This Chapter

▶ Experimenting with different forms of color

▶ Adding sensational scents to your soaps

▶ Wrestling with sensitive skin issues when you color and scent your soaps

Soap is a necessity if you want to promote a clean image. But if you're like most people, you want to enjoy what you wash with, as well as have it look (and smell) attractive in your bathroom and kitchen. Although coloring and fragrance don't necessarily add any special powers to your soap, they sure do improve its appearance and increase your satisfaction.

In this chapter, I show you how to color and scent your soap using a variety of methods. I also clue you in on the secrets of coloring and scenting your soap when you have sensitive skin.

The Ins and Outs of Coloring Your Soap

If you're like most soapmakers, you're probably hankering to try your hand at adding color. I don't blame you. In fact, the first bar of soap I ever made was done in my favorite color, purple — and I colored it easily.

Thanks to its translucent nature, melt-and-pour soap looks particularly stunning when you add vibrant colors. Matching your soap's color to your decor isn't difficult, especially when you use precolored melt-and-pour soap base. If you don't see precolored soap base that you like, you can take matters into your own hands — literally — and delve into the world of dyes and dried herbs and spices to come up with a color that appeals to you.

The coloring that works best for one soap doesn't necessarily work well for another — just like certain shades of clothing don't work well on all people. And, of course, each coloring technique has its little secrets of success, described in each section.

White is for wimps: Coloring options

If you don't color your soap, you end up with a translucent melt-and-pour bar and an opaque white remilled one. Chances are, you want to trade your blasé soaps in for soaps that sport a new shade — not that there's anything wrong, of course, with going au naturel in color!

In fact, coloring your soap is a lot like coloring your hair: You have to decide what type of product to use. Just as you can use natural hennas or permanent hair colorings, you must choose between several colorant options for soaps. Fortunately, the soap colorant decision is a fairly easy one to make, so you shouldn't have any trouble transforming your soap to the color of the rainbow you prefer. (Now, about that gray . . .)

No matter what type of soap you're making, you have the following main colorant options (see Figure 15-1):

- ✔ Herbs and spices
- ✔ Soap dyes

If you're looking for colorants that have been FDA approved, you can purchase them and see a listing at http://members.aol.com/pigmntlady/colors.htm.

You can even use certain essential oils to color your soap. And technically, you can use food colorings or wax crayons, but food coloring wasn't designed to work in soap. What you have in your cupboard is very diluted and doesn't offer much color. In addition, the color may alter over time.

The following sections outline your coloring options in more depth.

Easy does it: Melt-and-pour soap bases

If you want a little color, but you're new to soap making, then go buy some melt-and-pour soap base. Color is so easy when you go this route. All you do is substitute translucent or opaque (not see-through) colored base for your normal translucent base in your soap-making projects. (See Chapter 14 for some easy melt-and-pour projects.) You literally just melt and pour into your mold, and you have colored soaps.

Melt-and-pour soap base is available in the soap-making aisle of your local craft store and also at major discount stores. You have your choice of numerous colors. If you can't find the exact shade you want, then you may want to consider using soap dyes or mixing two colored soap bases together. (See the section "Dye another day: Soap dyes," later in this chapter, for information.)

Kids love making melt-and-pour soaps. Because you're not working with lye, also known as sodium hydroxide, melt-and-pour soaps are safe for kids to enjoy — as long as you take precautions with the hot liquid, of course. Precolored soap base gives you big results with little effort, something that kids really appreciate. If your child has his own bathroom, help him create matching soaps.

Dye another day: Soap dyes

Soap dyes are simply colorants formulated specifically to dissolve into your soap. The dye actually combines with your soap's molecular material. Although dyes change your soap's color, they don't change the soap's translucent nature. If you're not using precolored melt-and-pour soap base, then dyes are the next best thing.

Figure 15-1:
Soap dyes, herbs, and spices for the home soapmaker.

Dyes usually come in wax blocks or bottles (refer to Figure 15-1), although you can find them in powder and chip forms as well. You find mostly wax blocks or bottles at your local craft store. If you can't find the color you want, experiment with mixing colors or look in Appendix A at suppliers' Web sites to order those hard-to-find colors.

Soap dyes are different than candle dyes. I don't recommend interchanging them. That's because candle dye is specifically manufactured for wax, while soap dye is made for, well, soap — two very different ingredients. That said, I have heard of people who have had success and no detrimental side effects from coloring their soap with candle dyes. Like crayons, they work but have not technically been approved by the FDA for use in soaps or cosmetics.

Some folks are tempted to use fabric dyes in their soaps, but these should definitely be avoided.

The most common complaint regarding dyes is that they aren't always *color-fast,* or resistant to *bleeding,* or color seeping. If your soap lather is the same color as your soap, your dye isn't colorfast. To help combat this problem, make sure that you're not adding too much dye. More dye doesn't equal more color in this case; it equals more bleeding!

Getting spicy: Herbs, spices, and other natural colorants

If you want to keep your coloring agents as natural as possible, then you may want to dig into your garden or kitchen cupboard for some herbs and spices. These natural colorants give a subtle, earth-toned appearance.

If your style leans more toward vibrant, edgy colors, then herbs and spices probably aren't for you. I personally love the look of soap colored with herbs and spices. In addition to a slight coloring, you see a bit of speckling, which adds an interesting texture and feel to your soap. Try including annatto, cocoa, cinnamon, or your favorite ground-up flower or herb to your next batch of soap. (For suggested amounts, see the section "Time to create: Adding your color," later in this chapter.) You can even mash up fruits and vegetables to color your soap, but remember that these food items may affect your soap's shelf life. Use them sparingly and be sure they're finely pureed.

If what you're adding has a fragrance on its own, keep that in mind when you scent your soap.

Do you like the idea of using natural colorants in your soap but don't know where to start? Try these few ideas.

- ✔ Annatto gives you intense orange and yellow colors.

- ✔ Black-eyed Susans — yes, the same bountiful flower that's determined to take over your landscaping — gives you a pastel yellow color.

- ✔ Calendula flowers produce yellowish-orange colors.

- ✔ Chlorophyll capsules, available at your local pharmacy, produce — what else — green.

- ✔ Cocoa gives chocolate lovers a nice shade of brown, as well as a chocolate scent. (Warning — avoid if you're on a diet.)

- ✔ Paprika produces a brick red color.

- ✔ St. John's wort ends up as yellow.

If you see a flower you like, why not experiment with it to see what color you achieve?

Essentially color: Essential oils

Although you use essential oils primarily to add scent (see the section "Essentially your own: Essential oils," later in the chapter, for information), essential oils can also add color to your soap. Don't expect anything major, but do know that you can achieve nice, soft shades with some oils. For instance, you can use orange essential oil for a soft warm orange shade or patchouli, which will make the soap a brownish tan.

Your essential oil's color is a good clue to the soft hue that you can achieve in your soap.

Tell me a secret: Color clues

Certain knowledge can make your coloring adventures easier. For example, if you know that using a lot of color can cause your soap to bleed, then you know not to keep adding it in an attempt to achieve a darker shade.

Melt-and-pour soaps are simple to color. The color you see is pretty much what you get. If you're going for white instead of color, you can buy the base precolored white.

If you're adding both color and fragrance to your soap, add color first.

Colors tend to fade over time. If possible, keep your soap out of sunlight to make the color last longer.

Time to create: Adding your color

When adding color, easy does it. Add too much blue, and you end up looking like a Smurf. Add too little, and you may not get the color of soap you wanted, but at least your skin looks normal.

If you're using liquid soap dye to color your melt-and-pour soap, add the desired amount to the melted base, stir well, and then pour the mixture into your mold (see Figure 15-2). If you're using solid dye, shave off the desired amount and melt it with your melt-and-pour soap base. Using powdered dye is even easier; just combine a small amount of powder with the same amount of water or soap, stir, and add it into the melted soap base before pouring into your mold.

If you're using natural colorants, such as herbs and spices, start out with 1 to 3 teaspoons per pound of soap so that your soap still solidifies. How much you use depends on your tastes and the potency of the spice you're using. You may decide to go higher after you get some experience with that particular additive. Mix your colorant with a small amount of soap and then remix it to the main batch. Always be sure to make a note of how much you've used to obtain a specific shade, so you can duplicate it later.

Additives can contribute volume to the soap, so take that into account when you're estimating how much to melt for a particular mold.

Figure 15-2:
Simply add
your dye
to your
melted soap
base —
when you're
not using
precolored
soap base,
that is!

Scenting Your Soap

Fragrance is very important to most people. If the soap smells awful, you probably won't want to wash with it. Of course, something that smells wonderful not only invites you to wash, but can also affect your mood.

Fortunately, adding scent is easy: You just put in your desired amount, stir well, and mold; the process is the same whether you're using essential oils, fragrance oils, or herbs and spices (see Figure 15-3). The hardest part of scenting may be deciding what fragrance you want to achieve. But finding just the right smell is a fun and creative aspect of soap making. (For some great scent suggestions, check out Chapter 19.)

Essentially your own: Essential oils

You may have heard all about the health- and mood-enhancing benefits of essential oils. *Essential oils* are the oils extracted from plants. Essential oils are natural, while fragrance oils (see the next section) are synthetic or a blend of synthetic and natural ingredients.

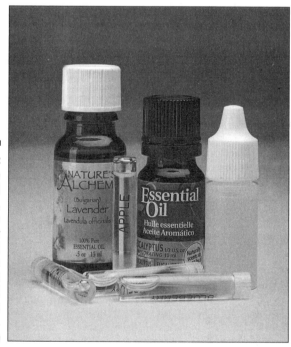

Figure 15-3: You can use essential oils, fragrance oils, or herbs and spices to add wonderful aromas to your soap.

I could write a whole book about the science of essential oils, known as *aromatherapy,* but instead I tell you the nuts and bolts of it in Chapter 19. (If you do want the longer version, check out *Aromatherapy For Dummies,* by Kathi Keville, published by Wiley.) But what you need to know right now for your scenting purposes is this: If you want to create a particular mood, then find the oil that matches it and consider adding it to your batch of soap.

In general, essential oils result in a stronger scent than you achieve with fragrance oils, which is good because essential oils are more costly than fragrance oils. How hard it is to extract the oil from the plant and how plentiful those plants are in nature determines how much each type of essential oil costs. Fortunately, a small bottle of oil should last through several batches.

Consider these tips when using essential oils:

- ✔ Although you can find fragrance oils in your local craft store, you probably won't find essential oils — or at least not high-quality oils if you do. Instead, visit your local health-food store or order online. (See Appendix A for some sources.)

- ✔ To scent your soap with essential oils, add the oil to your melting soap as the last step before you pour it into the mold.

- ✔ If you're just starting to scent with oils, don't delve into making your blends yet (see Chapter 19). Instead, try inexpensive oil.

- ✔ You don't need to adjust the liquid in your recipes when you use oils to scent your soap.

Finding fragrance oils

Companies manufacture *fragrance oils* with the goal of capturing a scent that's similar to essential oils or copying a fragrance that can't be obtained through essential oil extraction, such as in fruit scents. Although they're synthetic, they may contain some natural ingredients. Unfortunately, manufacturers don't list their ingredients, so knowing if any health benefits result from the use of fragrance oils is nearly impossible.

These oils are easy to find in the soap-making aisle of your local craft store. They're also less expensive than the real thing — in this case, essential oils. (See the preceding section for more on these plant extracts.) Quality, of course, varies among brands. Experiment to find a scent you're happy with. Be sure to check Appendix A for some reliable online suppliers of fragrance oils developed for use in soap. Some of those available online are superior to what is often offered at craft stores, and you will find a much greater variety.

Avoid potpourri oils when obtaining fragrance oils for soap making. They are not intended for use on the skin.

You don't need to use much fragrance oil to produce a nice scent. In general, you want to use about 1 to 3 teaspoons of fragrance oil per pound of soap. You add this oil as the last step before you pour your soap into the mold. Don't think that you can use more scent to achieve a more intense fragrance. The extra scent clouds your soap and can irritate sensitive skin. (And besides, do you think that people wearing excessive perfume smell better anyway?)

When working with fragrance oils, remember that although fragrance oils come in both liquid and block form, liquid is easier to use.

From your kitchen: Using herbs, spices, and extracts

Not only can you use herbs, spices, and other natural additives to lightly color your soap, but you can also create lovely aromas with them as well. (For more on using herbs and spices as a colorant, see the section "Getting spicy: Herbs, spices, and other natural colorants," earlier in this chapter.) The scent isn't as strong as when you use oils, but having the combination of color, scent, and texture all in one agent is a pleasant touch.

If you want your soap to have a definite scent, don't rely solely on herbs and spices. Their scent is too subtle to be used alone. Instead, combine them with essential or fragrance oil.

Check out your cupboard and garden. If you like a particular scent, grind it into powder using a coffee grinder, food processor, or mortar and pestle. Think cinnamon, oatmeal, peppermint, and lavender for starters.

Consider mixing liquid Vitamin E or Vitamin C with your herbs so that they don't darken down the road. (You can buy these at health-food stores.) These vitamins are great natural preservatives.

When You Have Sensitive Skin . . .

You may be turning to soap making to combat sensitive skin. Even though you're making soap at home, you still need to be careful with what you add to your soap. Many of the cautions I give are common sense. For example, if the item you're considering adding to your soap doesn't normally come into contact with skin, then don't use it.

In general, keep the following pointers in mind if you have sensitive skin:

✔ Certain essential oils are known to irritate skin. You may want to be careful with eucalyptus, juniper, orange, spearmint, peppermint, bergamot, pine, and rosemary, to name just a few. Fragrance oils can also give your skin grief.

✔ Dyes are common allergens.

Chapter 16

Going Beyond Basic Soap

*Y*ou don't have to settle for basic translucent soaps anymore — although as attractive as they are even when uncolored, I wouldn't exactly say that you're settling! But thanks to the simple techniques I describe in this chapter, you can take your soap from plain-Jane to beauty queen in a matter of minutes. And the best thing is that although these techniques fetch your soaps million-dollar looks, they require little effort. What a deal!

Matching Your Bath: Colored Soap

Who says melt-and-pour soap has to stay translucent? In fact, you can easily transform melt-and-pour soaps into stunning slabs of color. (You can see examples of colored soaps in the color photo section of this book.)

The easiest way to make colored soap is to buy a precolored slab of melt-and-pour soap base in the soap-making aisle of your local craft store. But you're not limited to those colors. You can purchase soap dyes and then mix and match them to create colors of your choice. (For more on working with color, see Chapter 15.)

To make colored soap, if you're not using a precolored soap base:

1. **Place your soap cubes in a microwave-safe bowl and cover; microwave and heat for 45 seconds.**

2. **Stir your soap.**

3. **Continue melting your soap in 15-second intervals, stirring in between each time, until your soap base is completely melted.**

4. **After your soap has melted, squeeze a few drops of liquid soap dye into the melted soap and stir until it dissolves completely.**

   If your soap isn't the color you want, add a few more drops of color until you reach the desired shade.

   If you're using a colored block of dye, slice off a small sliver of dye, place it in the melted soap, and stir until it dissolves completely. If the color isn't quite right, you can always add more dye, but remember, you can't take it out if you add too much in the first place.

5. **Pour your soap into the prepared mold.**

6. **Lightly spray the surface of your soap with rubbing alcohol.**

   The alcohol helps dissipate bubbles. Simply put your alcohol in an empty spray bottle and mist.

7. **Remove your soap from the mold after it cools and solidifies.**

8. **If you're not going to use your soap right away, wrap it in plastic to store.**

You now have *luminous* bars of colored translucent soap.

Jazzing Up Your Interior: Decorative Soap

Decorative soap may look fancy, but it doesn't have any dark secrets. Decorative soaps are really all about the mold. Just by changing your mold you can enjoy soaps in a variety of shapes, such as flowers, leaves, dolphins, shells, and even hearts. (You can see examples of decorative soaps in the color photo section of this book.)

If you can't find the shape you want in the soap-making aisle of your local craft store, check out the candy molds or even floating candle molds. Those work just as well. (For more on your soap-mold options, see Chapter 12.)

No matter what mold you use, you still can easily remove your soap. You don't even have to take any special precautions, other than making sure that you're particularly careful when applying pressure around delicate parts of your mold, such as the stem of an apple or a dolphin's tail.

Try to pair your decorative soap with a matching scent. For example, if you mold a soap in the shape of an orange, pair it with a citrus scent and avoid something confusing like watermelon!

Capturing Your Favorite Smells: Scented Soap

Adding scent doesn't make your soap look different, but it sure can affect your pleasure in the soap as you wash. And matching your scent to your soap's shape or even the room you'll be using it in is a particularly nice touch.

You can make a scented bar of soap by taking the following steps.

1. **Melt your soap base.**

2. **After your soap has melted, squeeze a few drops of liquid scent into your melted soap and stir until it disappears completely.**

   If you're using a scented block of fragrance, slice off the amount you want, place it in the melted soap, and stir until it dissolves completely.

3. **Pour your soap into your mold.**

4. **Remove your soap from the mold after it cools and solidifies.**

5. **If you're not going to use your soap right away, wrap it in plastic to store.**

Looking Inside Your Soap: Variegated Soap

Variegated soaps are simply translucent soap bases with embedded chunks or slivers of soap visible in them. (See the photo in the color section.) You can create these soap chunks or buy them premade at your local craft store.

 If you want to make your own soap chunks to embed in variegated soap, simply make your soap as usual and dice the bar into chunks that are the size you want. If you want a pleasing contrast, don't forget to use a different shade than the base color.

To make a variegated soap with premade colored soap cubes:

1. **Place your colored soap chunks in the freezer to chill for an hour or so.**

   Chilling the chunks makes them less likely to melt when you pour your melted soap base over them.

   If you're using store-bought soap slivers or chunks specially made for this task, then you can skip Step 1. They're designed not to melt, so no chilling is necessary.

2. **Melt your soap base.**

3. **Add color and then scent; stir well.**

   For more on color and scent, see Chapter 15.

4. **Fill your mold half full of soap.**

5. **After the soap starts to set, place the chunks where you want them to appear in your mold.**

6. **When the soap cools, pour your remaining soap over the preset soap chunks.**

   Your remaining soap should be warm, but not so hot that it melts the chunks. If you're using soap shavings specially made for this project, you don't need to wait.

7. **Remove your soap from the mold after it solidifies.**

8. **If you're not going to use your soap right away, wrap it in plastic to store.**

If you're making your own chunks for embedding purposes, consider using cookie cutters to form them into attractive shapes.

Inserting Small Soaps Inside a Larger Bar of Soap

In addition to embedding chunks or slivers of soap, you can embed entire small bars of soap inside a larger bar. You can buy premade small soaps at your local craft store, or you can create them yourself.

To make your own small bars of soap, pour your melted soap into small molds or use cookie cutters to cut out shapes from a finished slab of soap.

To embed your bar of soap, follow these steps:

1. **Place your small bar of soap in the freezer to chill for an hour.**

2. **Melt your soap base.**

3. **Add color and then scent; stir well.**

So that your embedded soap will be visible, consider using little or no color in the outer layer of soap.

4. **Pour a thin layer of melted soap in your mold.**

5. **After the soap starts to set, position your small bar of soap in your mold.**

6. **When the soap in the mold cools, pour your remaining soap.**

7. **Remove your soap from the mold after it solidifies.**

8. **If you're not going to use your soap right away, wrap it in plastic to store.**

Getting Creative: Embedding Items Inside Your Soap

There are any number of objects that can be embedded in a bar of soap. You can really let your creativity go wild with this if you know the criteria for choosing appropriate items.

Use your head when thinking of objects to embed. Avoid the following characteristics when choosing an embedment:

- A sharp item that may cut your skin, such as glass

- An item that can irritate your skin, such as certain poisonous plants

- An item that doesn't hold up to water, such as a dyed, fake flower

Some good items to embed include rubber bath toys — the yellow rubber ducky featured in a clear translucent bar of soap is a classic — and dried herbs. If you don't mind if they get wet and you have another copy, you can even embed photographs.

After you decide what you want to embed, make sure that you choose a mold deep enough to accommodate your embedment.

Think about colors when you embed your soap. If your soap is dark, you won't be able to see what's inside.

To place an embedment in your melt-and-pour soap:

1. **Melt your soap base.**

2. **Add your color and then scent; stir well.**

   For more on color and scent, see Chapter 15.

3. **Pour a thin layer of soap into your mold.**

   If your embedment is small, you may need to pour more soap to raise your item to the center position of the finished bar.

4. **After the soap starts to set, position your embedment.**

5. **Wait a few minutes and then add the remaining soap.**

6. **Remove your finished soap from the mold after it solidifies.**

7. **If you're not going to use your soap right away, wrap it in plastic to store.**

You don't have to totally embed an item in your soap. For example, you can partially embed a rubber fish in a blue soap so that it appears to be leaping out of the ocean.

Making Your Mark: Imprinted Soap

Imprinted soap is simply a bar of soap you've stamped when wet (see Figure 16-1). This technique gives you a nice sophisticated look and is actually one of the more-advanced ones in this chapter because it sounds easy to do but requires a bit more finesse. If you're up to a challenge, then you may want to try stamping your soap.

To make an imprinted bar of soap:

1. **Choose your stamp.**

   If you're making an imprint in your soap for the first time, try to choose a stamp that doesn't have a lot of intricate details. A smiley face and a simple shape are good starters. Visit your local craft store for many more ideas. For soap, look for stamps with sharper edges. Metal stamps work better than rubber.

2. **Melt your soap base.**

3. **Pour your melted soap into your mold.**

   A square or rectangle bar of soap works well. You may even want to try to match your mold's size to the approximate size of your stamp so that the edges aren't as visible.

4. **Wait for the soap to gel and then gently place your stamp in the mold.**

5. **Let your stamp remain in the mold for approximately 15 to 30 minutes.**

   If you remove your stamp too early, the soap is still liquid and runs back into the spot where your stamp was.

6. **Remove your stamp.**

7. **Gently smooth out any rough edges.**

8. **Let your soap continue solidifying.**

9. **Remove your soap from the mold.**

10. **Wrap your soap in plastic if you're not using it immediately.**

You can also create an imprint on a finished bar of soap, as long as your soap is at least room temperature. Simply position your stamp on your soap where you want it to appear and, using a mallet or hammer, hit the stamp several times to create an imprint.

Figure 16-1:
You use a stamp to make an imprinted bar of soap.

Creating a Design: Stenciled Soap

A stenciled soap is simply a bar of soap that has another shape outlined on it, thanks to the help of stencils (see Figure 16-2). Stencils work pretty much the same no matter what surface you place them on, and soap is no exception. The key is to make sure that the soap you're stenciling on is a lighter color than the soap you're using to stencil.

To stencil, all you need are a finished bar of translucent, white, or light-colored soap, a paintbrush, and melted soap in a darker color. Follow these steps.

1. **Using tape, attach your stencil to your finished bar of soap.**

   You want your stencil to be snug so that you don't paint underneath it and so that it doesn't move.

2. **Melt the soap base that you want to paint onto the stencil.**

3. **If you're not using a precolored soap base, stir in your color.**

   This batch of soap needs to be significantly darker than the finished bar of soap you'll be stenciling on.

4. **Using your paintbrush, paint your melted soap over the stencil.**

5. **After your soap hardens a bit, remove the stencil.**

6. **Let your soap continue to dry completely.**

7. **Wrap your soap in plastic if you're not using it right away.**

Figure 16-2:
You can stencil a shape on your soap using a contrasting color of soap.

Getting Fancy: Three-Dimensional Soap

Three-dimensional soap is actually soap that has a shape, such as in the form of a heart or duck. (You can see examples of three-dimensional soaps in the color photo section of this book.) Although you could try carving your soap into a shape, the easiest way to create 3-D soap is to pour it using a two-piece mold.

A *two-piece mold* comes in two pieces that are held together by plastic clamps. The mold also has a hole at the top or bottom so that you can add your melted soap.

A two-piece mold can be tricky, which is one reason why making 3-D soaps is a bit more advanced than other projects in this chapter.

You aren't limited to two-piece soap molds. In fact, I often use two-piece candle molds to create my soap shapes because they work the same way.

To create a three-dimensional bar of soap:

1. **Prepare your mold by sliding the clamp into place to hold the mold together and then place the pour spout side upside on top.**

   If your mold has a lot of intricate details, you may want to consider spraying it with vegetable oil or a releasing agent so that it the soap comes out easier.

2. **Melt your soap base.**

3. **Add your color and then scent; stir well.**

   For more on color and scent, see Chapter 15.

4. **Pour your soap into your mold through the hole provided.**

5. **Remove your soap from the mold after it solidifies.**

6. **If any excess edges exist, gently slice them away. Some potato peelers work well for this, if they don't take too big a bite when used.**

7. **If necessary, smooth out any rough edges remaining by using a damp finger or cloth.**

8. **If you're not going to use your soap right away, wrap it in plastic to store.**

If you want to use a mold that doesn't have a pour spout, simply pour each side separately. When they begin to gel, press the sides together firmly and clamp them together. When the soap cools, you should have a three-dimensional soap.

Rolling It Up: Soap Balls

Soap balls are a lot of fun and a great way to recycle shavings and leftover scraps from other projects. (see Figure 16-3). You can make soap balls in several ways:

- ✔ **Using a two-piece mold:** Simply follow the steps in the preceding section, "Getting Fancy: Three-Dimensional Soap." You can even make your own mold using tennis balls — see the sidebar "The game of love: Making a mold with tennis balls" in this chapter.

- ✔ **Using your hands:** After the soap cools, spray your hands with vegetable oil and shape the soap into balls. Place the balls on wax paper to finish cooling, rotating them occasionally so that you don't have a flat side.

- ✔ **Working with recycled soap shavings:** If you end up with shavings from other projects and wonder what to do with them, you can use them to make soap balls, or even take bars of soap and grate them specifically for that purpose. This can be done the same way you would grate cheese.

Put your grated soap or shavings in a bowl with some room to spare, and sprinkle with just enough water to help you mix it all together and have the shavings stick when you press them into a ball. If your soap is fresh, just wetting your hands should be enough. Mix with your fingers until all the shavings are slightly moistened and then grab a handful and start squeezing it with your hands and turning it over and over until it's as round as you can get it. You can even try "kneading" the soap like you would a ball of dough. Slightly moistening your palms at the end and smoothing the ball between them will give your soap ball a nice finish. Set the finished soap balls on racks or on a tabletop to dry and turn them in a day or two to expose all sides to air. If you want them to all be the same size, you may want to pre-measure your moistened shavings while they are still loose, and after squeezing they should be fairly uniform (a plastic ice-cream scoop works well for this).

The game of love: Making a mold with tennis balls

If you don't feel confident in your ability to hand-shape soap balls, you don't have to go out and buy a two-piece round mold. You can simply use scissors to cut an old tennis ball in half, gut the inside, and then pour your melted soap into each half. Then, use a rubber band to hold the sides together. When your soap starts to solidify, spray each surface with rubbing alcohol and put the ball back together. When the soap cools off, you'll have one solid ball.

Figure 16-3:
Soap balls
are always
popular with
family and
friends.

Making a Chain: Soap-on-a-Rope

If you've made soap balls (see the preceding section), then you can go a step further and make *soap-on-a-rope,* which is simply your soap balls threaded onto a rope. (See the photo in the color section of this book.)

You have two options when making soap-on-a-rope:

✔ Take your finished soap ball and make a hole in the center of it by using a dowel rod that's the approximate width of your rope. (A drill works well for this technique.) Knot the rope near the bottom to keep the soaps on and then thread your soap balls on.

✔ If you don't want to make a hole in your soap, then you need to hand shape your melted soap around your rope when you make the balls. For instructions on how to hand-shape soap, see the preceding section, "Rolling It Up: Soap Balls."

Chapter 17

Creating a Home Spa

In This Chapter

▶ Enjoying bath salts and bubble baths

▶ Concocting body lotion and massage oil

▶ Personalizing your shampoo and shower gel

*F*orget the last-minute trips to your local shopping meccas to buy spa-like items as gifts for your hard-to-buy-for relatives. This chapter tells you how you can make personalized home-spa items like bubble bath, massage oil, and shampoos, all of which make great gifts. Of course, you may like the results so much that you decide to keep them for yourself!

Disappearing in Bubbles

One of my favorite ways to relax is to take a long, hot bath. Of course, this habit can dry out your skin, but don't worry — you can add skin-soothing oils to your own special bubble baths to compensate for the overexposure to heat and water. You can also make bath oils that moisturize your dry skin.

To create a milk bath, purchase a milk bath base and mix in your essential oils. Then transfer to a covered container to store.

To create bath oil, follow these steps:

1. **Choose your favorite essential oil.**

   To find out all about aromatherapy, see Chapter 19.

2. **Choose your favorite carrier oil.**

   Some popular light carrier oils for use in the bath include sweet almond, coconut (virgin coconut oil has that wonderful smell), jojoba, and apricot kernel. Some of these can be found at your local grocery store if they have a selection of specialty oils near the regular cooking oils.

3. **Choose a colorant that complements your essential oil or blend of oils.**

   For example, if you're using a lavender essential oil, then opt for a lavender or purple-based colorant.

4. **Mix a few drops of your colorant with distilled water until you reach your preferred shade; set aside.**

   The amount of water you need to use depends on the bottle in which you choose to store the oil. Use equal amounts of distilled water and oil, so if you're using an 8-ounce bottle, opt for 3.5 ounces each of water and oil.

   Distilled water is not required, but you may want to use it.

5. **Mix your essential oil or oils with your carrier oil of choice.**

   Remember to use the same amount of oil and distilled water.

6. **Pour your colored water in a glass bottle — the more beautiful, the better — and then top with your oil.**

Before you use your bath oil, shake it up.

If you want a little lather in your bath, consider buying liquid soap bases to create lather and adding scent, colorings, and your favorite oils.

Relaxing with Bath Salts

If you're not too crazy about bubbles and oils, consider soaking away some time in a tub full of bath salts. You have two options when making these enjoyable salts.

- ✔ Use premade bath salts and add the finishing touches.
- ✔ Make your own from scratch.

You can purchase the bath salts in your local craft store and add your personal touch by scenting with essential oils, or you can make your own salts. To make your own, combine a variety of salts, such as Epsom salt, rock salt, and sea salt. Add some glycerin, essential oils, and colorants and you're good to go. Finally, place your mixture in a decorative jar or quaint see-through bath bag for storage.

Scrubbing Away with Bath Bags

Decorative bath bags not only look sophisticated, but they also feel nice. Whether you're creating them at home for personal use or giving them away as gifts, bath bags are a classy touch.

Although you can include plain bath salts inside the bags — well, not so plain if you follow the instructions in the preceding section, "Relaxing with Bath Salts" — why not make your own special body scrub?

To do so, combine your melt-and-pour soap with dried herbs and a coarse item, such as grated almonds, oatmeal, or cornmeal. (See Chapter 14 for recipes.) You can even add your favorite flowers, if you like, and of course, the finishing touch can be a few drops of your favorite essential oil or blend. (For aromatherapy ideas, see Chapter 19.)

Cleaning the Day Away with Shower Gel

You no longer have to buy whatever scent the store offers in shower gel — no more rain-fresh shower gel, faux citrus fragrances, and the like. Now, you can create your own shower gel with a scent that doesn't clash with your every-day fragrance — or your nose's sensibilities!

All you need to do is add a few drops of essential oil to a plain shower gel base, available at your local craft store or online. Then store your gel in a bottle and use as desired.

Getting Pampered with Massage Oil

Are you ready for a true spa experience? Then you're ready to create your own massage oil that you can enjoy in the privacy of your own home. Just take your favorite oil or oils — preferably ones with skin-softening abilities — add a preservative, such as liquid Vitamin E from a gel tablet, and then add essential oils. Sweet almond, apricot kernel, and grapeseed oils are good for massage because they're so light. Mix well and place in a bottle. You're ready to give a massage — or receive one!

Creating Your Own Shampoo

Why should your body receive all the pampering? Your hair deserves some special treatment, too.

The easiest way to create a shampoo is to take a plain, unscented, uncolored shampoo base (available from your local craft store or online) and customize it with essential oils and herbs. (See the sidebar "Maximizing what you've got" for hints on choosing herbs to match your hair color.) You can also add moisturizing oils, such as olive oil and coconut oil.

Maximizing what you've got

As a child, I remember my mom squeezing lemon juice on my hair before I spent a day in the sun to bring out any natural blond highlights. Was it an old wives' tale, or did lemon really brighten the blond? I discovered that my mom knew what she was doing.

If you want to bring out certain colors or features in your hair, use these few secrets. Chances are, now that you know what you're looking for, you may see these herbs and fruits listed on many shampoo bottles in your local store.

✔ Want to be a blonde? If you have dark blonde hair, try adding lemon or chamomile to your shampoo.

✔ Think you're really meant to be a redhead? Henna can enhance your natural red.

✔ Do you think dark hair is glamorous? Then try adding sage to your shampoo.

If you just want to condition your hair, go with rosemary. And for a nice, all-around shine, add parsley.

When you're creating shampoo, stay away from adding colorants — unless you don't mind your hair color taking on that hue!

Pampering Your Hands with Liquid Soap

Your soap-making adventures aren't limited to hard, molded soaps. You can actually make liquid soap.

The easiest way to make liquid soap is to buy a liquid soap base (available from your local craft store or online) and add your own essential oils and color. You can even add oils to help moisturize the skin.

If your liquid soap separates before you use it all, just shake it a bit to remix all the ingredients.

Sanitizing Your Cooking Area: Kitchen Soap

You can use melt-and-pour soap base to make everyday kitchen soap, using your favorite oils to soften your skin. Coconut and almond oils, in particular, work well if you want to create moisturizing kitchen soap.

To make your own kitchen soap from a melt-and-pour soap base, follow these steps:

1. **Combine 2 teaspoons of the oil of your choice, ¼ teaspoon lecithin, a few drops of essential oil, and 1 teaspoon liquid chlorophyll.**

   You can find these items at your local health-food store or online.

   You can use a combination of oils if you want.

2. **Melt 1 pound of melt-and-pour soap base.**

3. **Stir your liquid mixture into your melted soap.**

4. **Pour your soap into a mold.**

5. **Let your soap cool and remove it from the mold when solidified.**

6. **Wrap in plastic if you don't plan to use the soap immediately.**

Chapter 18

Solving Soap-Making Dilemmas

· ·

· ·

More than likely, if you're making melt-and-pour soaps, you won't encounter many problems. But just in case you do, this chapter is all about what can go wrong — what you should and shouldn't worry about and how to prevent problems from happening again in the future.

You Don't Look So Good: Appearance Problems

Chances are, even though your soap doesn't look quite right, you can still use and enjoy it. However, most people want their soaps to look as attractive as possible, so this section describes the various problems you may notice and what you can do to avoid them in the future.

I'm feeling thirsty: A little bubbly, please

If you notice bubbles in soaps you've made using techniques described in this book, they're the result of trapped air. Because air bubbles are more annoying than harmful, you can use your bubbly soaps without concern. Soapmakers who are using the cold process have to consider other problems when encountering bubbles that you don't need to worry about with melt-and-pour or hand-milled soaps.

To prevent air bubbles in the future in your melt-and-pour soaps, lightly spray the top of your soap with rubbing alcohol after you pour it into the mold. The bubbles should disappear instantly.

When your soap's in the clouds

If your melt-and-pour soap looks a little cloudy, a couple of factors may be at play:

- ✔ You added too much of an additive.
- ✔ You put your soap in the freezer.

Next time, add less additive and don't let impatience tempt you to put your soap in the freezer! (For more on additives, see Chapter 13.)

Feeling shaky: Cracked, brittle soap

If your melt-and-pour soap is cracking, you probably overheated your base or "overcooled" it. The soap is still usable, although it doesn't look very pretty.

Down in the dumps: Crumbly soap

If your melt-and-pour soap looks crumbly, you probably put it in the freezer.

Way down south in the land of cotton: Fuzzy texture

If your melt-and-pour soap seems to have cotton all over it, it just may. Actually, your soap may be sweating because it's attracting the moisture in the air, and that sweat may be attracting lint. Simply wipe the fuzz off the surface, rub the soap with alcohol, and then wrap it in plastic if you're not going to use it for a while. (For more on properly storing your soap, see Chapter 13.)

Streaking away

You can attribute a streaking soap mixture to these possible causes:

> ✔ Synthetic fragrances can cause streaking in soap.
>
> ✔ Your temperatures during mixing and melting were too cold.

The soap is still okay to use, although it doesn't look quite as attractive.

The wrong side of the tracks: When your soap is scummy

If your melt-and-pour soap looks, well, scummy, then somehow, some way, unwanted gook contaminated your soap.

Fortunately, though, your soap doesn't have a personality problem. If you can get by the soap's appearance problem or . . . ummm . . . unclean looks, you can safely use the soap. You can even scrape off the scum if it bothers you or rinse it until the scum disappears.

Stay Where You Are: Embedding Issues

If you've moved on to bigger and better things, or rather, decorative techniques, you may have tried embedding objects into your soaps. If you carefully placed your embedments in your soap only to have them fall out again and again, try spraying a little alcohol on the object before you add your soap. The alcohol encourages the soap to stick to the embedment and eliminates air bubbles.

If your embedments keep sinking to the bottom of your soap, try cooling your soap more before you pour it.

You're Not the Soap I Thought You Were: Color and Scent Calamities

You can spend all the time in the world creating the perfect color and scent for your perfectly molded soap, but unfortunately they may not last. As your soap ages, you may discover that your soap's color changes or its scent fades. I also devote an entire chapter to color and scent, so you may want to review Chapter 15 as well.

When color changes . . .

Just like candles, the colors in soaps fade when exposed to ultraviolet light. In addition, the additives you included when you made the soap may be taking effect and can cause the color to change.

If you're not going to use your soaps for a while, wrap them in plastic wrap and store them in a dark place. (For more on storing your soap, see Chapter 13.) If you want to have them on display, then you may want to make the color more intense to start with to accommodate the fading.

If you discover that your color is fading despite being stored in a dark place, then your soap base or additives are probably to blame. Take careful notes next time you make the soap and then experiment each time by changing one step in the recipe. Before too long, you should discover the problem. (The note-taking process is similar to the one you use in candle making; for more on taking notes, see Chapter 5.)

Fitting in with the crowd: Blending problems

If your colors are running together, then you may be using water-soluble dyes. Try switching to pigments. For more on your coloring options, see Chapter 15.

What's that I smell?

If you notice a funny smell, you may have burned your melt-and-pour soap by overheating it. If you used a thermometer and you're positive you didn't over-heat the soap, then your melt-and-pour soap base or commercial soap bar may smell of ammonia. Try experimenting with different manufacturers on your next few batches.

When your soap won't tan . . .

If you're trying to create a dark color and having problems, then the issue may be that you're using the wrong form of color. For example, dye only creates light colors, not dark, no matter how much you add. Check out Chapter 15 to find out which type of coloring agent works best for your soap.

That's Not How You Do It:
Soap That's Stuck

If you can't remove your soap from the mold, then first make sure that you used a flexible mold such as plastic. Glass or ceramic molds don't work. If your mold is flexible, you can try putting your soap in the freezer, although that may cause appearance problems, such as cloudiness.

In the future, make sure that you spray your flexible mold with vegetable oil before making that particular recipe again.

Or if you're using a mold with a flat bottom to create a slab of soap, lay a piece of freezer paper over one side, across the bottom and over the opposite side, and crease and tape it into place to get it as flat against the bottom and sides of the mold as possible. Put it plastic side up (it's paper with a plastic coating on one side). When it's time to unmold your soap, you only need to get it to release from two sides and then you can lift the slab out by the paper handles you've created on the other two sides. After you carefully turn the soap upside down, you can easily peel the paper off the soap before cutting.

Part V

Moving On in the Candle- and Soap- Making World

The 5th Wave   By Rich Tennant

@RICHTENNANT

"I appreciate you sharing your dreams and wishes for starting your own candle-making business, but maybe I should explain more fully what we at the Make-A-Wish Foundation are all about."

In this part . . .

If you decide you love candle making and soap making so much, why not take it to the next level? In this part, you discover more than just adding scent to your creations — you figure out the secrets of aromatherapy so that you can create candles and soaps that can actually alter or enhance your moods. Even more, you find a chapter on how to transform a hobby you adore into an actual business. Good luck!

Chapter 19

Experimenting with Aromatherapy

In This Chapter

▶ Figuring out which essential oil works

▶ Taking safety precautions when working with essential oils

▶ Knowing the therapeutic qualities of common essential oils

▶ Coming up with your own special blends

▶ Discovering scents that tantalize your nose and skin

*Y*our nose knows. Really. A scent that wafts through the air can do more than give your sense of smell pleasure: Scents can heal, improve your mood, lessen anxiety, and even reduce your stress level. The key is knowing which essential oil does what and then introducing it into the medium — candles, soaps, or home-spa products — best suited to its strengths. In this chapter, I tell you how aromatherapy can improve your life, as well as clue you in on which essential oils do what.

The information I provide in this chapter covers only the tip of the proverbial iceberg with aromatherapy. If you're fascinated by this topic, I strongly encourage you to pick up a copy of *Aromatherapy For Dummies,* by Kathi Keville (Wiley). She includes far more information about essential oils in her book than I could ever provide you with in one chapter. She also includes a detailed reference guide to essential oils.

A Little Moody Today? Choosing the Right Scent

Scent affects your mood. Cinnamon may make you hungry for apple pie. Vanilla may make you want to bake. And jasmine may remind you of your spouse.

But did you know that these scents also do other things? When you're delving into essential oils, you can actually achieve many other benefits as well. Need a lift for your mood? No problem. Choose an oil known for its uplifting powers. Can't go to sleep at night? Likewise, choose one famous for helping with insomnia. Want to host the party of the year? Then opt for an oil known to get people to loosen up and feel more comfortable.

Candles and soaps are great vessels for including aromatherapy in your life. *Aromatherapy* is simply when you use all-natural plant oils to affect your emotions by relaxing you, re-energizing you, and even healing you. Keep in mind, however, that a scented candle or soap isn't aromatherapy. To truly qualify as aromatherapy, the scent must be derived directly and exclusively from essential oils.

Keep the following in mind when scenting your candles and soaps:

- ✔ **Match your scent to your mood.** Ask yourself what your mood is or what you want it to be. Are you feeling tired or need to think clearly? Light a lemon candle. Feeling festive for the holidays? Try cinnamon. Or are you feeling a little romantic? Then light some jasmine candles. (I have one on each nightstand.) For information on the moods certain essential oils evoke, see the section "Your ABC Guide to Essential Oils," later in this chapter.

- ✔ **Remember the room.** When you're scenting candles or decorative soaps, consider where you plan to place them before you add scent. You want the scent to match the room — say, lavender in your bedroom or vanilla or cinnamon in your kitchen — and you also want the scent to match the other fragrances in the room. If possible, try not to burn different scents in the same room. For example, an invigorating peppermint candle in the bedroom probably wouldn't work very well, especially if you already have a lavender-scented candle burning there.

If your kitchen smells like a trash can or the burnt food you made for lunch, just light a candle scented with essential oil to help counteract the smell. You can also use a scented candle to lighten up your bathroom or citronella candles out in the yard to ward off insects.

- ✔ **Try to coordinate your scents to the color of your soaps and candles.** A lemon-scented soap is great in a yellow kitchen, while cinnamon naturally begs for red. The color that comes to mind first when you think of a fragrance is probably the one to choose, unless it clashes with the color of the room you want to use it in.

The best way to discover the most appropriate scent for you is to figure out what effects you want to gain and then choose the oil that provides that benefit and whose scent you like best. For information on the moods certain essential oils cultivate, see the section "Your ABC Guide to Essential Oils," later in this chapter.

Playing It Safe: Cautions When Working with Essential Oils

Essential oils are so powerful that some people consider them drugs. But unlike medications, essential oils aren't regulated, so using them responsibly and wisely is up to you. Not only do you need to pay attention to how you handle them, but you also need to consider what each oil does. (See the section "Your ABC Guide to Essential Oils," later in this chapter, for a list that covers the therapeutic benefits of popular essential oils.)

Remember these few tips when working with essential oils:

- **Be aware of whether your oil is toxic.** Some oils are toxic even when you use just a couple of drops. Others are poisonous when you use large quantities. Some of these oils include bitter almond, calamus, camphor, French tarragon, horseradish, hyssop, jaborandi, pennyroyal, mugwort, mustard, narcissus, parsley, rue, santolina, sassafras, tansy, tonka bean, and wormwood arnica. Many times, the chance of toxicity outweighs the potential therapeutic benefits.

- **Be careful not to splash the oil when you handle it.** If you splash the oil in your eyes, you need to flush them immediately with water. If you get oil on your skin, wash quickly with warm, soapy water. If you spill oil on your furniture or other items, wipe them down immediately with warm, soapy water to avoid damaging the finish

- **Citrus oils can cause sudden flare-ups in your candles, so use them sparingly.** You may even want to test a small amount first in a small test candle.

- **Consider how sensitive your skin is.** Certain oils irritate skin, so avoid using them in your soaps or at least use them sparingly. Common skin-irritating oils include allspice, birch, camphor, cinnamon, clove, oregano, savory, thuja, thyme, and turmeric.

- **Don't apply essential oils to your skin.** Always dilute them before using, which is the reason you can safely incorporate them into your soaps. What this advice also means to you as a candlemaker or soapmaker is that you should always wear gloves when handling them so that the oils don't come into direct contact with your skin.

- **If you're on medication, be careful about drug interactions.** Although interactions aren't common, they're not unheard of. Ask your doctor or pharmacist for possible drug interactions.

✔ **If you're pregnant or have epilepsy, asthma, or any other medical condition, ask your doctor if working with essential oils is okay.** You don't want to harm your unborn child or aggravate your medical condition. Even with oils that are considered safe, you may want to use them in a more diluted form if you have any medical issues.

✔ **If you're reusing your gloves, make sure that you clean them between each use.** Also remember to wash your hands after working with oils, even if you did wear gloves.

✔ **Never, ever ingest essential oils.** They're not meant to be ingested and are considered toxic.

✔ **Remember that kids have more sensitive skin than adults.** Dilute the essential oils even more and try to use only those oils that I cite as kid-friendly, such as chamomile, eucalyptus, or geranium.

✔ **Think about photosensitivity when you're using essential oils in your soap.** Just like some medications, some essential oils increase your chance of photosensitization, which basically looks like a rash, or increase your chances of getting sunburned. Common photosensitizing oils include angelica, bergamot, cumin, grapefruit, lemon, lemon verbena, lime, and orange.

Your ABC Guide to Essential Oils

Most people believe that the therapeutic powers of essential oils survive the candle-making and soap-making processes, despite the harsh conditions required. If you can smell a scent at the end of the process, then the therapeutic benefits may still be present.

Eek! Out-of-date oils

Just as you weed out rancid cooking oils from your kitchen cabinet, you need to periodically go through your stock of essential oils and throw some out. However, this housecleaning isn't because the essential oils spoil. The oils actually lose their scent and therapeutic powers over time.

To make your oils last, keep them exposed to as little oxygen as possible. Keep them tightly capped and undiluted in a small bottle. Avoid light exposure, so use either dark bottles or store them in a cabinet. When stored properly, the oils should last several years, unless you're dealing with oils such as lemongrass or orange, which last only about half that time.

As a result, liking the scent of the essential oil you choose and being aware of its purported benefits are important. Essential oils can help moisturize and heal skin, improve your moods, increase your energy level, decrease anxiety and stress, and even relieve physical woes.

Keep in mind that the quality of essential oils can vary greatly. Some manufacturers or retailers may say they're selling essential oils when they're really offering substitutions or adulterations. Always make sure that you buy your oils from a source you can trust. If you're not buying quality oils, you're not getting the full therapeutic benefits described in the following sections.

Angelica

If you want to be calm and alert and to increase your work performance, then you may consider angelica. It thins blood and clears your mind so that you can think better. It also energizes you, stimulating brain waves and reducing drowsiness.

If you suffer from headaches or mood swings, you may want to consider angelica, because it decreases your chances of headaches or becoming irritable. The oil also helps increase stamina and relieves depression.

This oil is photosensitizing.

Anise

If you want to add a little excitement to your bedroom, consider anise, an aphrodisiac known to spice up your sex life. This oil is especially adept at removing human odors — that may be why it's a favorite ingredient in soap designed for fishermen (and fisherwomen) and hunters.

Basil

Basil stimulates and clears your mind, improves your memory and stamina, gives you energy, and reduces drowsiness. It also helps prevent mood swings and headaches. If you want to pep up work performance, consider using this scent — but beware, an office romance may occur, because it's also a mild aphrodisiac! (Don't use that as an excuse, though!) This oil can also stimulate blood flow and warm your skin. It's also an antibacterial agent.

If you're using basil in your soap, use it only in small amounts because it can irritate your skin.

Bay

Although bay is mentally stimulating when inhaled, most of its benefits are more physical than mental. Use bay to relieve lung congestion, as well as treat viral infections. No wonder the camphorlike scent reminds me of the medicine cabinet!

Bay laurel

If you want to boost your memory, try bay laurel, which also has antibacterial properties.

Benzoin

If you're loaded down with work, then consider benzoin. This oil helps increase your work performance, stimulate brain waves, and increase your stamina to make the most of those long office hours. It also has mild antibacterial properties.

Although non-toxic and non-irritating in its pure form, use the liquid tincture of this substance with caution because it can be moderately toxic. The tincture often contains other ingredients that can cause contact dermatitis in some individuals.

Bergamot

Bergamot has a number of mental and physical benefits. On the mental front, it's calming and uplifting, which is good if you suffer from depression, stress, or mood swings. On the physical front, it thins blood, relieves muscle spasms, soothes irritated skin, helps insomnia, fights infections, and encourages healing.

This oil is photosensitizing.

Black pepper

A mild aphrodisiac, black pepper is another oil that can improve your on-the-job performance by energizing you, stimulating brain waves, and increasing your stamina. (It's probably an irritant if used in large quantities.)

You can mold or dip slim and elegant tapers.

A rolled beeswax candle makes a great first project or family craft.

You can use almost any container to make an attractive—and simple—container candle.

If you have an artistic side, consider painting your candles.

Just as you can sponge paint your walls, you can sponge paint your candles for a unique look.

An embellished wick makes a statement and gives your broken-heart candle extra pizzazz.

Floating candles are kind of a misnomer because wax naturally floats.

Frosted candles, with their mottled appearance, are a popular look.

Gel wax makes fantastic-looking container candles, thanks to its transparent nature.

To jazz up plain gel candles, consider adding embedments, such as wax chunks that look like fruit.

Soaps that you make are wonderful gifts for your family and friends.

Although translucent or solid white soaps look attractive, why not add a little color to your soaps so that they match your room?

You can add embedments, such as herbs and spices, to your soap.

You can embed paraffin wax shavings in your translucent soap, or you can add actual objects.

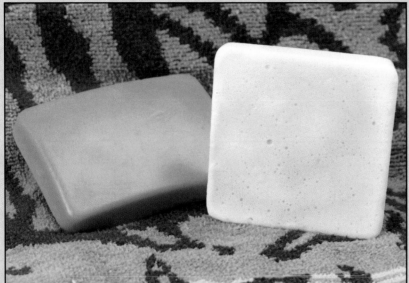

Try swirling a different color into your soap to achieve a marbled effect.

Certain molds make your designs jump out to create three-dimensional soaps.

You can use soap balls to create "soap on a rope."

Caraway

If you're suffering from a cold, are clumsy, or are battling a weight problem, you may want to try caraway. Caraway helps wounds heal, as well as relieves lung and bronchial congestion. It's even thought to speed up fat metabolism.

Cardamom

Not thinking clearly? Need more energy? Tired all the time? Then try cardamom. In addition to improving your work performance, it can spice things up between the sheets. It also improves mood, increases stamina, and decreases your risks of moodiness and headaches. It also has antibacterial properties (good for soap), and it helps treat viral infections — you know, the kind that antibiotics can't do anything about!

Carrot seed

Carrot seed is good for soap because it tones your skin and helps heal skin damage. It also battles infections, inflammation, and intestinal gas. Its stimulating property also tends to your mind, so consider this oil when you need a brainstorming session!

Chamomile

Chamomile is popular, and for good reason — it battles a cornucopia of mental conditions. If you're stressed or depressed, consider experimenting with it. Chamomile also relieves insomnia and reduces anxiety. Chamomile doesn't just stop at the mind, however. It can relax sore muscles, fight infection, and promote healing as well.

Because chamomile is so relaxing, it's also good for kids.

Cinnamon

Cinnamon isn't just for baking! As an oil, cinnamon adeptly handles a variety of tasks, including reducing inflammation and destroying infections, acting as an antibacterial agent, and reducing drowsiness. It also increases stamina and energy and functions as an overall pick-you-up. If you're prone to moodiness and headaches, it also helps prevent them. In addition to helping with depression, it also increases the chemistry in the bedroom!

If you have sensitive skin, be careful when using cinnamon oil because it can irritate your skin.

Citronella

Sure, you probably know that citronella works great in candles when it comes to repelling insects, but did you know that this essential oil also reduces inflammation, destroys infections, and helps with insomnia? Now you do!

Citronella essential oil can also irritate skin, so do a patch test if you plan to use it in soap. Better yet, skip it in soap altogether! Who wants to smell like insect repellant?

Clary sage

Clary sage helps ward off illness by destroying infections. If you overexercised in a quest to meet your New Year's resolution, then take advantage of clary sage's calming effects on muscle spasms and relaxing effects on sore and stiff muscles. Clary sage also tones skin and soothes irritated skin. This relaxing oil helps reduce anxiety and depression, relieves insomnia, and stimulates a good romp in the bedroom.

Clove

This powerful antibacterial oil helps you think better, energizes you, and reduces drowsiness. Clove oil also lessens your risks of moodiness and headaches. Not only does it stimulate your mind and blood flow and improve your memory, but it also works magic in the bedroom. (Can you see the sparks already?) It can also help you cope with depression.

Use this oil in small amounts so that you don't irritate your skin.

Coriander

Coriander's main benefits are threefold: It helps you fight off infections, tones your skin, and improves your sex life.

Cumin

This essential oil helps if you're battling infections or inflammation. However, cumin can irritate your skin, so use it in small amounts. Cumin is photosensitizing.

Cypress

If you couldn't disappoint Grandma and refuse that second bowl of home-cooked ham and beans, then don't worry. You can use cypress essential oil to cope with the resulting intestinal gas. At the same time, it also helps reduce infections and inflammation, and stimulates your mind. It eases depression and improves circulation.

Eucalyptus

The sharp smell of eucalyptus can clear up congested lungs, as well as treat infections and improve circulation. It's also an antibacterial agent. If you need to stimulate your mind and sharpen your reaction, then use this oil in a scented candle.

This gentle oil is good for children and those with sensitive skin, so consider using it in your soaps.

Fennel

If you're feeling overweight, skip the fad diets. Try fennel, which stimulates fat burning, as well as heals wounds, relieves congestion, and improves circulation. (But you still need to eat healthy and exercise to lose weight!)

Fir

If you can't stop worrying, then fir may help you out. Not only does this essential oil help reduce anxiety, but it's also known to be mentally stimulating and increase energy (so you can think about solutions to your worries). It also battles infections, inflammation, and intestinal gas.

Frankincense

This relaxing essential oil can put you to sleep — well, at least help you deal with insomnia. Frankincense has antibacterial qualities and also helps reduce pain. It can even improve your skin's appearance and heal damage.

Frankincense is a good oil for children because it's gentle.

Garlic

This antibacterial essential oil is good for treating viral infections. However, use with a gentle hand because garlic can irritate your skin. (And probably most of your friends!)

Geranium

This flowery oil is known for its relaxing effects on both the mind and body. Used in soap, geranium can help tone skin and soothe irritated skin. It also destroys infections and calms muscle spasms. You can use this oil with all complexion and hair types. It also has antibacterial qualities.

If your kids are always fighting viral infections, consider adding a little bit of geranium oil to your soap. Because of its gentle qualities, geranium is mild enough for kids.

German chamomile

German chamomile battles infections, inflammation, and intestinal gas. It also can stimulate your mind.

Ginger

Ginger isn't just the redheaded bombshell on *Gilligan's Island* or a cooking agent. (Am I dating myself here?!) It's a wonderful essential oil with many therapeutic qualities. Not only does ginger battle infections, inflammation, and intestinal gas, but it also reduces pain and improves circulation. Furthermore, it helps prevent moodiness and headaches, improves your sex life (I guess it would have to if your headache excuse has gone by the wayside!), and stimulates your mind. It also gives you energy and stamina, as well as reduces drowsiness.

Helichrysum

Helichrysum relaxes sore and stiff muscles and improves your skin's appearance.

Jasmine

Jasmine is renowned as a romance kindler, but it's also good for stimulating your mind and improving your work performance. Surprisingly, jasmine is also good for kids, who have more sensitive skin than adults.

Juniper

Juniper helps reduce anxiety. It also improves circulation and treats viral infections.

Lavender

Lavender is legendary for its calming effects. But it does more than relax you and battle stress, depression, moodiness, and insomnia. It's good for your skin, has a wonderful aroma, treats viral infections, relaxes tired muscles, and calms muscle spasms. It also works wonders on cuts and rashes.

Lemon

This citrus oil reduces infections, inflammation, and intestinal gas, while also stimulating your mind and memory. Lemon oil battles stress, depression, and insomnia and promotes relaxation and healing. It also has antibacterial qualities.

Lemon balm (melissa)

Also known as melissa, this oil reduces inflammation, infections, stress, anxiety, and depression. Lemon balm also relaxes sore muscles and helps relieve insomnia.

Use only in small amounts because lemon balm can irritate your skin. This oil is also photosensitizing.

Lemon eucalyptus

Similar to lemon, this oil reduces inflammation and infection and relaxes muscle. Lemon eucalyptus can, however, irritate skin, so be careful when using it.

Lemongrass

Lemongrass has the same therapeutic qualities as lemon eucalyptus (see previous section), but it also reduces pain and improves circulation. It has antibacterial qualities and fights viral infections as well. Again, be careful because lemongrass can irritate your skin.

Lemon verbena

Lemon verbena reduces inflammation and infections and relaxes muscles. It also works with depression. However, keep in mind that this oil can irritate skin.

This oil is also photosensitizing.

Marjoram

Marjoram relieves stress and reduces anxiety. It tones and soothes skin, fights infections, and relieves muscle spasms. It also has antibacterial qualities. (Just don't try spreading it on your toast, okay?)

Myrrh

Myrrh has antibacterial qualities, fights viral infections, and promotes healing, but it also spices things up the bedroom as well. (Wonder if the Three Wise Men knew that?)

Myrtle

In addition to its antibacterial qualities, myrtle relaxes muscles — it so relaxes them, in fact, that it also heats things up in the bedroom.

Niaouli

Niaouli battles infections and inflammation.

Nutmeg

This oil fights infections, inflammation, and intestinal gas. Nutmeg stimulates the mind, lessens anxiety, and improves your sex life. (With all these essential oils recharging your sex life, you and your partner should be *exhausted!*)

Orange

This citrus oil fights infections, inflammation, and intestinal gas and is well known for its mind-stimulating qualities. Orange also soothes nerves, reduces anxiety and depression, and quells insomnia.

This oil is photosensitizing.

Orange blossom (neroli)

Orange blossom oil fights infections, stress, depression, anxiety, insomnia, and muscle spasms. It also soothes irritated skin and promotes relaxation. If you want to get into the groove in the bedroom, try this oil.

Orange blossom is a good essential oil for kids because it's gentle.

Oregano

This strong-smelling oil stimulates the mind and blood flow, fights viral infections, and has antibacterial qualities. However, if you're using oregano oil in soap, use it in small amounts because it can irritate your skin.

Palmarosa

Palmarosa fights infections and tones skin.

Patchouli

This oil fights infections, inflammation, and intestinal gas. Patchouli also tones skin, improves your sex life, and stimulates the mind.

Pennyroyal

Although pennyroyal can help heal wounds, relieve congestion, and increase metabolism, it also can be potentially toxic. Unless you know what you're doing, you may want to stay away from it.

Peppermint

Peppermint oil makes you more alert and energetic and improves your thinking. It also makes you less likely to get a headache or mood swings. If you want to spice up your work performance or your sex life, you may want to try this oil.

Petitgrain

This relaxing oil helps reduce anxiety, depression, and stress. On a physical level, petitgrain helps battle infections and sore muscles, as well as tone skin.

Pine

This woodsy oil fights infections, inflammation, and intestinal gas, while stimulating your mind and increasing stamina. Pine also has antibacterial qualities.

Rose

If you want to relieve stress, depression, insomnia, anxiety, or moodiness, you may want to experiment with this flowery oil. Its wonderful therapeutic benefits don't stop there, however. Rose oil also battles infections, tones and improves skin, and adds some sparks under the sheets

Rose is a good oil for kids' sensitive skin.

Rose geranium

Rose geranium helps individuals suffering from stress, depression, moodiness, and insomnia and also improves your skin's appearance.

Rosemary

If you have a cold or your thinking is a bit sluggish, you may want to breathe in rosemary from a candle containing this oil. Not only does rosemary relieve lung congestion, but it also stimulates the mind (not to mention your metabolism!). It improves circulation and helps fight off viral infections.

Sage

This oil gives you energy and helps stimulate your mind. It also wakes you up and improves work performance and memory. If you're suffering from a cold and must go to work, try sage because it also helps with congestion and treats viral infections. You may just make it through the workday now!

Sandalwood

If you want to relax but be mentally alert, then sandalwood may be the oil for you. In addition, it fights infections, inflammation, and intestinal gas and even starts your libido purring like a feisty cat *(meow)*. If you're feeling stressed, you may find help with this relaxing oil, which also relieves insomnia.

Sandalwood is a good, gentle essential oil for kids.

Savory

Although savory has powerful antibacterial essential oil, it also may irritate your skin. Make sure that you use it in small qualities.

Spearmint

If you want some energy, try sniffing spearmint oil. This oil is also a good one for kids — but if you're already having trouble keeping up with them, you may want to skip it!

Tea tree

Tea tree oil is known for its medicinal qualities. It clears up congestion, battles infections, promotes healing, and has antibacterial powers. It even stimulates the mind so that you can do those crossword puzzles in your sick bed!

Thuja

Thuja oil thins out congestion and promotes healing. It also purportedly increases your metabolism. Use in very small doses because thuja can be toxic.

Thyme

Thyme has antibacterial qualities and battles viral infections. It also stimulates your mind and blood flow.

This oil can irritate your skin, so use it sparingly.

Valerian

If you need stress relief, you may want to consider valerian.

What's your type?

If you're using essential oils in soap, you may wonder which ones are good for dry or sensitive skin. No problem. The following list lets you know what works well with each skin type. Now finding the scent you like is up to you!

- ✔ **If your skin is normal:** Consider geranium, jasmine, lavender, orange blossom, rose, or ylang ylang essential oils.

- ✔ **If your skin is dry:** Think about basil, cedarwood, clary sage, cypress, eucalyptus, lemon, lemongrass, myrtle, palmarosa, patchouli, sage, sandalwood, tea tree, or vetivert oils.

- ✔ **If your skin is oily:** You may want to try carrot seed, cedarwood, frankincense, myrrh, palmarosa, peppermint, sandalwood, thyme, or vetivert essential oils.

- ✔ **If your skin is sensitive:** Experiment with chamomile, lavender, or ylang ylang oils.

Vanilla

Vanilla's comforting smell spices up your sex life.

Vetivert

Vetivert battles infections and has antibacterial qualities. It also tones skin and is known as a mild aphrodisiac.

Ylang ylang

Ylang ylang's fragrance is strong, but you can use it to relax your mind and muscles. It also helps kick up the romance factor. The relaxing qualities help you sleep and help fight depression. If you have irritated skin, you may want to give this one a try.

Ylang ylang is another gentle oil that's good for kids.

Playing Mad Scientist: Blending Your Own Scents

More than likely, you'll have no trouble finding a scent you like. But maybe you want to accomplish several things at once, so you may want to consider blending scents to get multiple therapeutic effects. Or maybe you want to achieve a unique, one-of-a-kind scent that's out of this world.

If you can't find an essential oil that has a scent you like or that has all the therapeutic benefits you want, don't be afraid to start concocting a recipe. Fortunately, creating your own signature isn't rocket science. You simply mix your favorite oils to create a blend. In general, the only guideline you need to follow is that you should combine fewer oils when you're first starting off.

You can create your own blend in almost any way. Really, the only rule is to choose the fragrances you like and to use a smaller amount of the stronger smelling oils when creating your blends.

To create a blend, find a clean glass bottle and glass droppers for each oil. (Use glass because essential oils eventually eat through plastic.) Create a blend by following these steps:

1. **Choose the oils that you want to blend.**

   You can choose as many oils as you like. However, when you first start creating blends, experiment with only two or three oils at a time. As you become more adept, you can blend as many oils as you like to come up with a scent you love.

2. **Place the same number of drops of each oil in your bottle.**

   Use a different dropper for each oil or you'll cross contaminate your oils. If you must use the same dropper, make sure that you thoroughly clean and dry it before adding the next oil.

   If one of the oils you're using is very strong, use fewer drops of that oil or it will overpower the others. Some strong-smelling oils include chamomile, cinnamon, clary sage, patchouli, rosemary, and ylang ylang, as well as other oils from spices and herbs.

   Another idea is to choose one oil as your main scent and use twice as many drops of it. The oil serves as your base scent, and the secondary oils just enhance it. In addition to your favorite scents, good base oils are those that already smell like a blend, such as rose or pine.

3. **Cap your bottle and shake it.**

4. **Sniff your scent and adjust the number of drops accordingly.**

   Just add a few drops at a time until you get the smell you like.

   Don't forget to write down how many drops and what oils you used. You don't want to forget how you made such a remarkable creation! (For more information on taking notes, see Chapter 5.)

If you want to create a blend but don't know where to start, consider these combinations:

- Chamomile, ylang ylang, and lavender
- Eucalyptus and lemon
- Lavender, rose, and lemon

Discovering Great Scents for Candles

Scented candles are a popular way to add fragrance to your home. Of course, you can buy scented candles, but you can also scent them yourself with essential oils. As the candle burns, the scent is released.

Just because a candle is scented doesn't mean that it has aromatherapy qualities. If it's scented with a synthetic scent, then it's not an aromatherapy candle. Only candles scented with essential oils have aromatherapy qualities. Scented candles and aromatherapy candles aren't the same. For details on how to scent your candle, see Chapter 6.

I'm not going to lie to you. Scenting your candles with essential oils is a lot of work that sometimes ends up with no fragrance whatsoever. If you don't want to make the effort, you don't have to miss out on the rewards of aromatherapy. You can purchase these candles instead. Just make sure that you're getting the real thing. (The best way is to start by purchasing from a reputable source — refer to Appendix A for a list of resources.)

You may want to begin with some of these popular aromatherapy scents. You can find out a lot more information about these scents by referring to the section "Your ABC Guide to Essential Oils," earlier in this chapter.

- **Chamomile:** This scent is known to relax and cheer you up. It also treats many woes, such as inflammation, tight muscles, skin problems (such as rashes), allergies, and menstrual cramps.

- **Citronella:** This scent is best known for repelling insects. If you're not fond of citronella, consider using eucalyptus, geranium, or sandalwood, which also ward off the bugs.

- **Lavender:** I know I mention this scent a lot in this book and for good reason. Not only is it one of my favorites, but it also relieves depression, anxiety, and stress. If you want to truly relax, then you need a scented lavender candle.

- **Rose:** There's nothing like the smell of the great outdoors, and rose is relaxing, to say the least.

- **Ylang ylang:** If you need cheering up or just want to relax but you're tired of mainstream oils such as lavender and rose, consider ylang ylang.

Sniffing Some Fantastic Smells for Soap

Soaps are wonderful when scented with essential oils. Not only can you receive the therapeutic qualities through smell, but your skin also reaps the benefits. In general, the longer the soap comes in contact with your skin, the more opportunity it has to improve your skin's condition.

Just remember to not use the oil directly on your skin and to think about your skin's sensitivity.

Essential oils moisturize and soothe your skin. They also battle sunburn, wrinkles, infections, swelling, and the like. Here are a few oils to get you started. You can find out a lot more information about these scents by referring to the section "Your ABC Guide to Essential Oils," earlier in this chapter.

- **Chamomile:** This relaxing oil is especially good for your skin and children.

✔ **Jasmine:** This sultry oil is another good one for kids.

✔ **Lavender:** This relaxing oil moisturizes skin and relaxes both muscles and mind.

✔ **Lemon:** If you have oily skin or hair, try experimenting with lemon. It also has antidepressant qualities.

✔ **Peppermint:** This tingly oil stimulates your mind, as well as relieving dry skin and hair. It also helps clear up congestion and relieves itching.

✔ **Rose:** This oil is relaxing and especially good for skin. It also has antidepressant qualities.

✔ **Rosemary:** This oil is good for almost all skin and hair types. It relieves both mental and physical pain and even improves memory.

Squeezing your plants for all they're worth

If you've ever shopped around for essential oils, then you know how much the prices vary, depending on the oil you opt for and how hard it is to extract the oil from that particular plant. In general, however, essential oils cost more than fragrance (synthetic) oils. (For more on the differences, see Chapter 6.) On the plus side, they're very intense, and only a few drops can scent your wax. However, if the cost is prohibitive or you just want to try to do it yourself, you can extract your own essential oils. These will not be as potent as oils you buy, which have been extracted with the use of expensive distilling equipment, but extracting your own oils at home can give you a great sense of satisfaction, especially if you use materials you grow yourself.

Although you can use several methods to extract your oils, the following steps cover the oil-infusion method:

1. **Mash your herb, spice, or flower to release its oil and place it in a plastic container.**

Don't use a metal container, or it will interact with the oils. However, essential oils can eventually eat through plastic, so don't store oils in plastic containers. Glass bottles, especially amber-colored ones, make excellent storage containers for essential oils or infusions.

2. **Pour either olive or safflower oil over your herbs until they're immersed and then cover the container.**

3. **Store at room temperature for 24 hours.**

4. **Using a strainer, strain and reserve the oil in a bowl placed underneath the strainer.**

   As you strain, don't forget to press your herbs with a spoon to get more oil.

5. **Repeat Steps 2 through 4 a half dozen times.**

   The more you repeat these steps, the stronger your essential oil will be.

Your essential oil is now ready.

Chapter 20

Turning a Hobby into a Business

If you're looking for something to do with all your extra soaps and candles, why not consider selling them? You can make a little money on the side as well as continue to enjoy making your crafts without running yourself out of house and home. In this chapter, I cover some points you need to consider if you're thinking about selling your wares.

Starting a business is a big decision that affects your personal, financial, and legal life. Use this chapter's advice as a general guide to areas you need to consider when starting out. Make sure that you touch base with an accountant or attorney for details and for the latest tax laws and rules and regulations.

Weighing Your Decision Carefully

Before you consider starting your own business, think about your motivation. What is your goal? Yes, doing something you love is great, but sometimes you can fall out of love with a hobby when it becomes a job. Plus, running a business takes time, and it involves more than just making your craft. You need to consider the financial, legal, and personal ramifications as well.

If you think you'd enjoy selling your products, then think about when you'll find the time to do it. Are you a stay-at-home mom just wanting some extra money on the side? Do you work full-time? If you don't have the time, starting a business may sound good in theory but not in practice.

After you start your business, you'll probably market your wares at local craft fairs. If you're busy a lot on the weekends — say that your kids are in sports or you travel often to visit your older parents who live out of town — then you may encounter problems unless you can find someone else to go in your place.

Knowing the Rules and Regulations

If only starting a business were as simple as making your candles and soaps and putting out a sign. Alas, if you're selling your wares on a regular basis, you're no longer considered a hobbyist but a businessperson. And that means that, more than likely, you fall under FDA (Food and Drug Administration) or FTC (Federal Trade Commission) regulations.

If you're a soapmaker, the agency that regulates you depends on whether your product is classified as a soap or cosmetic. If you're claiming special benefits of any kind, such as moisturizing or relaxing, then you fall into the cosmetic category and thus face stricter FDA regulations.

When the FDA rules

If you're a soapmaker and your wares are considered cosmetic, then you have to follow labeling guidelines and very strict production sanitation rules, which, unfortunately most home businesses can't meet. If you already wear gloves and hairnets and don't smoke, you're off to a good start. But you also need someone else around to double-check your measurements and to have your water tested.

On the other hand, the labeling part is easy because you basically just need your contact info and net weight of soap in ounces. (This regulation is true with FTC regulations as well.) But if you fall under the FDA domain, you must also list all ingredients, just like food labels do. Even if you're just labeling basic soap, if you list *any* of your ingredients, then you need to list *all* in descending order. You can't just list the essential oils and special additives without listing all the other ingredients, because listing only the special oils can give the impression that they're the primary ingredients when they likely aren't.

If you color your product, keep in mind that not all colorants pass regulations. Check with the FDA to find out if your colorant of choice passes its tests. You can access the FDA site at www.fda.gov.

Changing your name

Running your business as a sole proprietorship doesn't mean that you're limited to using your name as your business name. In fact, you can use a different name — said to be doing business as — as long as you register it with the government. (That way, if the law needs to track you down, it can!)

To register your business name, you need to complete some paperwork at both the local and state level and pay a fee. Contact your city or county clerk office to start the initial paperwork.

Keep in mind that unless you've trademarked your name, anyone can assume it to do business — not good if you've carefully built a reputation! (For more on trademarks, contact a patent attorney.)

Taxing matters

Don't forget that you have to pay taxes on your income. If you make at least $400, then you must file a self-employment tax form and pay your own Social Security. If you earn enough money, you must also pay estimated quarterly tax payments and have documentation to support any expenses you deduct on your tax return. People earning lower amounts from their sales may only have to file once a year.

But that's not all. More than likely, you must collect sales tax on any sales to a consumer (wholesalers and retailers excluded), including anything you sell at a craft fair or online.

To collect sales tax, you need a *free sales and use* tax permit. You can get this from the Department of Revenue. Visit the Web site www.irs.gov for more information or call your state comptroller or accountant to find out the details.

If you're making candles and soaps as a hobby and only occasionally sell a product to a friend or family member, then you don't have to collect sales tax. However, if you sell your wares with any regularity within your state of residence, you are required to do so.

The incorporation decision

Most crafts businesses are *sole proprietorships,* which means that individuals sell their wares under their own name and without creating a separate business entity. You don't have to do anything special to be a sole proprietor. The downside is that you're personally financially liable for anything that goes awry, so your personal assets are at risk in the case of a settlement or court ruling.

If the thought of liability bothers you, you may want to consider incorporating. However, incorporation comes at a cost, and you pay an initial fee as well as taxes on the business income and then on your wages. In general, though, you aren't personally responsible for paying the corporation's debts, although in some forms of corporation you may be. For more information on incorporating and its financial ramifications, see your attorney or accountant.

Zoning limitations

One thing that you need to think about is zoning. Because you're doing business in your home, you probably are in a residential area. That means zoning ordinances may not allow you to conduct a business in your home. Rules and regulations vary based on community, but you should definitely contact your local government before setting up shop — or you may be out of business sooner than you figured!

Creating a Business Plan

Even if you're running a small home-based business that just makes a few thousand dollars profit a year, consider drawing up some type of business plan. That way, you can focus on where you want to go and clarify any decisions you need to make.

To create a basic plan, write a description of your business, including what your product is, where your supplies and materials come from, what your costs are, and what the market is like (including both customers and competition). Also include a marketing plan that covers how you're going to sell your crafts.

When drawing up your business plan, think about your competition. Ask yourself the following questions:

- ✔ Who are my competitors?
- ✔ How much of a market is there for my products?
- ✔ What sets my products apart from the competition?

You may also want to consider including a *mission statement,* which talks about the purpose of the business and what sets it apart.

For more on coming up with a business plan and setting a mission statement, see *Business Plans For Dummies* by Paul Tiffany, PhD, and Steven D. Peterson, PhD (Wiley).

You can't reach any goal if you haven't established one.

Minding the Details

After you have your business plan in place, you need to take care of a few other details before you can actually start your business.

Pay attention to your paperwork

For starters, you need to have all your paperwork in order. That means designing and purchasing business cards and stationery, as well as organizing records of your expenses, inventory, and orders. Keep in mind that it's now very easy to produce business cards from your home with a good printer and word processing program. You can also find very attractive business card stocks at office supply stores if you don't want to come up with your own graphic theme.

Make sure that you include your Web site and e-mail address on your business card.

Also consider writing a *biography sheet* that you hand out with purchases. The biography sheet can help set you apart from the competition by talking about your specialized skills, as well as what makes your products unique. You should also talk about your business and mission. (Don't forget to include all this information on your Web site as well.)

Separate your home and business

Although you run your business out of your home, you may want to take measures to keep it separate from your household activities. For example, if you're going to accept phone orders, consider installing a second phone line. (You usually get a discount on the second line when you have multiple lines.)

Not only will you look more professional when your 8-year-old isn't answering the phone, but you'll actually be obeying the law, because you're not supposed to use a home line for business use. (You can avoid this by installing an actual business line inside your home; talk to your phone company about your options.) If you're on the go a lot, you may want to consider a cell phone for all your business calls.

You also need to have a separate business account, which doesn't include your spouse's name, to show that you're indeed a business. (That's in case the IRS ever comes after you! For more tax tips, contact your accountant.)

If you haven't done so already, contact your city or county clerk's office about getting a license. (See the section "Taxing matters," earlier in this chapter, for more on this topic.)

Insuring Your Business

Although you probably already have homeowner's insurance, you may be surprised to discover that after you leave the realm of hobby and enter the business arena, all things used to make a profit are usually exempt from this policy.

We discovered this when my husband was a photographer for a local newspaper. He had thousands of dollars in camera equipment, so we had to take out a special rider policy to insure the equipment. It paid off. Shortly thereafter, his equipment was stolen from his car, and we replaced it thanks to the insurance company. If we hadn't taken out that rider, we wouldn't have been reimbursed at all.

Although candle and soap making don't require such high-dollar equipment as photography does, you still don't want to be out your supplies — or your hard-made inventory — in the case of a mishap. Talk to your insurance company and make sure that you're covered. You may decide to purchase liability insurance as well, just in case a customer sues you.

Setting Your Price

Establishing fair pricing for your products can be a difficult task. Mark your price too high, and you'll be sitting on inventory for a long time. Mark it too low, and you won't make any money.

Don't mark your prices too low. Not only are you wasting your hard work, but you're also undermining the work of others by cheapening their labor. Pricing your products too low isn't fair to you, it's not fair to your competitors, and it's not fair to the industry.

To come up with a price, you need to know what it costs you to make the product, including materials, labor, and overhead. Follow these steps:

1. **Make a list of everything you use in the recipe and write down the cost of each item.**

   If you need to, break down the cost. For example, if you purchase an 11-pound block of wax but you're only using 1 pound, divide the purchase price by 11.

2. **Add up all the costs.**

3. **Divide that number by the number of candles or soaps you created.**

   This number is your supply cost.

You also need to figure out what your time is worth.

1. **Tally up your time involved in making the project.**

   Make sure that you include shopping and cleaning time as well.

2. **Multiply the amount of time you spent by an hourly amount, such as minimum wage.**

   Don't worry — you'll be able to give yourself a raise soon!

3. **Divide this number by the number of bars (and/or candles) as well.**

   This number is your labor cost.

Now add your supply cost and labor cost together. Then, depending on the market where you're selling, multiply that figure by 2 or 3 to come up with the price for a bar of soap.

Take a look at the price. Price your competitors. Are you in line? Chances are, you've come up with a fair price. If you're coming in low, you may want to boost your price up a bit to be more in line with the competition. If you're substantially higher, consider changing your ingredients or not selling the product in that area. After all, you do want to make money.

If you later discover that the price is too high or low, you can adjust it.

If you come up with an even dollar price, such as $5, consider pricing your product at $4.75 or $4.99. Even though the amount isn't that much different, there's something psychological about paying less.

Packaging Your Product

Looks count, at least when it comes to selling crafts. You want to package your candles and soaps creatively to go along with their attractive appearance.

Check out what other vendors are doing. It may jumpstart your creativity.

You can wrap your wares in fabric or tissue, enclose in transparent paper or bags, and tie with a ribbon. The prettier, the better! The more attractive and eye-catching the packaging and overall display of soap, the more value you're adding to the item for potential customers.

Always include a business card with anything you sell — or stamp your logo, phone number, and Web site on your package. Also consider packaging your products in a clear bag so that you create a walking billboard for your business.

Marketing Your Business

The key to a successful business is marketing. You want people to know about your product. You want people to like your product. And for that to happen, you need to get your product out on the market.

Even if your product is the best one out there, customers won't find it by themselves. You need to promote it.

To market your products, you have several resources at your disposal. You can sell your products at local craft shows and festivals (see Chapter 24), as well as church and school-based events. You can sell or consign your products at local shops. And you can sell your products online, if you like.

The following sections describe popular ways to market your crafts. Of course, the list isn't all-inclusive, and you may find other ways to market your wares.

Word-of-mouth sales

Word of mouth is still the best way to sell your products. Produce a quality craft and treat the customers right, and the money will follow. Friends, family, and customers gladly talk about positive experiences and quality products with others. (How do you think hairdressers get all their clientele?)

Show me your plastic! Credit card sales

If you want to bump up your sales, you can make an easy change: start accepting credit cards. Not only are people more likely to make a purchase if they can spend with plastic, but they also tend to spend two to three times as much as when they're parting with cold hard cash or a check.

To accept credit cards, you need to have *merchant status,* which means that you're not just any average Joe or Jane accepting credit-card payments at a garage sale. You can check with your bank or your local crafts organization to find out how to achieve this status.

If you have an Internet business, open a PayPal business account. It's as handy as using a credit card. PayPal charges a small fee per transaction, but your sales will increase if you provide this option for customers that use the Internet for their shopping needs. For more information, go to www.paypal.com.

Don't forget to reward your customers for referrals. Give them a small, complimentary product or a discount for each referral.

Consider giving your soap away free at local events a couple times a year. Don't forget to include a business card with the product or include contact information on the packaging.

At the same time, don't always give your wares away to family and friends. (You do want to make a profit, don't you?) As a compromise, perhaps you can offer a discount for these "preferred" customers.

Craft fairs

One of the most popular places to sell crafts is at craft fairs and festivals. Usually held outdoors, these shows feature vendors who rent space to sell their wares. The shows tend to draw crowds, because customers can see many crafts in one space. And besides, who doesn't like to shop outside?

Craft fairs are a good place to start if you're just beginning to sell your products, because you can easily gauge your competition, as well as your customers' response to your products. You see what sells, what doesn't sell, and you can also find out what people want.

Take advantage of face-to-face contact with your customers and talk to them. Find out what they like and what they're looking for. Incorporate their feedback into your business wherever you can.

These shows usually take place on the weekend, and if you're willing to travel, you can find one to participate in most weekends out of the year. They're a great opportunity to showcase your work and meet new customers at the same time. They're also a chance to get your name and product out into the marketplace.

One downside of craft shows is that you're subject to the weather and its effect on the show's turnout (not to mention your booth!). If you're under a tent, you're in better shape.

Finding craft fairs and festivals

Finding craft fairs is a little bit like a scavenger hunt. You know what you're looking for and you can find the information on them all around, but you seldom find it in the same spot every time. Here are a few ideas of places to look.

- ✔ **Ask your local craft store.** Many times, the store has a schedule of upcoming events. If not, the store's instructors often know of shows.

- ✔ **Check with your state's tourism department.** You can often request a brochure that lists all festivals and fairs in your state, along with contact numbers. Don't forget to check neighboring states as well.

- ✔ **Consider contacting churches and schools.** They commonly have holiday bazaars or fall or spring craft fairs to raise money for their organization or cause.

- ✔ **Go to craft Web sites on the Internet.** One good one is `www.procrafter.com`, the site of The American Craft Malls. Another is the CraftMark site at `www.craftmark.com`.

- ✔ **Look at advertisements in trade journals, such as *Craftrends*.** You can find these journals in your local newsstand stores, which carry hundreds of magazines on a variety of specialized interests, as well as your local craft store.

- ✔ **Scope out local newspapers.** The Arts and Entertainment section usually lists upcoming events, including fairs and festivals.

Reaching the inner circle

After you find a craft fair, you need to apply for booth space by completing an application form and submitting a fee. Depending on the type of fair you're applying to, you may need to submit photographs of your products or booth. You can enter one of two types of craft fairs:

- ✔ A *nonjuried craft fair* is basically first-come, first-served. If you get your application form in first, then you're in. If the show already has enough participants, you're out.

> ✔ A *juried craft fair* is one where you must submit photographs of your
> work and/or booth. The judge or jury then chooses the applicants
> whose work it likes best. If you're applying for this type of show, you
> may also need to pay an additional fee meant to reimburse the judge or
> jury for its time.

In both types, sometimes the amount of each type of craftsmaker is limited.
For example, if you sell candles, the festival may limit the number of candle
sellers to encourage diversity of crafts. If the fair already has its candle booth
quota, the fair organizers won't let you in even if they still have rental booths
available.

Figuring out the inner workings

Because you're renting space at the fair, you usually don't have to pay a commission to the organizer. That's great because you get the benefits of a shop,
if only for the weekend, without the shop rental.

You also need to think about your booth space. You want to be able to set it
up and tear it down easily. (For more tips, see Chapter 24.)

Place a guest book in your booth and ask customers to sign in. You can use
this book to create a mailing list. For more on mailing lists, see Chapter 24.

Trade shows

If you don't want to meet your customers or give up all your weekends, consider attending trade shows. *Trade shows* are where store buyers come and
buy a large quantity of merchandise from you.

Your prices need to be a little bit lower than normal because wholesalers
mark up your price when they resell it. For this arrangement to work, you
both need to make a profit.

You can locate trade shows through the same means that you find craft fairs
and festivals. See the section "Finding craft fairs and festivals," earlier in this
chapter.

Home shows and open houses

You're probably familiar with the workings of a home show. A representative
from a particular company, such as Pampered Chef, Avon, or PartyLite Candles,
comes into your home to show you and your guests new products and to let
you sample them. You then place an order and receive your items a few days
or weeks later.

Well, you can take this same concept and apply it to selling your candles and soaps. You can go into your customer's home, show off your products, and then book parties from your host's guests, or you can hold an open house in your own home.

Hosting an open house is probably easier because you don't have to lug your products around and risk damaging them. Plus, you're more comfortable in your own familiar surroundings. However, if you decide to host your own open house, then make sure that your area's zoning regulations permit such an event. Usually, they allow an open house if it's a rare occurrence, but if you host open houses often, you may run into problems. (See the section "Zoning limitations," earlier in this chapter.)

Local shops

If customer contact isn't your cup of tea, then limit it by focusing on selling to local shops. Sometimes, the shop owner will buy your product and resell it at a higher price, as trade show buyers do. Other times, they'll take your product on consignment and display it in their shop. After the item sells, you share the proceeds.

Because you're not the one selling directly to customers, the shop is responsible for collecting and paying sales tax.

The nice thing about this situation is that you get the benefits of a storefront without paying for it. However, your products may be nestled in the back of the store out of sight, and you may also risk losing your investment if the shop folds.

If you decide to sell or consign your products to a shop, consider these guidelines:

- ✔ If you've never sold or consigned to a particular shop, don't give too much in case the store goes out of business or disappears and you lose your inventory.

- ✔ Keep up on your inventory. If something is selling well, restock.

- ✔ Include your contact info on the packaging, and keep your business card and brochure in the shop. That way, future customers can contact you directly.

- ✔ Consider placing a guest book with your product so that you can create a mailing list.

Hey! I like your Web site!

A Web site is a smart investment for any business. But chances are that you're a crafty person, not a computer expert. Of course, the easiest thing for you to do is to hire someone to create your Web site for you. However, that may not be easy on your pocketbook because you generally pay at least a few hundred dollars to go this route. Try these less expensive options:

✔ **Become part of something larger.** You can pay to take out an inexpensive ad on an online craft site. Think about who visits the site, though, and whether those people are a good match for your customer base.

✔ **Create your own free Web site.** You can go to places like Geocities to create your own site. You're even walked through the steps. However, keep in mind that some search engines and directories don't include free listings.

✔ **Get your own domain and create a site.** The ending ".com" makes you official, at least in many people's eyes. Get your own domain name, and you look more professional. You're also listed on those search engines and directories. Of course, this option costs, and you must pay a yearly fee, as well as pay the host for your site.

Internet

When you don't have time to visit stores or you're looking for a hard-to-find item, you can turn to the Internet. Your customers do the same. If you're starting a business and you're serious about expanding it, you need to market and promote yourself on the Web.

Not only can you expand your client base, but you can also serve your existing customers better by keeping them abreast of new products and prices, and allowing them to place orders as well.

You can either become part of a larger site or create your own stand-alone page. If you create your own site, pay special attention to the keywords you choose because you want potential visitors to be able to find you.

If you want to increase your Web traffic, supply some of useful information that appeals to your target market. For example, if you sell soaps scented only with essential oils, you might provide a helpful reference chart of oils and their qualities. If people are also drawn to your site for information, you'll also gain customers and goodwill.

You also need to think about any orders you receive. How will customers pay for them? (Credit cards and PayPal work best — see the sidebar "Show me your plastic! Credit card sales," earlier in this chapter.) Don't forget to think about shipping and money exchanges, because a Web site virtually expands your customer base to the entire world. (PayPal now supports international money exchanges for many countries.)

Web sites don't run themselves. You need to update yours occasionally, so don't forget to allow for the time or costs to do so. If you include links to other sites, don't forget to check them periodically.

Advertisements

Although countless people are hooked up to the Web, many aren't. To reach those people, consider purchasing advertising in your local newspaper or national magazines. (Of course, the smaller the distribution base, usually the cheaper the ad.) When you get a new client, ask them where they heard about you. You may choose to make your ad larger next time!

You don't have to advertise in a publication. You can be your own best marketing tool. Hand out your business cards. Offer brochures. Use flyers to announce sales or new products. Get your name out there as much as possible!

Part VI
The Part of Tens

The 5th Wave   By Rich Tennant

"The combustion zone on your wick seems a little high."

In this part . . .

No self-respecting *For Dummies* book is complete without a trademark Part of Tens. This lighthearted part is short, sweet, and to the point. You find out more than 50 great tips in this particular part, focusing on great holiday decorating and gift ideas and fantastic projects for kids. You also get ten great tips for marketing your hobby at a craft show. Have fun!

Chapter 21

Ten Easy Holiday Decorating Ideas

In This Chapter

▶ Creating soaps for all seasons

▶ Making specialty candles

*H*oliday decorating doesn't have to be difficult or expensive, especially when you're using candles and soaps that you plan on making anyway. The ideas I give you in this chapter are particularly easy and fun to create. And the best part is, after you get into the habit of thinking about holiday decorations, you can look around stores and magazines and adapt your own ideas. The key is just to keep your eyes and mind wide open.

Be My Valentine, Please: Heart-Shaped Soaps

Valentine's Day may be for sweethearts, but I have a great decorating idea for you to spread the love with your entire family: a translucent soap complete with hearts inside it.

You may think this project requires a lot of work, but it's simple enough to do. You simply insert small, 1-inch or 2-inch, precolored heart-shaped soaps, available at your local craft store, in your mold.

Follow these steps:

1. **Using a knife, cut 1-pound melt-and-pour soap base into 1-inch cubes or smaller, place them in a microwave-safe bowl, and cover.**

2. **Place your soap in the microwave and heat for 45 seconds.**

3. **Stir your soap.**

4. **Continue melting your soap in 15-second intervals, stirring in between each time, until your soap base is completely melted.**

   5. **Pour a thin layer of soap in your mold.**

   6. **Arrange your hearts in the mold.**

   7. **Spritz with alcohol to prevent air bubbles.**

   8. **Wait a few minutes so that your soap begins to solidify and then pour the rest of the melted soap.**

After your soap solidifies, you have a bar of soap filled with love — heart-shaped soaps, that is!

Make sure that you choose a mold large enough to accommodate your hearts.

You can easily use this technique to make candles with heart embedments. (To find out how to make a chunk candle, see Chapter 8.) You can also purchase two-piece heart-shaped candle and soap molds to create a three-dimensional heart. Just make sure that you color your candle or soap red or pink! (For more tips on coloring your candles and soaps, see Chapters 6 and 15 respectively.)

Cutting It Up for the Holidays

If you make tons of cookies and candies, you probably know that you can find a cookie or candy cutter for just about any shape. That generalization is especially true when it comes to the holidays.

Why not take this a step further and use these cutters to make decorative seasonal soaps? You can either cut your shapes out of finished soap or you can melt soap specifically for this task.

To make your own shapes:

   1. **Place an old cookie sheet on your counter.**

      If it's not so old, line it with aluminum foil or wax paper.

   2. **Melt your soap in the microwave as you normally would to make melt-and-pour soap.**

   3. **Stir in your color.**

      Think seasonal. Red or green work well for Christmas, pink or red for Valentine's Day, and lavender or green for Easter.

   4. **Pour your melted soap in a thin layer on the cookie sheet.**

      The amount of soap you pour will depend on the desired finished depth of your shapes.

   5. **When the soap solidifies, cut out your shapes.**

After you have your shapes, embed them in your soap. To do so, follow the steps in the preceding section, substituting your shapes for the hearts.

If an idea works well for soaps, you can generally apply it to candles. This craft is no exception. To embed shapes in your wax, follow the chunk candle instructions in Chapter 8.

Making Easter Eggs in a Basket

Who says an Easter basket has to be full of chocolate and candy? If you're like me, you probably don't want your family stocking up on too much sweet stuff during the holiday seasons, and Easter is no exception. So if you make a basket for your kids, what are your other options? Here's a hint: Think soap!

Melt your soap and color it in springlike, pastel shades. Then pour it into some two-piece egg molds, available at local craft stores. (If you can't find these molds, then try using gelatin molds, which show up around Easter in department stores.) When you remove the mold, you have egg-shaped soaps.

Opaque melt-and-pour bases look especially attractive.

As a finishing touch, fill an Easter basket or decorative Easter pail with grass and top with your eggs. And you don't even have to worry about them spoiling, so leave them out as long as you'd like!

Painting Festive Holiday Candles

If you have any artistic talent whatsoever, you'll love this decorating idea — painted candles. And if you don't have much talent, don't despair. As long as you can spell or draw simple lines, you, too, can have your very own decorative candles.

All you need is a white or light-colored finished candle. (Store-bought candles work fine if you don't want to make your own.) Plan your design, grab your paintbrush, and start painting something festive, such as Christmas trees, Stars of David, shamrocks, flags, or bunnies, depending on the occasion. (For details on your paint choices, see Chapter 7.)

If you're short on artistic talent, paint words, such as "Ho, Ho, Ho," or draw simple designs, such as snowflakes or flowers. You also have the option of stenciling a design on your candle.

For instructions on how to paint your candle or how to stencil, see Chapter 7.

Trick-or-Treating: Jack-o'-Lantern Fun

What's Halloween without costumes, parties, trick-or-treaters, and, of course, the jack-o'-lantern? This year, though, you can decorate your home with a twist — a jack-o'-lantern that truly lights up your room. Better yet, no carving is required!

All you need is an inexpensive glass jar shaped like a jack-o'-lantern face. (You can find these in local craft stores around Halloween.) Then, either buy pre-colored orange gel wax or color your gel wax orange. (You color gel wax the same way you color paraffin wax; see Chapter 6 for detailed instructions.) Melt and pour into the mold. When it sets, you have your very own jack-o'-lantern. Of course, you don't get to enjoy eating the pumpkin seeds!

Don't limit this decorating idea to just Halloween. You can use it for almost any season, as long as you find a glass that works with your theme. Then just color your gel wax to match the season.

Say, Cheese: Wearing Your Smile on Your Soap

Grandparents especially will love this decorating idea. Make copies of your kids' photographs and embed them in translucent soaps. Because you have a copy of the photograph, it doesn't matter if someone uses the soap and gets the photos wet — although I bet some grandparents would never dream of washing their hands with their grandchild's face!

To make this personalized craft, follow these steps:

1. **Melt your soap in your microwave as you normally would to make melt-and-pour soaps.**

2. **Pour a thin layer of soap in your mold.**

   Make sure that you choose a mold tall enough to accommodate your photograph.

3. **Wrap your photo in plastic wrap and center it vertically in your mold.**

4. **Wait a few minutes so that your soap begins to gel and then pour the rest of the melted soap.**

Going Back to Basics: Simple Votives

You don't have to do anything fancy to decorate for the holidays. Why not just let the color of your candles mark the season? For example, color votives red and green to celebrate the Christmas season. Use red, white, and blue to signify July 4th. Red, white, and pink mark Valentine's Day.

Don't limit yourself to votive candles. Have fun with multiwick candles, tapers, and pillars.

Adding scent is an especially nice touch. Apple scents scream fall, while bayberry brings to mind the Christmas season. (For more detail on adding color and scent, see Chapter 6.)

Mold One for Me: Soaps for All Seasons

One of the things I particularly enjoy about soap making is the variety of molds available. Want spring flowers? No problem. Want to celebrate summer with dolphins and shells? Gotcha covered. Leaves to signify autumn? That, too. Pretty much, you name it, you can find it, especially when you consider that you can choose from among soap molds, candle molds, and candy molds, or even make your own molds.

The only thing special that you need to do with this craft is to plan ahead. Think of the next season or holiday and then go shopping for your mold.

Layering One for the Fourth

Although red, white, and blue are a natural for the Fourth, you may have trouble thinking of ways to use the colors together. That's where a festive Fourth of July–layered candle fits the bill.

To make a layered candle, all you need to do is melt your wax and dye your colors. (You only need to dye red and blue wax, because white is wax's normal color when left uncolored.) Then layer it in your candle mold. (A pillar one works well.)

For detailed instructions, check out Chapter 8.

Stenciling Shamrock Candles

St. Patrick's Day isn't necessarily a big decorating holiday, but why not go ahead and decorate this year by placing a light green candle with a dark green shamrock stenciled on its surface in your living room. You can even use stamps in place of stencils to add your design to soaps.

All you need is a finished candle, your paint, paintbrush, and stamps or stencils, and then just follow the instructions for stamping or stenciling your soaps in Chapter 16.

Chapter 22

Ten or So Great Gift Ideas for Family and Friends

In This Chapter

▶ Working magic with relaxing candles and soaps

▶ Making special kits for your loved ones

▶ Living the high life with foot oil and body lotion

M ost people love personal gifts — especially handmade crafts. Not only do such gifts show your recipients that you spent time on them, but if you personalize the gifts with favorite scents and color, it shows that you pay attention and care as well. Unless you're showering your family and friends with an overabundance of the same crafts year after year, candles and soaps are almost always a surefire hit. In this chapter, I give you great ideas to kick off your gift giving. (And who says you have to save gifts just for birthdays and holidays?)

Serving Up Decorative Soaps in a Glass Bowl

Decorative molds abound, so you can make some beautiful decorative soaps in all shapes and sizes. Melt-and-pour soap's translucent nature causes it to look fantastic when colored. Take advantage of this beauty and create some personalized soaps whose shape and color match your recipient's taste. Don't forget to add some soothing scent (see Chapter 15) and then serve them up in a glass bowl or jar. The result is stunning.

Harmonizing Sand and Shells with Surf — er, Make That Candles

Buy a beautiful, flat stoneware candleholder that's large enough to hold several candles. Make three different size candles, using the same color but different shades. Arrange them on the candleholder, scatter some sand around them, and then strategically place shells in the sand. This gift is the next best thing to receiving a beach vacation!

Presenting a Candle Gift Basket

Make a batch of candles in your friend's favorite color and buy a basket to accommodate them. Then wrap up the entire basket — handle, candles, and all — in translucent cellophane paper in your favorite color. Who wouldn't want such a lovely gift?

Softening Skin and Hearts: Body Lotion

Almost everyone enjoys body lotion, especially in winter. (Think Christmas gift!) Buy a body lotion base, available at your local craft store, and customize it with your relative's favorite essential oil — or one you think she can use, to relax a little bit. (See Chapter 19 for the lowdown on essential oils.) Then transfer it to a beautiful bottle, tie a bow around the neck, and present it to your relative.

Cooking Up Something: A Kitchen Gel Candle

One year I received a store-bought gel candle, complete with fruit embedments, as a Christmas gift. The natural home for it seemed to be the kitchen. Not only did the candle put me in the mood to cook, but it also put me in the mood to eat — fortunately, healthy food, because all those strawberries, bananas, and watermelons looked so scrumptious.

You can make a gel candle with embedments of your friend's favorite foods — no French fries, please — shaped from paraffin wax. If you're choosing something mainstream, such as oranges, you can probably find the embedment in your local craft store. If not, you can use cookie cutters and cut your own embedments out of wax. To find out how to make a gel candle with embedments, see Chapter 8.

Finding Fun in a Toy Soap Bar

If you have a little one on your gift list, then place a toy in the middle of a translucent bar of soap. Rubber bath toys work best, and also try to make sure that they're large enough not to fit into a child's mouth when the toy's compressed. To find out how to embed a toy in soap, see Chapter 16.

Taking It Easy: Foot Oil

Who doesn't like a foot massage? Although this idea isn't technically soap, it does fall into the home-spa category and uses many of the same oils. Although my recipe calls for mixing eight drops of almond oil with eight drops of lavender essential oil, you can really substitute any oils. You can even do four drops each of two different base oils or two different essential oils. Then just rub the oil onto clean, dry feet, don socks, and go to bed. (Did I mention this was a gift for yourself?) When you find an oil combination you like, you can double, triple, or even quadruple the recipe.

Showing Off Patio Candles

Unlike most presents, this gift belongs outside. To make a patio candle, melt your wax, color and scent it, and pour it into three small terra cotta pots. Place the pots in a large terra cotta saucer and then arrange shells around the pot. Secure the shells in place by pouring a very thin layer of hot wax or using glue. Then add sand.

This gift is great if you're on a tight budget but want high-dollar results. Terra cotta saucers and pots are inexpensive, and if you've ever collected shells at the beach, you know they're free. The wax is the most expensive part of the project, and you can even get around that cost, if necessary, by using recycled wax. (See Chapter 2 for details on recycling wax.)

Concocting a Home-Spa Kit

Who doesn't like to be pampered? If you can't afford to send your sister to a day spa, then treat her to her own home-spa kit. Include body lotion and foot oil (see the "Taking It Easy: Foot Oil" section earlier in this chapter), as well as massage oil, bath oil, and shower gel. Don't forget to include some aromatherapy votives! (For home-spa recipes, see Chapter 17.)

When Sleep Is Elusive: Good-Night Votives and Soap

If your loved one is having trouble sleeping, then give a goodnight kit. Include aromatherapy soaps and a dozen votive candles. Make sure that you match the scents to the mood — you want your loved one to be totally relaxed before hitting the sheets. For more on essential oils, see Chapter 19.

Remember, you should always extinguish your candles before you go to sleep for the night.

Making Magical Mosaic Votives

Go to any craft store, and you can find many soap-making and candle-making kits. But a kit that lends a truly remarkable effect is one that guides you through making mosaic votive holders. Using the kit, paste bits of glass onto a votive candleholder, basically creating a stained-glass effect. (You can also do this without a kit, but I suggest trying it this way first.) If you can't find the kit at your local craft store, check out the supplier Web sites in Appendix A. The results are sensational.

Chapter 23

Ten Super Projects for Kids

- -

In This Chapter

▶ Making candles without heat

▶ Getting creative with paint and glitter

▶ Helping out with simple soaps and embedments

▶ Concocting bath salts and lip balm

- -

This subject is one that is near and dear to my heart. As the proud parent of a 4-year-old and a 1-year-old, I know how challenging finding crafts suited to their talents *and* their safety can be.

Not every candle or soap project in this book is appropriate craft fare for a young one — in fact, most of them aren't because of the heat involved — but in this chapter, I give you ten projects that you can share with your little ones. If your kids are like mine, they want to be just like Mommy, and the crafts in this chapter give them that chance.

Making a Bead Wax Candle

If your child really wants to make a candle, don't despair. You really can let her do it without exposing her to hot wax. The secret is a simple bead-wax candle. (You can see photos of both the wax and finished product in Chapter 2.)

All you do is buy a bag of bead wax and a decorative glass container. (You can find such containers for under a $1 at your local craft store.) Let your child place the wick on the bottom of the container and then help her carefully pour the wax in the container. (For more on wicks, see Chapter 4.)

Making a bead wax candle is a great craft for toddlers who don't always have a lot of coordination but can usually hit a wide-mouthed jar. And besides, it's a lot like playing in sand because bead wax has the same texture and look (just ignore the color!). Just make sure that you place the finished candle out of their reach, or it won't be a candle for long!

Let your child choose where the candle is going to go and then help her match the color of the bead wax to the room.

Rolling Around in Beeswax

The first candle I ever made was a beeswax candle, and boy, did I feel a sense of accomplishment because it was so simple and looked so nice. Any child who loves working with his hands will enjoy this simple project. And rolling a beeswax candle doesn't involve any heat.

Your first step is to buy a sheet of beeswax. (Let your child choose the color.) Line your kitchen table or counter with aluminum foil and help your child align a wick at the end of the beeswax sheet. Then let him roll up the candle.

You may want to make sure that the candle edges align, but even if they don't, you can cut off the uneven edges at the bottom so that the candle can stand.

Pouring a Liquid Gel Candle

This project also requires no heat. I discovered this project by mistake. I mistakenly bought a product at a local craft store that I thought was colorant. When I got ready to use it, I discovered that it was actually colored liquid gel. (Don't ask me how I made this mistake!)

All you do is squeeze the liquid gel out of the tube and into a container. Then you insert a tabbed wick. (I suggest, though, adding the wick first and then straightening it to minimize the color on your hands.) That's it. The candle actually can burn at that point. (For more on wicks and instructions on how to tab your own, see Chapter 4.)

The hardest part of this project is simply choosing a container to pour the gel into! (For more tips on choosing a container, see Chapter 3.)

Creating Painted Artwork

Most children enjoy painting, so why not forego the paper and give them a finished candle instead? I personally love seeing my children's artwork around me, but I also like things to be functional. A painted candle fits the bill!

This craft can be messy. Make sure that you line your work area with newspaper or foil and deck your child out in an apron.

All you need is a white or light-colored candle, some paint — the more colors, the better — and a paintbrush. Then let your little Picasso do his magic! (For more on your paint options, see Chapter 7.)

Creating Candleholders

My daughter Katie went to a playgroup party where she decorated a baby food jar to be used as a tealight candleholder. Of course, she had a great time making it, and, what's more, I get to proudly display it in my office.

To make this candleholder, you need a clean baby food jar with the label and remaining adhesive completely removed. Let your child decorate the jar with stickers and glitter glue. When the jar dries, tie a ribbon around the top of the jar for decoration. Pop in a tealight candle, and you have an instant gift for the grandparents.

Plan your decorations around a theme. If it's Christmas, use Christmas stickers, red and green glitter glue, and red or green ribbon. For St. Patrick's Day, think green. And for the Fourth of July, what's better than red, white, and blue with star stickers?

Helping Out with Precolored Melt-and-Pour Soap

Working with melt-and-pour soap base is a lot safer than working with hot wax. As long as you take the same precautions you'd take if you were cooking, then why not let your child help out? Just make sure that you're the one handling the hot stuff.

Divvy up the tasks as follows:

- ✔ You cut up the soap chunks, while your child selects a mold from your collection.
- ✔ You melt the soap, while she chooses the color and fragrance.
- ✔ Your child stirs in the color and scent.

  ✔ You pour the soap into the mold.

  ✔ Your child removes the soap from the mold — with a little thumb strength from you, if necessary!

What teamwork!

Bagging Up Bath Salts

Venture into the soap-making aisle of your local craft store, and you probably see some beautiful mesh bags. You may wonder what they're for — to hold bath salts. The great thing is that you can even buy the bath salts in that same aisle.

When you get home, why not have your child fill a bag? She can add fragrance and substances, such as dried herbs and flowers. Then help her pile her concoction in her very own bag.

Making Up a Batch of Lip Balm

My daughter started off loving nail polish, and now she has moved on to lip balm. Even my 1-year-old son, Carter, loves the stuff and knows what to do with it, thanks to his big sister.

If your kids are anything like mine, then they'll like the thought of making their very own batch of lip balm. All you do is buy the base at your local craft store and then add color. It's that easy. You store it just as you would store-bought lip balm.

Quack, Quack! Embedding Rubber Toys

If you've ever seen a rubber toy embedded in a bar of soap, you have to admit it's cute. And if it's cute to an adult, just think how much a rubber duck embedded in a bar of soap will tickle your children.

This craft is another one that requires full parental participation. (I describe the other one in the section "Helping Out with Precolored Melt-and-Pour Soap," earlier in this chapter.)

You can find the basic steps in Chapter 16, but I suggest divvying up the tasks as follows:

- ✔ You melt the soap, and your child finds a rubber toy to embed.

- ✔ You pour the melted soap, while your child positions the embedment.

- ✔ You pour the rest of the soap into the mold, and your child gets to remove the soap from the mold.

- ✔ You get to help all your child's friends make similar soaps because they admire your child's soap so much.

Getting Creative with Soap Chunks

Who says those precut, precolored soap chunks have to go in something? Why not let your child come up with an innovative project for them? Perhaps he can find a decorative container to fill with matching soap chunks for the bathroom. Maybe she wants to use them to make roads for her toy cars. Or maybe he wants to glue them to paper to create a happy face for such a great parent who gives him soap chunks to play with. Who knows? Let your children inspire you with their ideas.

Chapter 24

Ten Musts for Attending a Craft Show

In This Chapter

▶ Getting the lowdown on a potential show

▶ Setting up your booth

▶ Using your people skills and a mailing list to build up clientele

*I*f you decide to take the plunge from hobbyist to entrepreneur, then one of the best places to market your candles and soaps is a local craft fair or festival. You meet new people, get your product out, and can take the pulse of the market. But attending a craft fair isn't as easy as signing up and showing up. This chapter gives you ten things to consider when attending a craft show.

Asking the Right Questions

Not every craft show is right for you. (Besides, you'll wear yourself out if you try to attend them all!) The clientele may not be right. The area may be having tough economic times and folks may lack disposable cash. Or maybe the show's size doesn't warrant the money you'd have to spend traveling.

When you look into a craft show, especially if it's one you haven't attended before, you need to ask the right questions. Figure 24-1 helps walk you through it.

For tips on locating a craft fair, see Chapter 20.

Quizzing Show Organizers

Show schedule

What are the dates of the show?_____

What are the show's hours?_____

Application process

How much does it cost to apply and rent space?_____

When's the application deadline? _____

Is it a juried or nonjuried show?_____

Show background

Is this show an annual event?_____

Who is sponsoring the event?_____

If it's an annual event, how many people attended the show last year?_____

How many exhibitors will be at the show?_____

How is the show marketed to the public?_____

_____

Figure 24-1:
Ask the right
questions
when inves-
tigating a
craft show.

Show setup

Will you be outside under a tent or inside a building?_____

What happens in the case of bad weather?_____

How much booth space do you have?_____

Starting Locally

What an exciting life! Every weekend in a different city, meeting different people, making money . . . maybe.

Before you jump into the national craft show scene, participate in fairs and festivals in your region. That way, you familiarize yourself with how the shows work, figure out what sells and what doesn't, are able to adjust your prices accordingly, and can scope out the competition. Why pay big money for travel expenses to learn the ropes of the craft show scene?

To find out how to locate a craft show in your area, see Chapter 20.

Selling Out Isn't Necessarily Good

Great! You sold out all your new die cut soaps. You may be happy not to pack them up, but don't automatically think that *selling out* is a good thing.

Selling out is actually a sign that you didn't make enough inventory. You may have even underpriced your items. If you know an item is popular, make extras so that you don't run out and miss potential profit.

Plan ahead before going to your show. For example, if you're going to a show that you've been to before and you know that scented soaps are more popular than container candles, you may want to bring more scented soaps.

If you think you underpriced your products, see Chapter 20 for more tips on pricing.

Thinking About How You Set Up Your Booth

Selling at shows is a lot like having a garage sale — everyone always seems to come at once. As a result, the more prepared you are, the better you can serve your customers.

Keep these pointers in mind when you set up your booth:

- You need to have tables set up and covered by tablecloths, as well as chairs to sit in.
- All your products should be on display and easy to see.
- Your guest book should be open and ready. (Don't forget pens!)
- Business cards, brochures, and even your biography sheet should be available. (See Chapter 20 for more on what to include in these items.)
- Your cash box should be well stocked with plenty of coins and one-dollar bills.
- You need bags to sack up your orders. (See Chapter 20 for more packaging tips.)

Remembering the Weather

Many times, craft fairs and festivals are located outdoors. More people tend to come to outdoor events because of the weather, and striking up conversations with attendees is easier because of the casual atmosphere.

But the outdoor factor is only good when the weather is nice. If it's too hot, too cold, too windy, too sunny, or too rainy, you'll encounter problems. Uncooperative weather affects show attendance, and, depending on where you set up, weather can affect your display.

Ideally, you'll be under a tent to shelter you from the rain and sun. And, of course, a tent usually makes the area warmer, too, which helps in the case of rain. But if it's windy, you want to make sure that you have plenty of heavy items to hold down your papers and also protect your products from blowing away. (Fortunately, candles and soap tend to be heavy enough to avoid that problem!) And as far as too much heat, consider setting up fans if you have access to electrical outlets.

If you're going to a show that requires that you provide your own tents and tables, don't be tempted to skimp. Buy lightweight, quality equipment. If you're not sure where to start your search, ask acquaintances and friends who frequent these shows what they suggest. Or attend a craft show on your own and talk to the show's vendors.

Showing Off Your Wares

Don't be shy when strutting your stuff — your candles and soap. Place them prominently on display. Use a bio sheet to tell everyone why your products are unique (but be careful about making cosmetic claims when it comes to soaps, unless you want to reclassify them as cosmetics, which means you must meet certain standards). Give out samples occasionally.

Best of all, use clear bags so that other festivalgoers can see your products and ask about them. This tip really does work. I gleaned another great idea at a festival where everyone was carrying around large baskets, but the vendor wasn't in the best location. Because everyone asked customers about the baskets, he couldn't keep the baskets in stock and people lined up to buy them as his trucks unloaded. The baskets never even made it to his booth!

Take something to do at your table. You might have some slack time on your hands and if people see you labeling soaps or beveling edges on bars . . . it will pique their curiosity and draw them to your table. Then you can likely explain a bit about what you do.

Creating a Mailing List

Put out a guest book for customers to sign. You can use those names to create a mailing list to notify customers of discounts, new products, sales, and upcoming craft fairs and festivals where you'll be, as well as holiday gift ideas. You may even want to include a coupon to attract customers. When you have the names, your only cost is the paper to print your information on, as well as postage. Your guest book should ask for your customer's name and complete address. Don't forget to also request an e-mail address. (You can send out e-mails occasionally to save on postage and be good to the environment.)

Make sure that your guest book has a Yes/No spot so that customers can indicate whether they want to be on your mailing list.

Chatting with Your Customers

If you're manning the craft show scene, you probably like people. Take advantage of all this personal contact and actually talk to your customers. Find out what products they're looking for and their likes and dislikes. Are there any particular colors they want? Is there anything they detest? Consider this market research for your company! Don't just sit back on your duff and expect customers to know everything about your products.

Offering Rewards to Loyal Customers

Many times, people who attend craft shows attend other shows as well. If you notice familiar faces or you're getting referrals from others, reward your loyal customers with complimentary tealights or miniature soaps. You may even want to offer a discount to reward your customers.

They'll remember your gestures and, chances are, keep sending business your way.

Being There

I'm not talking about being a shoulder to cry on — but you can if you want! I'm advising you to *actually* attend craft shows and market your product. That way, people can put a name with a face and product. Talk directly with people about your candles and soaps.

Many times, repeat customers are coming to buy from you as much as they are the product and are disappointed if you've sent someone in your place.

Part VII
Appendixes

The 5th Wave   By Rich Tennant

@RICHTENNANT

"I sell my candles through gift shops and stationery stores, whereas Philip's market is mostly lighthouses."

In this part . . .

Do you live far away from a large city and can't find the items I mention in this book? Do you have stores nearby, but they're too general to fit your needs? Or maybe you don't have Internet access? Whatever your obstacle to obtaining supplies or advice is, don't get discouraged. Appendix A serves as a great resource list for both candle-making and soap-making suppliers. If you want to read more on candle and soap making, check out Appendix B. It lists additional resources for your reading pleasure. And for those of you who do have Internet access, I include a Web site in both appendixes whenever it's available.

Appendix A

Candle-Making, Soap-Making, and Aromatherapy Suppliers

In This Appendix

▶ Finding candle-making suppliers

▶ Buying soap-making items

▶ Locating essential oils and aromatherapists

▶ Taking advantage of one-stop shopping for your candle- and soap-making needs

S ooner or later, you're going to want to buy supplies or materials that you can't find in your local craft store. Thanks to this appendix, your search for online candle- and soap-making suppliers is much easier because I give you a few to start with. I even give you resources for essential oils.

Keep in mind that many more suppliers exist. By getting online and doing a search on the Internet, you can locate other suppliers and compare prices and shipping costs. The lists in this appendix are by no means meant to be all-inclusive.

Whenever these suppliers offer additional information, I indicate that as well. For informational Web sites (that don't sell merchandise) where you can find candle- and soap-making tips, check out Appendix B.

Candle-Making Suppliers

Want a specialty wax or mold? Tired of hitting store after store searching for one in your area? Then you're in the right spot. Check out these online candle-making suppliers.

The Candle Maker

www.thecandlemaker.com

You can order supplies, such as starter kits, wax, wicks, molds, and even fragrance oils. The company has been in business for more than 30 years.

Cierra Candles

www.cierracandles.com

This Internet/mail-order candle-supply company boasts customers around the world.

Craft Catalog

www.craft-catalogs.com/Candlemaking.asp

You can find wicks, molds, dyes, and scents at this site. The more you order, the bigger your discount.

Earth Guild

www.earthguild.com/products/candle/cndhub.htm

This Asheville, North Carolina-based site is well suited to first-timers looking to buy complete starter sets. You can also purchase candle-making materials and books.

From Nature with Love

www.from-nature-with-love.com

If you want to order natural ingredients, such as oils and candle supplies, then check out this site. Click on the "Candle Supplies" link, and you see a page with all the products listed in categories on the left side of the screen. You can also take advantage of a search catalog for products.

Gel Candlemaking.com

www.gelcandlemaking.com

Because gel wax has a higher melting point (200°F), making gel candles requires that you take more safety precautions than when you use other types of waxes. This site focuses on safety issues. It also offers a very detailed guide to gel candle making. The guide's topics are divided into sections with a table so that you can easily locate the subject you want.

General Wax and Candle Company

www.genwax.com

Supposedly the largest candle-making site on the Internet, this site does seem to live up to its name. Not only can you order products, but you also can research subjects as well, including waxes and different types of candles. If you want to know something about candle making, you can probably find it here.

Lone Star Candle Supply

www.lonestarcandlesupply.com

This site offers scents, waxes, wicks, molds, dyes, and scents. You can even sign up for an e-mail mailing list that gives you periodic new product updates and specials.

The wax section is particularly helpful because you can find descriptions of different types of wax, as well as each wax's melting point and flash point. You also find the benefits of each wax and guidelines for using it, as well as a special notes section that comments on the wax's stickiness and softness.

Your orders should arrive in one to two business days. If you think it's taking too long, you can even track your order's status online.

Moonglow Candles and Suppliers

www.moonglowcandles.net

This easy-to-navigate site is well organized. You can see photographs of molds, as well as subscribe to a newsletter. If you're interested in working with soy wax, you may want to take a peek at the site's discussion of soy.

Pacific Northwest Candle Making Supply

www.nwcandlemaking.com

This site offers everything from wicks and waxes to molds and fragrances. You can even see photographs of each product.

The site has a catalog box divided into categories on the left side of the page for an easy search of products. If you get carried away with your order, you can even take advantage of wholesale prices when you spend $300 or more.

The Wax House/Scentmasters

www.waxhouse.com

This site's home page has a "Catalog" button that you click to search their product listings. In addition to placing orders, you can find information on additives, books, bulk wax, dyes, wicks, and scenting oils.

Soap-Making Suppliers

If you want some soap supplies or materials, then check out these online resources.

Brambleberry.com

www.brambleberry.com

This thorough soap-making site is a good source for supplies. It has sections on fragrance oils and molds, as well as a product catalog. The site also has nifty soap kits to choose from, including a build-your-own-kit section.

Cedar Vale Natural Health

www.cedarvale.net/soaps.htm

This simple and easy-to-use site doesn't look fancy, but its simple layout is easy to understand. Products — and you have many choices — appear in alphabetical order in a table format on the home page. Click on the product you want, and an order form appears.

Snow Drift Farm Natural Products

www.snowdriftfarm.com

This soap-making site offers fragrance oils, waxes, molds, herbs, preservatives, antioxidants, and soap kits. If you're a bargain shopper, then give the site your e-mail so that you can receive information on sales and specials. A nice feature about the site is that it offers products that haven't been tested on animals.

SoapCrafters

www.soapcrafters.com

Recipes may be found here, as well as soap-making supplies, such as herbs, incense, fragrances, and oils. This easy-to-navigate site has a search engine so that you can quickly and easily look up specific items.

Soaper's Choice

www.soaperschoice.com/

Located in Chicago, Illinois, this is a good source for all types of soap-making base oils and exotic butters. They also carry two types of melt-and-pour soap base in 25-pound blocks.

Sweetcakes!

www.sweetcakes.com

They're probably the most reliable fragrance oil provider and test all their scents before offering them. Some suppliers are cheaper, but you'll rarely be disappointed with the quality of fragrances purchased here. They carry other supplies as well.

The Pigment Lady at AOL

members.aol.com/pigmntlady/

This is a great source of cosmetic-grade colorants! The site also has some instructions on how to use them.

TKB Trading

www.tkbtrading.com/

This is an excellent site for melt-and-pour soapmakers.

Well, Naturally Products Ltd.

www.wellnaturally.com

This site offers oils, fragrance oils, herbs and spices, soap bases, and molds. The site isn't cluttered and has its categories featured right on the home page.

Aromatherapy Product Suppliers

When you get your candles and soaps looking like you want, chances are you'll want to experiment with scent. If essential oils are in your plans, check out these suppliers.

Aromatherapy Marketplace

www.halcyon.com/kway

This site not only has products for sale, but you can also peruse articles and basic aromatherapy information, such as essential oil uses and beginning aromatherapy know-how. This site has plenty of good information.

Aromatherapy Outlet.com

www.aromatherapyoutlet.com

Who says you can't get deals on essentials oils? Just check out this site, which offers incense, oils, candles, and body-care products, and see what the monthly special is.

A Garden Eastward

addy.com/brinkley/index.html

This has wonderful essential oils and blends for soap making, or anything you like!

Lavender Lane Inc.

www.lavenderlane.com/

This site offers pure essential oils, as well as dried flowers and soap-making supplies and recipes. If you're buying something at the site for the first time, you receive a first-purchase discount. Steer your friends there, and you receive a referral discount. The site also offers recipes.

Nature's Gift Aromatherapy Products

www.naturesgift.com

This site has a catalog and information about aromatherapy organized by topics. You can also purchase kits and accessories and read client testimonials, if that's your thing.

Precious Aromatherapy

www.aromatherapy.com

Do you have a question about aromatherapy? Then click on the "About Aromatherapy" link at this site to find your answers. In addition to offering supplies for sale, you also find a "Resource Guide" link in case you want to hunt down more info.

Uniquely You

www.uniquelyyoublends.com

Not only can you buy essential oils, but you can also read good, solid information on aromatherapy at this site. Take advantage of the "Women's Healing" link to find out information specific to women's health.

One-Stop Shopping: Candle and Soap Sites All in One

The vendors listed in this section offer both candle- and soap-making supplies. If you want to place just one order, check out this list.

BitterCreek South Candle & Soap Supply, Inc.

www.bittercreeksouth.com

Formerly Sissie's Candlemaking Supplies, this site is now under new ownership. It offers basic candle-making supplies and instructions, as well as ingredients for melt-and-pour soaps.

Holly Hobby

www.hollyhobby.com

This site offers candle- and soap-making products and illustrated instructions, as well as soap recipes. A photograph as well as a short product description for each item makes it easy to locate exactly what you're looking for. Based in Arizona, this site is mail-order only and has no retail location.

Joann.com

www.joann.com

A spinoff of Jo-Ann Stores, Joann.com offers the same candle- and soap-making products that you can find in their stores. If you want a lot of choices, you won't find them here. However, you can save yourself a trip to the store and buy from a source you're familiar with.

Liberty Natural Products

www.libertynatural.com

At this site, you have access to supplies for all three categories: candle making, soap making, and aromatherapy. Just click on the "Product" link, and you're transported to the products page with an aromatherapy category. You can also order bulk ingredients, such as oils, herbs, soaps, and waxes. You have several choices, especially when it comes to essential oils.

Lynden House International, Inc.

www.lyndenhouse.net

At this site, you don't find additional info, but you can order a variety of candle- and soap-making supplies in one spot. In particular, you can order supplies for your home spa. (See Chapter 17 for some home-spa recipes.)

Natures Garden

www.naturesgardencandles.com/

This wholesale candle- and soap-making supplier is small, but it has an abundance of helpful information on fragrances. For example, this easy-to-navigate site tells you which fragrances are body safe for soap and which ones are safe for gel candles.

Although the information centers mostly on fragrances and waxes for soaps and candles, you can buy other items, such as wax, wicks, and candle- and soap-making kits. If you want more information on fragrance, this spot is the one for you.

Rainbow Meadow

www.rainbowmeadow.com

This site is a nice, clean site, but it can take a while to load if you have a slower connection. After you're in, you can order products relating to aromatherapy, soaps, and candles. Clicking on the online catalog reveals the links for the products. You can purchase fragrance oils, natural perfume oils, waxes, melt-and-pour soap bases, and soap molds, to name just a few items.

Wholesale Supplies Plus

www.wholesalesuppliesplus.com/default.asp

At this site, you can order both candle- and soap-making supplies, as well as access a candle and soap teacher link that answers frequently-asked questions (FAQ) and gives instructions on certain techniques, such as embedding and suspending items.

In addition, the fragrance finder and color finder search engine helps you limit your search of fragrances for your specific use. The search engine helps you eliminate fragrances and colors that don't work well in your particular projects and then offers available suggestions to shorten your searching time.

Wicks and Wax Candle and Soap Making Supplies

www.wicksandwax.com

This Canadian site accepts fax, phone, and mail orders, but has no online ordering features. When you've browsed their online inventory and are ready to place your order, also keep in mind that the billing is done in Canadian currency. Fortunately, the site has a universal currency converter.

Appendix B

Additional Resources for Avid Candlemakers and Soapmakers

. . . .

In This Appendix

▶ Finding out even more about candle and soap making

▶ Looking at a few cold-process soap-making resources

▶ Experimenting with essential oils

. . . .

*S*urprisingly enough, you don't find a lot of specialized magazines on the topics of candle and soap making (you mean you've never heard of *Candle Making Monthly* or *Soap Making Digest?*), although you may come across articles in general interest craft magazines. So in case you want to stay abreast of the latest and greatest in the candle- and soap-making world or to expand your horizons beyond this book, this appendix offers a list of resources that can keep you reading for a long time. In addition to interesting candle- and soap-making Web sites, aromatherapy sites are provided.

If you're interested in finding candle- or soap-making suppliers, check out Appendix A. Many of the sites in Appendix A also include great reading material.

Reading More about Candle Making

I'm barely touching the surface in this list, because you can find so much candle-making material on the Web. But these sites are good ones to get you started. (Also don't forget to check out the suppliers listed in Appendix A, many of which include good information about candle making.)

The Candle Cauldron

www.candlecauldron.com

This site offers many descriptions and is an excellent reference site. You can find information about waxes, wicks, scent, and molds, as well as access a dictionary that defines common candle-making terms. Be sure to visit the safety page, where you find tips about candle safety.

Family Crafts

http://familycrafts.about.com/cs/candlemaking

If you want information on candle crafts, tips, patterns and a list of additional online resources, see this site. If you also enjoy making soaps, you're in luck — see the list in the section "Perusing the Web for Your Soap-Making Pleasure" for the direct link to the soap-making portion of the site.

Michaels

www.michaels.com/art/online/home

Surprisingly enough, this spinoff of the popular Michaels craft store doesn't sell products online. Instead, you find neat project ideas (just like the free project sheets available in the Michaels stores) that indicate the recommended skill level. The site also gives instructions on candle-making and soap-making projects. If you like what you see, check out the store locator to find a store in your area.

National Candle Association

www.candles.org

The National Candle Association Web site is practically an encyclopedia of information about all things candles. You can find information about the candle industry, ingredients, waxes, and more. Information on how to become a member of this national organization is also provided.

Pitter Patter Craft Library

www.homeschoolzone.com/pp/candlemaking.htm

You don't have to homeschool your children to take advantage of this site's candle-making craft ideas, which feature holiday candles, as well as cute teddy bear candle projects. You can also sign up for a newsletter.

Perusing the Web for Your Soap-Making Pleasure

If you haven't absorbed your fair share of soap-making material in this book and find yourself wanting more, then the following Web sites can help satiate your desire for more reading.

Family Crafts

http://familycrafts.about.com/cs/soap/index.htm

If you have young ones in your family, then you may like this site, which offers soap-making projects and information. You can also find information on candle making. (For the direct link to the candle-making portion of the site, see the section "Reading More about Candle Making.")

Soap Center

www.halderman.net/soap

If you're looking for supplier links, instructions, recipes, and tips, check out this site.

SoapMaking

http://waltonfeed.com/old/soaphome.html

This site discusses soap making and has many links to other sites.

Finding Some Information about Cold-Process Soap Making

I don't cover cold-process soap making in this book because it can be dangerous if you don't take proper safety precautions. But if you've had a great time making melt-and-pour and hand-milled soap and are curious about making cold-processed soaps, take a look at these Web sites for more information.

The Complete Guide to Soapmaking

`www.colebrothers.com/soap`

Not only does this site give good information on cold-process soap making, it also provides helpful tips if you're having problems. What's particularly helpful about this site is that you can click the "Troubleshooting" link for help with soap-making problems. The informative table separates information by problem, cause, and solution. You can look up your problem to find out what may be going wrong and how you can fix it.

Miller's Homemade Soap Pages

`http://millersoap.com`

This is one of the most highly trafficked sites on soap making on the Internet. While its focus is on making soap by the cold-process method, the site also has instructions on hand-milling soap and some information and suppliers listed on the links page that apply to melt-and-pour soapmakers.

Sabrina's Soapmaker's Resources

`http://ziggurat.org/soap/`

This is a *wonderful* soap-making site that is not only comprehensive but a delight to read!

Soap Recipes

http://members.aol.com/oelaineo/soapmaking.html

If you're looking for some cold-process soap recipes to try out, check out this site. It also has links to other soap-making sites.

Tracking Down Aromatherapy Resources

Essential oils can be difficult to find, and finding someone knowledgeable about them even harder. With these Web sites, you can become an aromatherapy expert in no time.

Aromatherapy

www.aromanotes.com

If you want to discover more about aromatherapy, go to this site and subscribe to its newsletter, _Grade A Notes Essential Oils Newsletter._

Aromatherapy Today

www.aromatherapytoday.com

You find a journal, books, and articles about aromatherapy at this Australian Web site.

AromaWeb

www.aromaweb.com

This informative site has articles, recipes, and a listing of essential oil profiles. You can find out about many essential oils and their possible uses.

The Guide to Aromatherapy

www.fragrant.demon.co.uk

This site contains descriptions of essential oils, as well as a symptoms guide that walks you through the use of oils for therapeutic benefits. You also find a glossary and books available for sale.

HealthWorldOnline

www.healthy.net/clinic/therapy/aroma

You can find out about many uses for oils and herbs at this informative Web site.

The National Association for Holistic Aromatherapy

www.naha.org

The National Association for Holistic Aromatherapy, a nonprofit organization that focuses on public awareness, hosts this site. You find an aromatherapy journal full of articles, as well as an "About Aromatherapy" link that covers common questions.

What Is Aromatherapy?

www.cpinternet.com/~cappy90/aroma.htm

If you have questions about aromatherapy, this site is for you. In addition to the questions and answers, you find information about aromatherapy organized by topic.

Index

• *Y* •

• *Z* •

Notes

Notes

Notes

Notes

FOR DUMMIES®

The easy way to get more done and have more fun

PERSONAL FINANCE

0-7645-5231-7

0-7645-2431-3

0-7645-5331-3

Also available:

Estate Planning For Dummies
(0-7645-5501-4)
401(k)s For Dummies
(0-7645-5468-9)
Frugal Living For Dummies
(0-7645-5403-4)
Microsoft Money "X" For
Dummies
(0-7645-1689-2)
Mutual Funds For Dummies
(0-7645-5329-1)

Personal Bankruptcy For
Dummies
(0-7645-5498-0)
Quicken "X" For Dummies
(0-7645-1666-3)
Stock Investing For Dummies
(0-7645-5411-5)
Taxes For Dummies 2003
(0-7645-5475-1)

BUSINESS & CAREERS

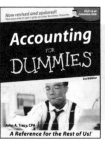

0-7645-5314-3

0-7645-5307-0

0-7645-5471-9

Also available:

Business Plans Kit For
Dummies
(0-7645-5365-8)
Consulting For Dummies
(0-7645-5034-9)
Cool Careers For Dummies
(0-7645-5345-3)
Human Resources Kit For
Dummies
(0-7645-5131-0)
Managing For Dummies
(1-5688-4858-7)

QuickBooks All-in-One Desk
Reference For Dummies
(0-7645-1963-8)
Selling For Dummies
(0-7645-5363-1)
Small Business Kit For
Dummies
(0-7645-5093-4)
Starting an eBay Business For
Dummies
(0-7645-1547-0)

HEALTH, SPORTS & FITNESS

0-7645-5167-1

0-7645-5146-9

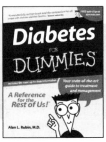

0-7645-5154-X

Also available:

Controlling Cholesterol For
Dummies
(0-7645-5440-9)
Dieting For Dummies
(0-7645-5126-4)
High Blood Pressure For
Dummies
(0-7645-5424-7)
Martial Arts For Dummies
(0-7645-5358-5)
Menopause For Dummies
(0-7645-5458-1)

Nutrition For Dummies
(0-7645-5180-9)
Power Yoga For Dummies
(0-7645-5342-9)
Thyroid For Dummies
(0-7645-5385-2)
Weight Training For Dummies
(0-7645-5168-X)
Yoga For Dummies
(0-7645-5117-5)

FOR DUMMIES®

A world of resources to help you grow

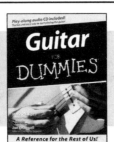

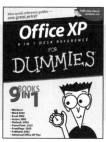

FOR DUMMIES®

Helping you expand your horizons and realize your potential

INTERNET

0-7645-0894-6

0-7645-1659-0

0-7645-1642-6

Also available:

America Online 7.0 For Dummies
(0-7645-1624-8)

Genealogy Online For Dummies
(0-7645-0807-5)

The Internet All-in-One Desk Reference For Dummies
(0-7645-1659-0)

Internet Explorer 6 For Dummies
(0-7645-1344-3)

The Internet For Dummies Quick Reference
(0-7645-1645-0)

Internet Privacy For Dummies
(0-7645-0846-6)

Researching Online For Dummies
(0-7645-0546-7)

Starting an Online Business For Dummies
(0-7645-1655-8)

DIGITAL MEDIA

0-7645-1664-7

0-7645-1675-2

0-7645-0806-7

Also available:

CD and DVD Recording For Dummies
(0-7645-1627-2)

Digital Photography All-in-One Desk Reference For Dummies
(0-7645-1800-3)

Digital Photography For Dummies Quick Reference
(0-7645-0750-8)

Home Recording for Musicians For Dummies
(0-7645-1634-5)

MP3 For Dummies
(0-7645-0858-X)

Paint Shop Pro "X" For Dummies
(0-7645-2440-2)

Photo Retouching & Restoration For Dummies
(0-7645-1662-0)

Scanners For Dummies
(0-7645-0783-4)

GRAPHICS

0-7645-0817-2

0-7645-1651-5

0-7645-0895-4

Also available:

Adobe Acrobat 5 PDF For Dummies
(0-7645-1652-3)

Fireworks 4 For Dummies
(0-7645-0804-0)

Illustrator 10 For Dummies
(0-7645-3636-2)

QuarkXPress 5 For Dummies
(0-7645-0643-9)

Visio 2000 For Dummies
(0-7645-0635-8)

Available wherever books are sold. Go to www.dummies.com or call 1-877-762-2974 to order direct.

FOR DUMMIES®

The advice and explanations you need to succeed

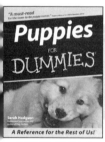

FOR DUMMIES

We take the mystery out of complicated subjects

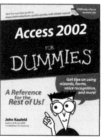

Making Candles & Soaps For Dummies®

Cheat Sheet

Identifying Common Appearance Problems when Making Soap

Chances are, even though your soap doesn't look quite right, you can still use and enjoy it. However, most people want their soaps to look as attractive as possible. Check out this list of common appearance problems and how to solve them.

- **Bubbles mar the appearance of your soap:** Those bubbles are the result of trapped air. To prevent air bubbles, make sure you lightly spray the top of your soap with rubbing alcohol after you pour it into its mold. The bubbles should disappear instantly.

- **Your soap looks cloudy:** You may have used too much of an additive, or you put your soap in the freezer to hasten hardening. Try using less of an additive next time, and despite your enthusiasm, let the soap harden at room temperature!

- **Your soap is cracked and brittle:** You most likely overheated your base or "overcooled" your soap. You can still use the soap, although it doesn't look very pretty!

- **Your soap looks crumbly:** You probably put your soap in the freezer. Remember to let the soap harden at room temperature.

- **Fuzz covers your soap:** Your soap may be sweating because it's attracting moisture in the air, and lint may be attracted to the sweat. Simply wipe off the fuzz, rub the soap with alcohol, and wrap it in plastic if you're not going to use it for a while.

- **Your soap is streaked:** The temperatures during mixing and melting were too cold. Synthetic fragrances can also cause streaking in soap. You can still use the soap, but it just doesn't look very attractive.

- **Your soap looks scummy:** Unwanted gook somehow contaminated your soap, but you can still safely use it. Simply scrape off the scum if it bothers you, or rinse the soap until the scum disappears.

Your Basic Soap-Making Supplies

When making melt-and-pour soap, you can get by pretty inexpensively. Follow this list to know the important supplies.

- **Double boiler or microwave:** You need a heat source to melt your soap, so a double boiler is ideal. You can even use a microwave.

- **Flexible molds:** You don't have to buy soap molds, although you can if you prefer. You can use candy molds, candle molds, or any flexible item as a mold. (Don't use ceramic or glass molds.) Make sure the mold is flexible enough so that you can remove the soap without breaking it.

- **Glass or heat-resistant plastic bowls:** You use these bowls to melt your soap. Seeing through your bowls so that you can see how close the soap is to being melted is helpful.

- **Melt-and-pour soap base:** You can buy this precolored. It's usually translucent, although you can now find it in opaque.

- **Releasing agent:** You can buy this in your local craft store, or use vegetable oil or nonstick cooking spray.

- **Spoons:** As the soap melts, stir it. Opt for metal or wooden spoons. Although wooden spoons don't last forever, they're cheap to replace.

For more information about Wiley Publishing, call 1-800-762-2974.

For Dummies: Bestselling Book Series for Beginners

Making Candles & Soaps For Dummies®

Cheat Sheet

Your Basic Candle-Making Supplies

You don't have to buy tons of supplies to make candles. Here's an overview of the bare essentials:

- **Double boiler:** You can improvise by placing a smaller pot on a trivet inside a larger pot.
- **Mold:** You can buy fancy metal molds at your local craft store, or you can use household items, such as metal cans or yogurt cups.
- **Mold sealer:** You can use this item to seal your wick hole so that no wax leaks out.
- **Releasing agent:** Spray on your mold a releasing agent, such as vegetable oil, before you add your wax, and your candle will be easier to remove.
- **Thermometer:** You need to melt your wax to 190°F, and this tool helps ensure that you reach the correct temperature.
- **Wax:** You have many options to choose from, but the most common waxes are paraffin, beeswax, and gel.
- **Wick:** Buy them preprimed and pretabbed, and you won't need to take any extra steps.

Types of Candles

You may wonder what each type of candle is called. The following list helps demystify the terminology.

- **Container:** Container candles burn in the actual container that you pour them into. In essence, the container is your mold.
- **Pillar:** Pillar candles are sturdy and thick. They can be short or tall and square or round. Some pillar candles are huge and contain multiple wicks. These candles are usually referred to by their diameter and height, as in a 3- by 5-inch pillar candle.
- **Taper:** Taper candles are long and slim. Taper candles are usually a standard size at the base so that they fit into standard candle holders.
- **Tealights:** Tealight candles are the same diameter as votives but are just 1 inch high. They're usually used under something, such as a pot of simmering potpourri or a lampshade.
- **Votives:** Votive candles are short, small candles that are only 2 to 3 inches high and ½ inch in diameter. Unlike pillar candles, votive candles are classified according to how long they burn. Most votives are 10-hour or 15-hour candles.

For Dummies: Bestselling Book Series for Beginners